Praise for THE CHRIST-CENTERED MARRIAGE

The ineffectiveness of most churches is due to the ineffectiveness of our marriages. I have tried all kinds of counseling, but the process in *The Christ-Centered Marriage* deals directly with the source of our conflict and brought a life-changing transformation.

—INVESTMENT BROKER

Excellent! God used this process to resolve all known strongholds that bound us. We are experiencing purification and holiness in all areas of our marriage.

—HOMEMAKER

Yes, it was difficult. Through honest and vulnerable discussion, the Lord led us through problems, anguish, hurts, fears, all the way to forgiveness, resolution, love and commitment.

—HOMEMAKER

It opened my eyes to the spiritual force that would destroy our marriage and gave us the tools to win.

—ATTORNEY

I have been to marriage seminars, attended your conference and read your books, but this broke the strongholds in our marriage and allowed us to continue in ministry.

—REGISTERED DIETITIAN

Praise for
THE CHRIST-CENTERED MARRIAGE

This cuts through the "religion" of society and puts us back on Christ's team, in the Word, focused on Him, and entering into His work.

—MARRIAGE INSTRUCTOR FOR PRISON FELLOWSHIP

This was my last resort and I was so apprehensive. But this real, honest, heartfelt, truthful, godly way softened my heart, gave me back my hope and a desire to truly love my husband.

—CHILDREN'S MINISTRY ASSOCIATE

The Lord got to the heart of our dysfunction. Most of our work on our marriage has been 90 percent psychological and 10 percent spiritual. This was 100 percent spiritual without ignoring the psychological.

—METHODIST PASTOR

Freedom is found in Christ individually first—then as a couple. This method and material got us beyond the surface into the cancer and then finally free.

—TEACHER

This process gets to the heart of marital issues, provides a format for dealing with them, and brought the truth of God's Word coupled with God's strength and the strength to resolve them

—MISSIONARY

Praise for
THE CHRIST-CENTERED MARRIAGE

This was a powerful and meaningful experience for us. The Lord performed a significant work in our marriage. This gave us a clean slate. After 20 years we wanted a fresh start and we got it.

—A COUPLE

The material was excellent. It addresses issues that destroy our marriages and then challenges us to deal honestly with each one.

—ENGINEER

Finally a very practical way to apply God's principles to our marriage.

—PRISON FELLOWSHIP

It provided the most solid biblical, practical, helpful, life-changing information and experience of anything we have done together.

—NUTRITIONIST

Excellent. You dealt with all the major issues a successful marriage should be built on. It was a challenging and liberating experience.

—PASTOR

NEIL T. ANDERSON

the CHRIST CENTERED MARRIAGE

DISCOVERING AND ENJOYING YOUR FREEDOM IN CHRIST TOGETHER

CHARLES MYLANDER

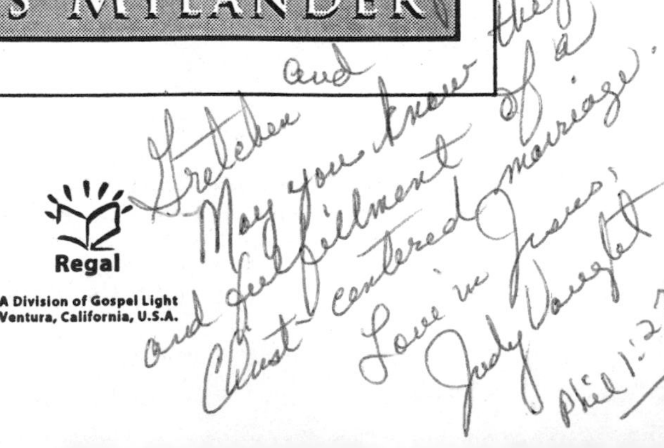

Regal
A Division of Gospel Light
Ventura, California, U.S.A.

Regal Books
A Division of Gospel Light
Ventura, California, U.S.A.
Printed in U.S.A.

Regal Books is a ministry of Gospel Light, an evangelical Christian publisher dedicated to serving the local church. We believe God's vision for Gospel Light is to provide church leaders with biblical, user-friendly materials that will help them evangelize, disciple and minister to children, youth and families.

It is our prayer that this Regal book will help you discover biblical truth for your own life and help you meet the needs of others. May God richly bless you.

For a free catalog of resources from Regal Books/Gospel Light please contact your Christian supplier or call 1-800-4-GOSPEL.

Cover design by Barbara LeVan Fisher
Interior design by Britt Rocchio
Edited by Virginia Woodard

Library of Congress Cataloging-in-Publication Data
Anderson, Neil T., 1942-
The Christ-centered marriage / Neil T. Anderson and Charles Mylander.
p. cm.
Includes bibliographical references.
ISBN 0-8307-1871-0 (trade)
1. Married people—Religious life. 2. Marriage—Religious aspects—Christianity. I. Mylander, Charles. II. Title.
BV4596.M3A55 1996 96-8783
248.8'44—dc20 CIP

6 7 8 9 10 11 12 13 14 / 03 02 01 00 99 98

Contents

Introduction

A Cultural Revolution

The Nifty Fifties

"Boys, get up," Mom called from downstairs.

My brother and I (Neil) didn't want to leave our warm bed. It was cold in the upstairs loft we shared as a bedroom in that old farmhouse in Minnesota. The floor was like ice, and you could scrape frost off the inside walls in the winter because the second floor had no heat. We would wait until the last minute (before Dad said something), then grab our clothes and race downstairs. We dressed in front of the register that poured heat into the first floor from a wood-burning furnace in the basement. Mom always got up at five in the morning to start the fire. Chores had to be done before we ate breakfast. Then we walked our quarter-mile lane to catch the school bus that took us to school in our little country town.

I have great memories of my childhood. Our social life was centered around church, 4-H, school and family gatherings. We didn't have a perfect family—nobody does—but we stayed together. The decade of the '50s was a good time to be raised. Our parents were survivors of the Great Depression and World War II. Patriotism was at an all-time high. The Fourth of July, Memorial Day and Veterans Day were community celebrations. When the National Guard shot off their rifles, a bunch of us boys would race to get the spent cartridges. Families that prayed together stayed together. Only one in a thousand church-going families experienced a divorce.

The Shocking Sixties

Then came the '60s. Our country was pulled into a war that was all wrong. At the same time, the problem of racial segregation could no longer be ignored. Something had to be done, but there were no popular answers. Some of our boys went to Canada to avoid the draft. Many of our neighbors moved to the suburbs to avoid busing their children. Our country was being torn apart. Neighbors turned against neighbors, and fathers against sons. The use of illegal drugs spread among our college and high school campuses, and the era of "free sex" was ushered in. The Beatles claimed they were more popular than Jesus was.

The silent victim of this cultural revolution was the family. The public debate was about war, racism, teenage rebellion, sex, drugs and music. The devastating effect on the family wouldn't be detected until later. The Church and our Christian schools were caught off guard. We offered family-oriented ministries because our churches were filled with families. Churches focused their ministries on the "married only once" family in which the father worked and the mother stayed home to raise their children.

Family Pressures Changed

Today, that model comprises less than 7 percent of the population in an average church. It wasn't as difficult to raise good families in the '50s, because society basically supported traditional family values. "Father Knows Best," "Ozzie and Harriet" and "Leave It to Beaver" were popular television programs. Foul language and explicit sex were forbidden on television and in the movie theaters.

Pastoral counseling in our seminaries was taught by godly pastors who knew how to pray and apply the Word of God. Few if any classes were taught about marriage or emphasized the need for premarital counseling. The practical application of ministry focused on preaching, teaching, evangelizing and discipling. We finally realized we had to do something to save our families. Social pressure was ripping them apart.

The Catholic church began "Marriage Encounter," and the process spread to Protestant denominations. Evangelical seminaries started offering classes about the family, marriage and premarital counseling, parenting and divorce recovery. I remember people debating whether we should offer a class about divorce recovery or single parenting.

Some argued, "Isn't that giving permission for those who are considering divorce, like putting a stamp of approval on it?" Others said, "It is our Christian duty to forgive and help these people. What's done is done."

Programs, retreats, books, tapes, graduate-degree programs about marriage, family and child (MFC) counseling began throughout the country. Godly pastors were replaced in our pastoral counseling classes by clinical psychologists, all of whom received their doctoral degrees from secular schools because no Christian schools offered doctoral degrees in psychology in those days. Many of these counselors were and are godly people concerned for the family and committed to helping them become healthy and functional again. On the other hand, many concerned Christians are troubled by the influence of secular psychology on the Church, as well as the demise of evangelism and discipleship.

Never in the history of the Church has such a concerted effort been exerted to save the family. The most popular radio ministry today is Focus on the Family: James Dobson is having an amazing influence on the Christian family. Gary Smalley's series about marriage and communication, which was made popular through his "infomercials," is the best-selling video series of all time—secular or sacred. Books and tapes about marriage and family are consistently the best-sellers. Why? Because strengthening the family is the greatest felt need of our time.

I'm thankful for all this concerted effort to help troubled marriages and families, and I want to acknowledge the incredible contribution these Christian authors and speakers—particularly my friend Norm Wright—have made. Radio hosts and family advocates such as John Neider and Dennis Rainey are providing tremendous information for the Body of Christ. Many more have been called by God to speak and minister to families.

In all honesty, however, we need to ask a hard question:

Generally speaking, how are we doing? Has the family as a whole become stronger in the United States? Have our marriages become better? Certainly we can point to the cultural war as a factor, but have we missed something? We have searched the Word of God to find the answers for how a husband should love his wife, how a wife should be submissive to her husband, how a mother should mother, how a father should father and how together they should raise their children. Consequently, we have available some excellent biblical instruction for the following family disciplines that relate to God, society, marriage and parenting:

Marriage and Family Disciplines

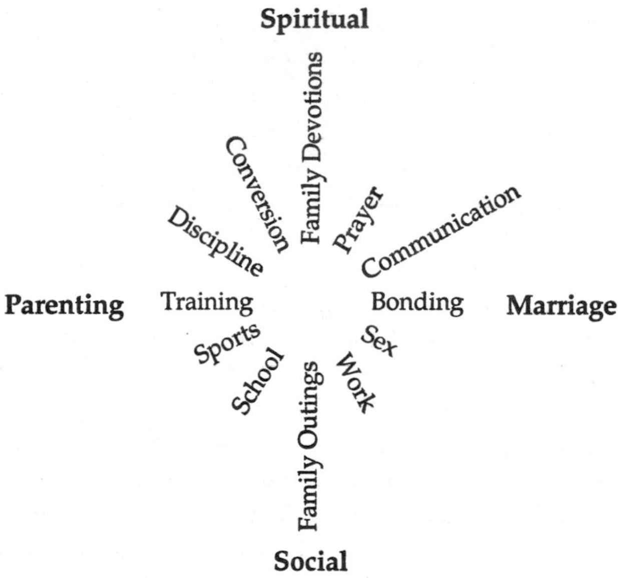

DIAGRAM I.1

Each discipline is like a spoke that forms an important Christian family wheel. How did we learn these disciplines? Our concordances directed us to some wonderful Old Testament passages, and to the second half of Paul's Epistles. There we received biblical instructions for the father, mother, parents and children. I have presented messages, or conducted seminars, workshops or conferences about every one of those spokes in the diagram.

When you read or listen to what I or any other committed Christian leader has to say about these issues, ask the following: Are they telling the truth? Are they biblically correct? In most cases I'm sure we are. Some of us, including Chuck and myself, go out of our way to make sure that what we are saying is biblically accurate.

However, something can be right but not complete. Someone could biblically and accurately communicate all that God has to say about parenting, marriage and all the related disciplines, and yet our best efforts to respond may leave us far short of what God desires for our marriages. What's wrong then? Better yet, what's missing?

In too many cases, the result is a subtle form of Christian behaviorism that sounds like this: "You shouldn't do that. Here is a better way to do it."

In response, we huff and puff our way into burnout. We may not be legalists in a pharisaic sense, but in too many cases, all we have done is gone from negative legalism (don't do this and don't do that) to positive legalism (do this and do this and do this and do this, ad nauseam). Nowhere is this more likely to occur than in marriage counseling:

> Mr. Jones, you shouldn't treat your wife that way. You are supposed to love your wife as Christ loved the Church. And Mrs. Jones, if you would just show your husband a little respect, maybe he would pay more attention to you. Do you suppose you both could do that for each other? Good! Now let's meet again next week at this same time and see how you are doing.

That may be good advice, and in the right circumstances appropriate, but in many cases it would have little or no effect. Why? Because we are just trying to force two people to behave a certain way without resolving the deeper inner conflicts most people have. It is not that most Christians don't want to behave appropriately. In many cases they can't because of unresolved internal conflicts. It would be similar to having a star quarterback play in the Super Bowl when he has the flu and a 103 degree fever. Believe me, he would love to play and win the game. People don't like to lose or fail on the most important assignment in their lives.

RESOLVING CONFLICTS

A month after one of my "Living Free in Christ" conferences, a friend called me. She had a friend who also attended my conference. Prior to the conference, this lady would call my friend three times a week for prayer. She had other prayer

---

A CHRISTIAN MARRIAGE IS A SPIRITUAL UNION WITH GOD THAT IS INTENDED TO BE A VISIBLE EXPRESSION OF THE RELATIONSHIP THAT GOD HAS WITH THE CHURCH, WHICH IS THE BRIDE OF CHRIST.

---

partners whom she called regularly for encouragement and counsel. In addition, she was seeing a Christian counselor at least once a week. This network of Christian support was keeping her going.

During the conference she realized she was trusting and relying on everyone but God. She decided not to call any of her friends and not to see her counselor for a month. Instead she memorized a list of Scripture references showing who she was in Christ, and decided to depend upon Him. A month later, my friend said she could hardly recognize this woman. She was a different person because she had resolved her personal and spiritual conflicts and was now living free in Christ.

Don't get me wrong. We all need friends and family to support us, and I am certainly not against good Christian counsel. Good Christian friends and counselors, however, will not take the place of Christ in your life. Friends can and should encourage us in our faith and help us live a life that is dependent upon our heavenly Father. What is missing in the previous diagram, however, is the life of Christ. The title and diagram should look like this:

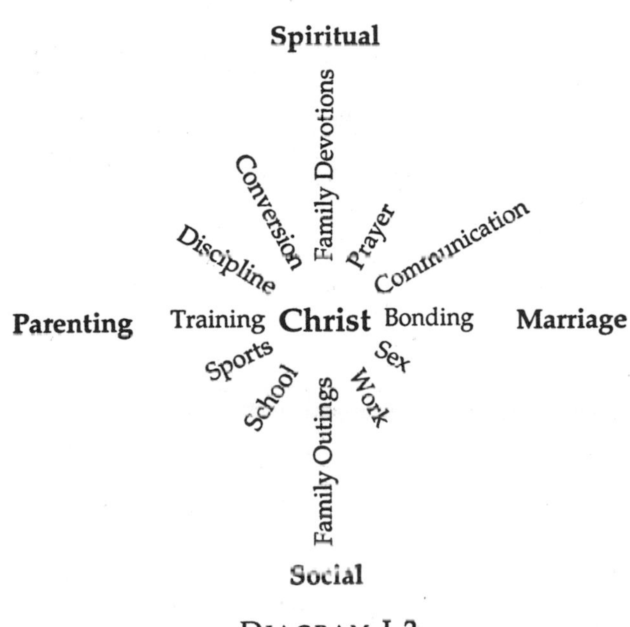

DIAGRAM I.2

MAINTAINING A CHRISTIAN MARRIAGE

We have a tendency to live according to the law or godly principles that expect us to respond in obedience. Every born-again Christian is alive in Christ and should—in the power of the Holy Spirit—live by faith according to what God says is true. Then we will not carry out the desires of the flesh (see Gal. 5:16-18). A Christian marriage is a spiritual union with God that is intended to be a visible expression of the relationship that God has with the Church, which is the Bride of Christ. They are so intertwined that Paul switches from one to the other in Ephesians 5:25-27:

> Husbands, love your wives, just as Christ loved the church and gave himself up for her to make her holy, cleansing her by the washing with water through the word, and to present her to himself as a radiant church, without stain or wrinkle or any other blemish, but holy and blameless. In this same way, husbands ought to love their wives as their own bodies.

TO MAINTAIN A CHRISTIAN MARRIAGE WE HAVE TO BECOME ONE IN CHRIST.

We cannot do in the flesh what God by His power can do through us. What makes this so subtle is that all the spokes in the wheel may be totally biblical and necessary. We will add some of our own spokes in this book, but our real purpose is to connect you and your spouse to the hub of the wheel, which is Christ, so that His life will flow through you. Surely we want people to behave according to God's standards, but they never will if they are trying to live by godly principles in their own strength.

Let's look at a parallel concept. John 15:8 says, "This is to my Father's glory, that you bear much fruit, showing yourselves to be my disciples." Our tendency is to read that passage and conclude that we have to bear fruit. We don't! We have to abide in Christ.

Bearing fruit is the evidence that we are abiding in Christ. "I am the vine; you are the branches. If a man remains [abides] in me and I in him, he will bear much fruit; apart from me you can do nothing" (John 15:5). We try to bear fruit without abiding in Christ, and we can't.

Without Christ we are not simply handicapped. Without Christ we are not simply limited in what we can do. Without Christ we can do nothing! We are incomplete without Him, and so are our marriages. To maintain a Christian marriage we have to become one in Christ. Just saying that won't change anything. It has to be individually appropriated through repentance and faith.

Here is our presupposition for this book: *If you will enter into the first half of Paul's Epistles, you will do the second half instinctively.* The response seen in the second half will become the natural or supernatural thing to do. The first half of Paul's Epistles establish us in Christ. If people are established free in Christ first, they will grow and their marriages will come together. We want people to behave like Christians, but many don't have a clue about who they are in Christ. We want husbands to act like husbands when they are not free in Christ, and the same for wives.

I'm tempted to say to many struggling couples, "Forget your marriage; you are so torn up on the inside that you probably couldn't get along with your dog right now. But if you are willing to resolve your personal and spiritual conflicts first and get radically right with God, then there is great hope for your marriage."

A Troubled Marriage

A pastor asked if I (Neil) would spend time with a couple on his staff. I was the last resort. If I couldn't help them, they would become divorced. Talk about hopeless! They were like two armadillos heading in opposite directions with their tails tied together. Both were defensive against the other person's propensity to claw.

Finally I told the couple to forget about their marriage. In no way would any words of advice from me change anything for them. So I asked the wife if she had a place to go for a couple of weeks. She said she did. I gave her a set of tapes that would help her realize who she was in Christ and how she could resolve the bitterness and pain she was experiencing. I encouraged the husband to do the same at home. Then I asked them not to work through the material for the purpose of saving their marriage, but rather for the purpose of finding their freedom in Christ. They said they would.

I didn't see or hear from the couple for three years. Then

one Sunday I went to a restaurant after church with my family. There was the husband with his three children, but no wife. The absence of his wife was painfully obvious. Then to my surprise, she came in and sat with her husband and children. She had been parking the car. After recognizing me, they shared what they had done. Both had found their freedom in Christ and agreed that now they could resolve their differences.

THE PURPOSE OF THIS BOOK

I have had the privilege of helping thousands find their freedom in Christ and, in many cases, it saved their marriages. But I have also discovered, as has Chuck, that issues still need to be resolved as a couple. That is what this book is all about: setting your marriage free in Christ. We will start with God's perfect design for Adam and Eve, and then explain how the Fall and individual sin affects the marriage and family. Then we will show Christ's plan to restore a fallen humanity and the institution of marriage. We will discuss male and female differences, conflict resolution, communication, finances, sex and finally a plan for forgiveness, resolution and restoration.

The last chapter is a step-by-step procedure for resolving your personal and spiritual conflicts. You can work through the process as a couple on your own as Chuck and I have done with our wonderful wives. Others are studying through this material in their churches and then scheduling a weekend retreat to facilitate the process.

I was reading Chuck's part in this book on an airplane when the person next to me asked if I was writing a book. I told him I was, and what it was about. He laughed and said, "I should be the one writing the book. I have a lot of experience, having been married three times." Not wanting to pursue the conversation anymore, he started to flirt with the airline attendants. He probably could write a book about how not to be married. I couldn't help but think, *What a tragedy that he never learned how to live with his spouse.*

Every married couple will experience difficulty; some run from it, others grow by it. Some couples manage their conflicts and learn to get along; others learn how to resolve their conflicts and grow together.

This is not a theory book. We have both been married many years and are now enjoying our adult children and grandchildren. We are convinced Christ can resolve the conflicts that are keeping couples from having wonderful relationships together in Christ. We are not wonderful counselors. The Lord Himself is the wonderful Counselor, and only He can set a captive free.

God loves His Church, and marriage was His idea. If you are willing to face the truth and walk in the light, your marriage can be what God wants it to be. The will of God will never lead you where the grace of God cannot enable you to be all that He wants you to be. If you are ready to put Christ back into the center of your lives and the center of your marriage and home, there is great hope for you. The Lord has an answer because He is the answer. He is the Bondage Breaker, and will help set your marriage free.

Chapter One

God's Perfect Design

The Lord God said,
"It is not good for the man to be alone.
I will make a helper suitable for him." But for Adam no suitable helper was found. So the Lord God caused the man to fall into a deep sleep; and while he was sleeping, he took one of the man's ribs and closed up the place with flesh. Then the Lord God made a woman from the rib he had taken out of the man, and he brought her to the man. The man said, "This is now bone of my bones and flesh of my flesh; she shall be called 'woman,' for she was taken out of man." For this reason a man will leave his father and mother and be united to his wife, and they will become one flesh. The man and his wife were both naked, and they felt no shame.

—GENESIS 2:18,20-25

COMPANIONSHIP—A UNIVERSAL NEED

He was a good student. His grades were above average, and his questions were on target. He came from a good family. His parents were missionaries, and he was planning to serve the Lord in the same way he had been taught. He did seem to be a little obsessed with finding the right answer, and he was rather uptight. I (Neil) remember thinking at the time that if I tiptoed up behind him and tapped him with a little hammer he would break into a thousand pieces. He was a good student, though, dedicated to the cause of Christ, motivated to do the right thing and disciplined to accomplish it.

He was also a loner. I never saw him associate with the other students. I passed it off as another example of a missionary kid who had trouble socializing with his own peer group, having been raised in another culture. Too many seminary students, too many people like him, come and go without making any lasting friends or personal connections. I always try to go out of my way to greet such people, but in all honesty, the conversations are usually trite and superficial. I had all but forgotten about him when I read in the paper that the police discovered this frightened young man cowering in a closet of a suburban home after having murdered his parents, whose bodies were found in the living room.

For too many people, life is like riding around in those bumper cars at carnivals. "Hi, how are you doing?" Bump! Bump! "Fine, thanks for asking." Bump! Bump! "Good to see you again." Bump! Bump! "Nice day, isn't it?" Bump! Bump! The little cars are our protection to keep others from getting too close to us. We keep bumping into each other superficially and then one day somebody slips off and kills his parents in utter despair and insanity. It is not good for man to be alone.

It is not good for anybody to be alone. A book may be a good companion for a season. We can have a vicarious relationship with our favorite television characters once a week, but they never talk back. A walk in the park is refreshing, but we cannot carry on a two-way conversation with a tree. We can worship creation for a while, but it will not satisfy our needs for the Creator. Sitting in a beautiful house alone will eventually lead to loneliness. Even attending a social function alone can be a lonely experience in the midst of a crowd. We all have an inner longing for some reciprocal human contact that doesn't violate our fragile existence. Those who think they don't are most needy. It is a sad commentary about humans if dogs really are our best friends!

At times we need to be alone with our thoughts, but sooner or later we need to share with somebody else what we are

---

Adam needed someone who was his equal in creation; someone who was spiritually alive and created in the image of God—someone like himself.

---

thinking, seeing, hearing or experiencing. Life was meant to be shared. One of the most basic instincts upon seeing a beautiful sunset or hearing some inspiring music is to share it with someone else. We photograph special times and places because we want to share them with someone—anyone. We may look at our old photos for a nostalgic moment alone, but they usually are viewed when friends or relatives visit.

An Eternal Need

It seemed as though Adam had it all. God formed him out of the dust of the ground and then breathed life into him. Adam was physically alive. His ability to feel, think and experience the environment around him was synchronized with his physical body. He was a living, breathing, walking and talking man created in the image of God. His soul was in union with his body. More important, he was also spiritually alive. His soul was in perfect union with God.

Adam knew who he was and why he had been created.

Adam's purpose and responsibility was to rule the rest of God's creation. God placed him in the "Garden of Eden to work it and take care of it" (Gen. 2:15). He was afforded a tremendous amount of freedom as long as he remained in a dependent relationship with his Creator. Adam seemed to have a perfect life and could have lived forever in the presence of God. He was completely accepted by his heavenly Father and had no concept of insecurity. All his deepest needs of life—identity, acceptance, security and significance—were met in creation and sustained by the presence of his heavenly Father.

All that God had created was good, but something was missing for Adam. It wasn't good for man to be alone; but he wasn't alone—God was there. That is true, but our relationship with God is not based on equality. It is based on His sovereignty and our necessity. Without Him we don't exist. He is the Creator, we are the creation. He is the Infinite, we are the finite. He is the Potter, we are the clay. Yet we are unique from all the rest of creation. God spoke and the heavens were formed, but God did not speak man into existence. He took dust and breathed His own life into it (see v. 7). This synthesis of divine breath and earthly dust is what sets us apart from the animal kingdom and describes our basic nature.

Human superiority may be why God paraded all the animals in front of Adam and had him name them. No animal form of life could fulfill Adam's need to belong. It wasn't that the giraffe was too tall, or the elephant too big or the monkey too silly. Physical compatibility was not what Adam or any man needs today. Adam needed someone who was his equal in creation; someone who was spiritually alive and created in the image of God—someone like himself.

God could reason and communicate with His own trinitarian self. Notice the inner communication within the Godhead in the creation account: "Then God said, 'Let *us* make man in *our* image, in *our* likeness'" (1:26, italics added). Although this represents the Hebrew plural of majesty, it also suggests com munion among Father, Son and Holy Spirit. The animals could interact with each other, but Adam was alone. Adam could not be mentally, emotionally and spiritually compatible without one of his own kind. So God created a suitable helpmate for him.

Like Adam, the woman was not spoken into existence as was all the rest of creation. Unlike Adam, however, she was not an independent creature taken from the dust. She was related to man in creation. God formed the woman from a part of the man. Adam knew the difference instantly and proclaimed, "This is now bone of my bones and flesh of my flesh; she shall be called 'woman,' for she was taken out of man" (2:23). The woman was not created to have an independent status from man, and no longer does man have an independent status from her. They were not created to be in competition with each other. Eve came into being by the power of God, from man, for whom she is called to be a helpmate. She is the only suitable helper for him.

Adam was drawn to Eve the moment he saw her. They saw each other as male and female, yet one flesh. They recognized both their differences and their oneness. God used their masculinity and femininity to both differentiate them and unite them. They were naked and unashamed. Sexual attraction and passion were present before the Fall. Sex was not evil, it was God's plan. The Fall only perverted what God had created to be good.

A Covenant Relationship

The Lord bestows favor and honor upon those people whose walk is blameless (see Ps. 84:11). The man is honored by the acknowledgment that the woman was created for him. The woman is honored by the acknowledgment that the man is incomplete without her. In humility, the woman acknowledges that she was made for man. In humility, the man acknowledges that he is incomplete without the woman. Both share an equal dignity, honor and worth because of their created purpose; both share a common humility and honor before God and each other. Each is necessary for the completion of the other. Both absolutely need God, and both necessarily need each other. They were created to live in an interdependent relationship with each other, and a mutually dependent relationship with God.

Relationships are the heart of life, and the relationship

between the male and the female is the earthly expression of the relationship between God and humankind. Interestingly, the first comment in Scripture about the creation of Adam and Eve relates to our sexuality: "Male and female he created them" (Gen. 1:27). Even our sexuality relates us to the image of God. Because adultery and fornication are forbidden, marriage represents the essence of life, which is relationship. It has its source in the eternal fellowship of the triune God: Father, Son and Holy Spirit.

Many close and wonderful relationships are described in Scripture, such as that between Jonathan and David. But we can experience only two covenant relationships in this life. Both are based on God's Word and rooted in His character. The first and foremost is our covenant relationship with God. The second is the marriage between a man and a woman. All other meaningful relationships are contractual or mutually convenient. Two people can have a covenant relationship with God, and consequently have fellowship or spiritual kinship one with the other. They don't have covenant relationship with each other, however, unless they are married to each other.

Contracts are usually drafted to protect all parties involved in case any of them default or fail to fulfill their sides of the bargain. They can be written contracts, which are legally binding, or verbal agreements, which are sealed with a handshake. In either case, the innocent parties can seek legal action for a breach of contract, or simply be no longer obligated to fulfill their sides of the agreement should the others not fulfill theirs. Contracts ensure that all involved fulfill their word, and provide an escape clause should the contract be broken.

Covenants are promises to fulfill our own word irrespective of the other person, and are made to last regardless of the circumstances. Contracts provide for natural disasters or human failures that are beyond the right or ability of either party to control. Covenants don't make such provisions because honoring them is not dependent upon things we have neither the right nor the ability to control. I am eternally grateful that the covenant relationship I have with God is not based on whether I can perfectly keep my end of the bargain. He will keep His word whether I do or not.

Wedding vows are a covenant commitment to stay faithful as a husband or wife, for better or for worse, for richer or for poorer, in sickness and in health, until death separates the two. I made a covenant commitment to my wife, which I intend to keep whether my wife does or not. She did the same. Nothing, nor anyone other than ourselves on planet Earth, can keep us from being the husband and wife God created us to be.

At some point in church history, the tradition of exchanging rings was inaugurated. Rings were a visible sign that sealed the covenant. They were to be publicly worn so that others could see these two people had become one in Christ and were not available for anyone else. The rings would also serve as a reminder to the couple of the vows they made publicly.

A covenant relationship is unique from all others not just because it is based on love, but because it is a lifelong commitment. We are commanded to love all humankind. Marriage is based on commitment, but what makes a marriage work is love. The following paragraphs were written by Michael P. Horban:

Marriage License—A Learner's Permit

It's a wise groom who has to be dragged to the altar. He knows what love is. It's death! If the lovers don't know this, they're headed for trouble. Never will you have your way again. You can't be happy if the other person isn't. No matter who wins the argument, you lose. Always. The sooner you learn this, the better off you'll be.

Love is an exercise in frustration. You leave the window up when you want it down. You watch someone else's favorite television program. You kiss when you have a headache. You turn the music down when you like it loud. You learn to be patient without sighing or sulking.

Love is doing things for the other person. In

> marriage two become one. But the one isn't you. It's the other person. You love this person more than you love yourself. This means that you love this person as she or he is. We should ask ourselves frankly what that impulse is that makes us want to redesign the other person. It isn't love. We want the other person to be normal, like us! But is that loving the other person or ourselves?
>
> Love brings out the best in people. They can be themselves without artificiality. People who know they're loved glow with beauty and charm. Let this person talk. Create the assurance that any idea, any suggestion, any feeling can be expressed and will be respected. Allow the other person to star once in a while. A wife's joke doesn't have to be topped. Don't correct your husband in the middle of his story. Cultivate kind ways of speaking. It can be as simple as asking them instead of telling them what to do.
>
> Don't take yourself too seriously. Married life is full of crazy mirrors to see ourselves—how stubborn, how immature we really are. You may be waiting for your wife to finish because you never lifted a finger to help her.
>
> Love is funny. Its growth doesn't depend on what someone does for you. It's in proportion to what you do for him or her. The country is swarming with people who have never learned this. So are divorce courts.[1]

All other relationships are intended for mutual convenience, such as friends, roommates, coworkers and neighbors. These relationships are important, too, and in many ways necessary for life; no man is an island. They are not covenant relationships, though, and many disappointments come when we begin to live as if they are. We develop expectations from others that we have no right to assume. Some people can be deeply hurt when a roommate moves out, or a friend starts to drift away because of other interests. Engagements can be broken, but marriage is supposed to be for life once the vows are said.

Our children are also born to leave. The psalmist said, "Your wife will be like a fruitful vine within your house; your sons will be like olive shoots around your table. Thus is the man blessed who fears the Lord" (Ps. 128:3,4). A major difference exists between a vine and an olive shoot. A vine is connected to some other form of life and cannot operate independently of it. An olive shoot is not; it is similar to a potted plant. It was created separately and intended to be transplanted some day. The child is not a part of the mother's body in the womb, although it is carried and nurtured by the mother.

Convenience relationships are similar to attaching two pieces of paper with a paper clip. They can be easily separated by being careful, and will leave little imprint on each other. In attempting to tear them apart without removing the paper clip, however, some damage will occur. Most surface relationships are similar to Post-it Notes: They stick together for a short time and no damage is done when they separate. Very little imprint remains on either of them.

In contractual relationships, the two pieces are stapled together. Both pieces are free to do their own thing except where they are stapled together. Damage is done when one is torn from the other, although the individual content of each page is left intact.

In covenant relationships, the pages are glued or bonded together. The two have become one. Lasting damage will be done to both if they are separated. "For this reason a man will leave his father and mother and be united to his wife, and they will become one flesh. The man and his wife were both naked, and they felt no shame" (Gen. 2:24,25).

Criteria for a Successful Marriage

Most conservative scholars credit Moses for writing the first five books of the Old Testament. In Genesis 2:24,25, Moses both narrates and instructs. Adam and Eve did not have parents to leave, but they were naked and unashamed. Marriages would be a lot easier if neither spouse had any ancestral baggage to bring into the marriage, and it would be a piece of cake if neither had sinned.

The following points reveal three essential criteria for a successful marriage:

- First, both the husband and wife need to leave Mom and Dad—physically, emotionally, mentally, spiritually and financially.
- Second, they need to bond together in such a way that they become one.
- Third, they need to have no unresolved issues between themselves and God, so that intimacy and transparency are the norm for their relationship.

Let's briefly look at these three criteria, which will be further explained throughout the remainder of this book.

Leaving Mom and Dad

It does not take long for newly married couples to realize they did not marry a single person having no ancestral heritage. They usually become painfully aware of this during the engagement period. Some probably wonder, *Can't I just have this wonderful person without the family and all their problems? I can handle the parents, but do I have to accept that brother and weird uncle?*

Since Adam and Eve, nobody marries a new creation without ancestral or cultural baggage. We marry into three or four generations of family heritage, including all the accompanying customs, habits and patterns of doing things. Some family traditions can be healthy, others are destructive. The cycles of abuse that pass from one generation to another are some of the most attested social phenomena of our times.

In what ways have you not left your mom and dad, and what patterns of behavior have you brought into your marriage that are not productive for a stable relationship? Separation from parents and from destructive behavior patterns comprise the first two issues we attempt to resolve in setting a marriage free. We cannot change our family heritage or fix the past, but we can all be free from the past by the grace of God. Please keep in mind, this is not a license to dishonor our parents or an admonition to cut off all family ties.

Listen to the interchange between Jesus as an adult and His mother, Mary, in a public setting:

> And on the third day there was a wedding in Cana of Galilee, and the mother of Jesus was there; and Jesus also was invited, and His disciples, to the wedding. And when the wine gave out, the mother of Jesus said to Him, "They have no wine." And Jesus said to her, "Woman, what do I have to do with you? My hour has not yet come." His mother said to the servants, "Whatever He says to you, do it" (John 2:1-5, *NASB*).

Jesus was not being impertinent. "Woman" was a term of respectful address, but He was also saying to His mother that He was no longer subject to her, but rather to His heavenly Father. She immediately stepped back and told the servants to obey Jesus. If you think for a moment that Jesus no longer respected or cared for His mother, then listen to His words on the Cross:

> When Jesus saw his mother there, and the disciple whom he loved standing nearby, he said to his mother, "Dear woman, here is your son," and to the disciple, "Here is your mother." From that time on, this disciple took her into his home (John 19:26,27).

What a wonderful model! Jesus showed respect and concern for His mother, and even provided for Mary after His departure by asking John to look after her. Our role as parents is not to raise good little children who will do our bidding as long as we can control them. It is our responsibility to raise responsible adults who will learn to do the will of God. Remember, they are potted plants, not vines.

I have talked to older adults who are still trying to earn the approval of their parents. Many young adults are financially dependent upon their parents. Some parents use money as a way of controlling their adult children. I talked with a middle-aged lady who made decisions about her home and family based on whether she thought her mother would approve. The mother was dangling a sizable estate over her head. The mother had already disinherited one of her children whom she could not control or manipulate.

We are usurping God's place in our adult children's lives when we try to control and manipulate them with conditional love and acceptance, threaten them with disinheritance or insist they honor us. Parents need to repent of such attempts at controlling their children, and their children need to renounce it as a sin. Consider the following questions:

1. Does the approval of relatives (or any mortal) mean more to you than the approval of God?
2. Are you still trying to live up to the expectations of your parents or siblings?
3. Is your relationship with God the most important relationship in your life?
4. Is your relationship with your spouse the second most important relationship in your life?
5. Would you be willing to sever any other relationship that would threaten your relationship with God or your spouse, even if it included members of your immediate family?
6. In what ways have you not left your mother and father:
   Physically?
   Spiritually?
   Mentally?
   Emotionally?
   Financially?

A young wife and mother of two children wept openly as she considered the need to forgive her mother. "I can choose to forgive her now, but what do I do this Sunday when I go over to her house and she verbally abuses me all over again?" I encouraged her to put a stop to that. "But aren't I supposed to honor my mother?" she asked.

How would it honor her mother to allow her to systematically destroy her daughter's present marriage and family by her verbal abuse? If the daughter does not free herself from such abuse and set scriptural boundaries to protect herself and her family from further damage, she will likely do the same to her children and grandchildren. The primary thrust of honoring mother and father in the Old Testament was to financially look after them in their old age (see Exod. 20:12; Deut. 5:16).

Both Chuck and I are parents and we love our adult children. We and our wives support them in all that God leads them to do, but we have relinquished all control of them. They are no longer our children, they are children of God. We want them to have self-control, which comes from abiding in Christ. We will lend physical, spiritual, mental, emotional, as well as financial, support—when it is appropriate or possible—by the grace of God.

Our prayers are that we will never do anything that would supplant God's place in their lives. They will honor us most by becoming the people God wants them to be. We have done the best we could to raise children who would leave us and cleave to someone else. We gave away our potted plants. Someday they will do the same. We were not perfect parents; they will undoubtedly have to renounce some less than perfect habits they picked up from us.

The Bible does not elaborate on what it means to leave mother and father. Physically leaving mother and father in nomadic tribes may be inadvisable for the sake of survival and safety. Financial separation may not be possible when it comes to family owned businesses. However, to protect the covenant relationship of marriage, contractual agreements should be made (written or verbal) to ensure that the newly married couple have their own tent (or space) and financial freedom. The Holy Spirit will convict one or both spouses when there is an unholy attachment to a parent that is keeping them from having a oneness in Christ.

Becoming One

The second essential ingredient for a successful marriage is oneness. Bonding is not a given. You can have a house full of Christians and not have a Christian home. Two people can live together and be legally married according to the government, but they are just two people living together. Somehow the

Lord intends that the two become one. Jesus provides the best commentary about this important issue in Mark 10:7-9:

> For this reason a man will leave his father and mother and be united to his wife, and the two will become one flesh. So they are no longer two, but one. Therefore what God has joined together, let man not separate.

This mystical union between a man and a woman is both spiritual and physical. Adam and Eve were to be fruitful and multiply (see Gen. 1:28). Becoming one flesh certainly includes the idea of a sexual union, which may result in a child. The two become one in procreation.

Sexual union can also be abused. Paul teaches that a man can join himself to a harlot and become one flesh (see 1 Cor. 6:16). They are not married, however; not in the eyes of God. Jesus said, "What God has joined together" (Matt. 19:6). Adam and Eve were spiritually alive. Their souls were in union with God. In marriage they were joined by God.

Most Christian ministries understand the threefold process of marrying as leaving, cleaving and becoming one flesh. The marriage must also be in accordance with the laws of the land, because all authority has been established by God. It includes a public declaration in front of witnesses to take each other as husband and wife. Then they exchange vows, which establishes the marriage as a covenant relationship. Finally, they consummate their marriage by becoming one flesh.

The glue that holds the two together is the relationship that each spouse has with God. The strongest architectural design is an equilateral triangle (i.e., all three sides are equal):

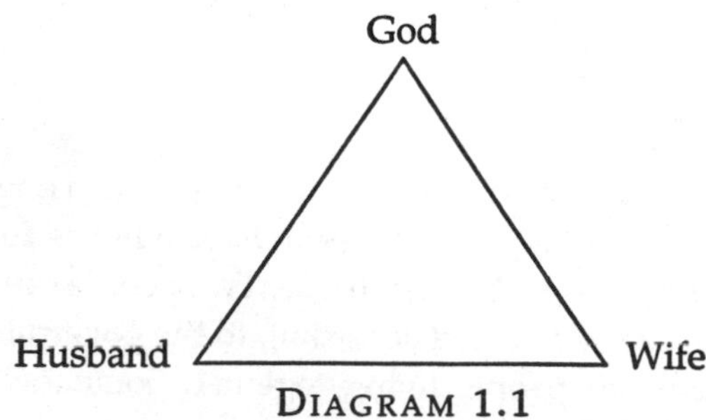

DIAGRAM 1.1

Should either side of the triangle be broken or weakened, it dramatically affects the strength of the marriage. That is why we are not to be unequally yoked.

> Do not be yoked together with unbelievers. For what do righteousness and wickedness have in common? Or what fellowship can light have with darkness? What harmony is there between Christ and Belial? What does a believer have in common with an unbeliever? (2 Cor. 6:14,15).

BONDING TAKES PLACE BETWEEN A MAN AND A WOMAN WHEN THERE IS A TOTAL COMMITMENT OF BODY, SOUL AND SPIRIT TO EACH OTHER WITHOUT RESERVATION.

Bonding takes place between a man and a woman when there is a total commitment of body, soul and spirit to each other without reservation. Adam and Eve bonded in the presence of God. Together they were naked and unashamed. There were no dirty parts of their bodies, and a sexual relationship between a husband and a wife was not separated from an intimate relationship with God. There was no sin, nothing to hide, therefore no reason to cover up. They were naked and unashamed! That was God's perfect creation and design for marriage. Such was the case for Adam and Eve, but such is not our case.

Developing Intimacy

The Fall of humankind clipped two sides of the triangle. Sin separated us from God. A man and a woman were left alone to relate to one another without God. Only in Christ can we be restored, and only then can our marriages become what God intended them to be.

Before we look at the consequences of the Fall and what must happen for our marriages to be free in Christ, let me ask you a question: *Would you be willing to work toward intimacy and transparency before God and your spouse?* We are called to walk in the light (see 1 John 1:7) and to speak the truth in love (see Eph. 4:15). If that is not possible between you and your spouse, what we say in this book will be of little consequence to you.

IN CONCLUSION

Chances are that some may not be willing to proceed from here if those are the criteria; consequently, we have learned to help people be free in Christ individually first. Hundreds of people have spoken to me about their marriages at my conferences about living free in Christ. Many of them have tried marriage counseling and have had little success. After listening to them, my advice is always the same. "Forget about your marriage for this week; come to counseling for yourself. Once you have resolved your own personal and spiritual conflicts in Christ, then the two of you will be able to work through the process of setting your marriage free."

We have included the personal "Steps to Freedom in Christ" in appendix A. From experience, we have learned that about 85 percent can work through the individual Steps on their own. The chances of gaining your freedom in Christ and maintaining it will be greatly enhanced if you read my books *Victory over the Darkness* (Regal Books) and *The Bondage Breaker* (Harvest House). The other 15 percent need the help of a trained encourager. That process is explained in my book *Helping Others Find Freedom in Christ* (Regal Books).

I heard an old godly pastor refer to a time when he was newly married. He had sown some wild oats and done other things of which he was ashamed. He had never told his wife and, frankly, he was ashamed to tell her now. He didn't want anything to come between them, though, and he always feared she would find out about some of his escapades from another source. So one day he wrote down all those things he had done.

For whatever reason, he lacked the courage to just confess it to his wife face to face. So he asked her to sit and listen while he read all that he had written. Without looking up, he asked her what she thought.

"Charlie," she said, "there isn't anything you could share with me that, just by having you share it, wouldn't cause me to love you more."

I love that last line. Would you be that kind of spouse—one who is willing to share, one who is willing to forgive and accept the other person, "warts and all"? If that is your heart's desire, then close this chapter with the following prayer:

> *Dear heavenly Father, I acknowledge You as the Lord of my life. Thank You for my own salvation. I deserved eternal damnation and You gave me eternal life. I want to be merciful as You have been merciful to me, and to forgive as You have forgiven me. Now I ask You to give me the grace to accept my spouse in the same way that You have accepted me. Give me the courage to speak the truth and the grace to do it in love. I desire to have an intimate and transparent relationship with You and my spouse. I commit myself to be the husband/wife that You created me to be. I desire our marriage to be one in Christ, an indissoluble union in which we are free from our pasts. Lead us into the truth that will set us free in Christ. In Jesus' precious name I pray.*

Note

1. Michael P. Horban, *The Pentecostal Evangel*, no. 3099 (September 30, 1973).

CHAPTER TWO

The Curse of the Fall

So the Lord God said to the serpent, "Because you have done this, Cursed are you above all the livestock and all the wild animals! You will crawl on your belly and you will eat dust all the days of your life. And I will put enmity between you and the woman, and between your offspring and hers; he will crush your head, and you will strike his heel." To the woman he said, "I will greatly increase your pains in childbearing; with pain you will give birth to children. Your desire will be for your husband, and he will rule over you." To Adam he said, "Because you listened to your wife and ate from the tree about which I commanded you, 'You must not eat of it,' Cursed is the ground because of you; through painful toil you will eat of it all the days of your life. It will produce thorns and thistles for you, and you will eat the plants of the field. By the sweat of your brow you will eat your food until you return to the ground, since from it you were taken; for dust you are and to dust you will return."

—GENESIS 3:14-19

- If you want to see what your fiancée will look like in 20 years, just look at her mother.
- Like father, like son.
- He's a chip off the old block.
- What can you expect from him, given who his parents are?
- He's the spittin' image of his old man.

I (Neil) grew up with those clichés. Is there any truth to them? Are we destined to be like our parents?

HEREDITY OR ENVIRONMENT?

"Not me! No way am I going to be like my old man." How often I have heard that sentiment expressed. The tragedy of that statement is that the "old man" is still the one determining who he is or is not going to be. The son's guiding principle is, *I'm not going to be like him.* That kind of thinking alone will set up most people for failure.

To what degree are we products of our pasts? Are we just biological products of our parents? Have our personalities and habits been totally shaped by our upbringing? Educators have asked these questions for centuries. The secular debate is usually about the prominence played by the environment, as opposed to genetics. Our hormones and genetic code dictate certain physical features and predispose us to certain strengths and weaknesses.

On the other hand, nobody questions that the homes in which we were raised, the schools we attended and the communities in which we played all affected how we think and the ways we developed. Chances are we will discipline our children in the same ways we were disciplined, and relate to our spouses in the same ways our mothers and fathers related to each other. They were the only models we had during our early development. Unless we make concentrated efforts to reprogram our minds and retrain our habits, we will bring into our marriages all that we have been taught in the past.

Are our struggles only confined to the less-than-perfect worlds in which we were raised and the fleshly lusts of our fallen natures? Do we not also have to contend with the devil? Don't we inherit spiritual bents toward certain sins?

For instance, Abraham lied about his wife to save his own neck. He told the Egyptians that she was his sister (see Gen. 12:10-20). His son Isaac did exactly the same thing (see 26:7). Isaac's son Jacob lied about everything, and 10 of his sons lied about selling Joseph into slavery. Jacob's son, Joseph, however, was given three major opportunities to save himself by lying, but he would not. How do we explain all that? Coincidence? Modeling? I doubt it was the latter, because Isaac wasn't around when his father lied.

Did Abraham teach Isaac to lie about his wife? I seriously doubt that Abraham said to Isaac, "Listen, son, if your life is ever threatened because others lust after your wife, just tell them she is your sister. I tried it once. It turned out to be a bad decision, but maybe it will work for you."

A well-known pastor committed adultery a few years ago. It was a devastating experience for him, his church, his marriage, his family and the thousands who had looked to him as their spiritual leader. Not too many knew, however, that his father was a pastor who had committed adultery and left the ministry. His older brother also was a pastor who had committed adultery and left the ministry. How do we explain that? Bad genes? I would suspect that this gifted pastor at some time would have said, "That is never going to happen to me!" But it did.

In what ways are we products of our pasts, and how have the sins of our ancestors affected us and our marriages? Struggling with these theological issues will cause this chapter to be difficult to read for some, but please bear with us. We must biblically understand the problem to realize that Christ is the answer. We will reveal from God's Word the cosmic spiritual battle, the importance of ancestral bloodlines, how iniquities are passed on from one generation to another and what to do about them.

EFFECTS OF THE FALL

The first sin, and its domino effect throughout the generations, began with Adam and Eve. The Lord commanded them not to eat from the tree of the knowledge of good and evil (see Gen. 2:17). They were instructed that they would die if they did. Satan was not planning to silently watch God's plan of creation remain uncontested, so he questioned and twisted the Word of God and tempted Eve (see 3:1-6) through the same

ALL THE PERSONAL ATTRIBUTES INHERENT IN CREATION (SPIRITUAL LIFE, IDENTITY, ACCEPTANCE, SECURITY, SIGNIFICANCE) WERE GONE, AND EACH BECAME A GLARING NEED.

three channels that exist today: "The lust of the flesh, and the lust of the eyes, and the boastful pride of life" (1 John 2:16, *NASB*). Deceived by the craftiness of Satan, Adam and Eve defied God; thus they declared their own independence—and they died.

Adam and Eve did not die physically; they died spiritually, although eventually physical death would also be a consequence of sin (see Rom. 5:12). The effect, however, was immediate. All the personal attributes inherent in creation (spiritual life, identity, acceptance, security, significance) were gone, and each became a glaring need. Adam's self-perception became one of shame and guilt. In response, he covered his nakedness and hid from God. The Lord immediately took the initiative by confronting Adam:

> "Where are you?" And he said, "I heard the sound of Thee in the garden, and I was afraid because I was naked; so I hid myself." And He said, "Who told you that you were naked? Have you eaten from the tree of which I commanded you not to eat?" And the man said, "The woman whom Thou gavest to be with me, she gave me from the tree, and I ate" (Gen. 3:9-12, *NASB*).

When Adam and Eve lost their relationship with God, they were immediately overcome with guilt and shame. Adam tried to defend himself by blaming his wife for his own choice. Fear was the first emotion expressed by fallen humanity: "I was afraid because I was naked, so I hid" (v. 10). Before the Fall, Adam was naked and unashamed; now he wanted to hide and cover up. To a certain extent we all do. It would be embarrassing to be seen naked by the public, but what we primarily fear is someone finding out who we really are and what we have done. Jesus explained why:

> Everyone who does evil hates the light, and will not come into the light for fear that his deeds will be exposed. But whoever lives by the truth comes into the light, so that it may be seen plainly that what he has done has been done through God (John 3:20,21).

Facing the truth is the first step toward freedom.

An even more devastating effect of the Fall was that Adam and Eve were darkened in their understanding, because they were excluded from the life of God (see Eph. 4:18). When Adam tried to hide from God, his actions revealed that he had lost his true understanding of God. How do you hide from an omnipresent God? The Lord did not create humankind to live independently from Him. This is most evident in the natural person's inability to understand the things of God.

> But a natural man does not accept the things of the Spirit of God; for they are foolishness to him, and he cannot understand them, because they are spiritually appraised (1 Cor. 2:14, *NASB*).

The consequences of the Fall wreaked havoc on Adam and Eve. Because they were no longer spiritually alive, they now had no choice but to find their identities and purposes for living in the natural world. Women would bear children in pain and men would work by the sweat of their brows (see Gen. 3:16-19). Even today, women have a tendency to acquire their identities and fulfill their purposes by bearing children, and men have a tendency to acquire their identities and fulfill their purposes in their work or careers. This concept has also been taught as the norm in many of our churches. When you meet a man, what is the first thing you want to know about him? And who always carries pictures of children and grandchildren?

What if a woman never gets married or never has any children? What if the man is fired or can't find a job? Do they lose their identities? Do they no longer have a purpose for being here? Finding our identities in the things we do and searching for significance in the natural world is part of the curse of the Fall.

Another issue Adam and Eve faced after the Fall was "Who should rule?" because neither now had a relationship with God. The curse pronounced upon the woman said, "Your desire will be for your husband, and he will rule over you" (v. 16). Trouble in paradise was already present, and it gets worse!

Satan had usurped the role of God's people and become the rebel holder of earthly authority. The devil tempted Jesus by showing and offering Him the kingdoms of the world if He would just bow down and worship him: "I will give you all their authority and splendor, for it has been given to me, and I can give it to anyone I want to" (Luke 4:6).

Jesus never corrected Satan's claim and referred to him as the "ruler [prince] of this world" (see John 12:31; 14:30; 16:11). Paul called him "the prince of the power of the air, the spirit that is now working in the sons of disobedience" (Eph. 2:2, *NASB*). Consequently, "the whole world is under the control of the evil one" (1 John 5:19).

God's plan of redemption was implemented immediately. The Lord cursed the snake and foretold the downfall of Satan: "I will put enmity between you and the woman, and between your offspring and hers; he will crush your head, and you will strike his heel" (Gen. 3:15). "He" (an individual from the woman's seed, namely Christ) will deal a death blow to Satan's head at the Cross, while "you" (Satan) will strike Christ's heel.

This cosmic battle is the background for the drama that unfolds in the pages of Scripture and continues into our present day. Enmity will occur between the spiritual descendants of Satan and those who are in the family of God. We are either children of God (see John 1:12) or "sons of disobedience" in whom the evil one is now working (see Eph. 2:2). We are either in the domain of darkness or the kingdom of His beloved Son (see Col. 1:13).

THE MESSIANIC LINE

The rest of the Old Testament is hardly preoccupied with marriage; in fact it is a rather shameless parade of adultery and polygamy. Nobody asks if Abraham was compatible with Sarah, or how Solomon treated his wives. The Old Testament was obsessed with the Messianic line. The burning question was, "When would the child, the seed of the woman, be born to carry on the redemptive line?" We get bored reading about the generations in Genesis 5 and 11, the long summaries in 1 Chronicles and the genealogies in the Gospels of Matthew and Luke. The main issue in these passages, however, is the perpetuation of the seed (Eve's offspring), the step-by-step and generation-by-generation movement toward the coming Messiah.

Ironically, the genealogies become irrelevant after the birth of Christ. We know the family line of Jesus in detail, but we can't give the name of the apostle Paul's mother and father. Since Christ's birth, it is no longer the first birth that is important, it is the second birth.

The Song of Solomon gives us the only picture of affectionate love in the Old Testament. Here we have the man and the woman relating to each other as lovers. It draws us back to the shameless sex and mutual affection God intended a husband and wife to have for each other. There is no mention of childbearing, or preserving the bloodline in this Song of Songs—only the uninhibited, transparent, intimate relationship between two people in love. The concept of "one flesh," so eloquently illustrated in this book of Scripture, is more than a sign, it is an expression of true marriage.

The intended bonding that takes place between a husband and wife is for pleasure as well as procreation. The romantic relationship between Solomon and the Shulamite woman reveals what God intended us to have in our marriages. The law also ensured that a new marriage was afforded ample opportunity to bond correctly:

> If a man has recently married, he must not be sent to war or have any other duty laid on him. For one year he is to be free to stay at home and bring happiness to the wife he has married (Deut. 24:5).

To redeem fallen humanity, God established a covenant relationship through which He could bring forth the Savior. So He sovereignly chose Abraham and called him into the Promised Land. The Lord told him:

> I will greatly multiply your seed as the stars of the heavens, and as the sand which is on the seashore; and your seed shall possess the gate of their enemies. And in your seed all the nations of the earth shall be blessed, because you have obeyed My voice (Gen. 22:17,18, *NASB*).

Paul points out in Galatians 3:16 that the use of the singular for seed clearly establishes Christ as the ultimate means by which the nations of the world will be blessed.

How unfortunate for the world that Abraham and Sarah could not wait for God's timing. Sarah believed she could help God keep His Word by offering her handmaiden to Abraham. The two conceived, and the world has continued ever since to live in the conflict created between the descendants of two semitic peoples: the descendants of Isaac (the Jews) and the descendants of Ishmael (the Arabs). When we take matters into our own hands instead of trusting God, tragedy always follows.

THE FIDELITY OF MARRIAGE

Not many generations passed before the descendants of Abraham found themselves in bondage to the Egyptians. So God raised up Moses to set His people free and to provide them with the Mosaic covenant and the law to govern their relationships in the Promised Land. The law required them to maintain a clear distinction between man and woman:

> A woman shall not wear man s clothing, nor shall

> a man put on a woman's clothing; for whoever does these things is an abomination to the Lord your God (Deut. 22:5, *NASB*).

Specific instructions were given to those who would go into the Promised Land. Seven nations greater and stronger than they would occupy the land, but...

> The Lord your God shall deliver them before you, and you shall defeat them, then you shall utterly destroy them. You shall make no covenant with them and show no favor to them. Furthermore, you shall not intermarry with them; you shall not give your daughters to their sons, nor shall you take their daughters for your sons. For they will turn your sons away from following Me to serve other gods; then the anger of the Lord will be kindled against you, and He will quickly destroy you (7:2-4, *NASB*).

Those who had a covenant relationship with God were not to marry those who did not, nor make any covenant with them.

The Lord gave Moses the Ten Commandments that specified holy living for the children of Israel. Of the Ten Commandments (see Exod. 20:1-17), five had direct or indirect bearing on the fidelity of the marriage relationship. The seventh commandment, "You shall not commit adultery," required that sex stay confined within marriage. To commit adultery was a sin against the marriage partner as well as against God (see Gen. 39:9).

The ninth commandment, "You shall not give false testimony," would also be violated in the case of adultery because a marriage ceremony is an oath made before God and man; it is a covenant relationship made before witnesses. An adulterer gives false testimony. He or she breaks the marriage vow and usually tries to cover up the sin by lying.

An adulterer also steals, which violates the eighth commandment. He or she takes the most precious possession that another person has. The sexual pleasure gained in a moment will be soured by the fact that something was stolen from another.

The tenth commandment says a man is not to covet his neighbor's wife, manservant or maidservant. To covet means to desire something that doesn't belong to us. Woe unto them who strive to get what they should not and cannot have! How blessed are those who are thankful and content with what God has entrusted to them.

Finally, an adulterer dishonors his mother and father, which violates the fifth commandment. Adulterers bring shame to their families, as well as pain. Weddings and funerals that bring together broken families are always painful.

Even the first commandment to have no other gods is violated by an adulterous affair because it elevates sexual pleasure above our relationship with God. God is a jealous God. He will have no other gods before Him—not the god of this world nor the god of our appetites. Nevertheless, the commandments of God are not restrictive, they are protective. God's intention was to prevent fallen humanity from sowing even more seeds of destruction and thus enlarging the realm of the kingdom of darkness.

SATANIC INTERFERENCE

As God's plan of redemption unfolded, Satan tried to prevent the seed of Abraham from coming. When God first delivered His people from bondage in Egypt, Pharaoh ordered all the sons two years old and younger to be thrown into the Nile and drowned (see Exod. 1:22). But God preserved Moses and raised him up 80 years later to set His people free. When Christ was born, Herod gave a similar order (see Matt. 2:16), but the Lord warned Joseph in a dream, so Joseph took his family to Egypt (see Matt. 2:13-15). Unable to prevent the birth of the Messiah, Satan persuaded the heart of Judas (see Luke 22:3), one of the Lord's own, to betray Him. That devious plan played right into God's hand. The grave could not hold Jesus, and His resurrection sealed forever the fate of Satan (see Heb. 2:14,15). I wonder what great deliverance God has in store for His Church as we watch the "kings" of this world slaughter the lives of the unborn children through abortion. What is Satan trying to prevent now?

Just as the redemptive plan of God began to unfold after the Fall, so did the plan of Satan:

> When men began to increase in number on the earth and daughters were born to them, the sons of God saw that the daughters of man were beautiful, and they married any of them they chose. Then the Lord said, "My Spirit will not contend with man forever, for he is mortal; his days will be a hundred and twenty years." The Nephilim were on the earth in those days—and also afterward—when the sons of God went to the daughters of men and had children by them (Gen. 6:1-4).

Who were these "sons of God"? I disagree with the view that these were human figures. For one thing, the term "sons of God" is used almost exclusively in the Old Testament to mean angels. This interpretation attempts, but fails to explain away the clearest meaning of the text. Additionally, until the mid-second century A.D., all Jewish and Christian interpreters agreed that "sons of God" in Genesis 6:1-4 were fallen angels.[1] The fact that Jude 6 and 7 describe a group of fallen angels confined because of this unique sin appears to support this interpretation. Although angels no longer procreate after their kind (see Mark 12:25), apparently they did before the judgment of the Flood. On this unique occasion they cohabited with human women to produce offspring.

> The Lord saw how great man's wickedness on the earth had become, and that every inclination of the thoughts of his heart was only evil all the time (Gen. 6:5).

I'm not sure I would have accepted this interpretation several years ago. It goes against the grain of my western education and natural world view. However, for those who believe in the virgin birth of our Lord Jesus Christ, the idea that a spirit can "know" a human is not absolutely impossible. Further, because I have counseled many people who have encountered sexual spirits, I am inclined to take this passage literally. The

Latin terms for male and female sexual spirits are *incubi* and *succubi*. Every period of history records some reference to them. Mythology is replete with these stories and images. They have caught the fancy of many artists and sculptors. They are demon spirits that visit men and women during the night and subject them to sexual depravity, lust and terrifying nightmares. It is far more common than I would ever have imagined. We don't hear about it because most fear no one would believe them, and because such occurrences are horribly disgusting and embarrassing. These encounters will never produce any offspring, but they do result in sexual bondage.

How did God respond to these cohabitations?

> Then the Lord saw that the wickedness of man was great on the earth, and that every intent of the thoughts of his heart was only evil continually (v. 5, *NASB*).

The Lord put an end to that wicked generation by bringing the Flood. If that seedline had continued, who knows what the human race would look like today. Noah and his family alone were spared. The Lord said:

> I will never again curse the ground on account of man, for the intent of man's heart is evil from his youth; and I will never again destroy every living thing, as I have done (8:21, *NASB*).

He hasn't until this day, but He did have to destroy Sodom and Gomorrah because of their incredible sexual perversions.

GODLY AND GODLESS BLOODLINES

The second of the Ten Commandments is:

> You shall not make for yourself an idol in the form of anything in heaven above or on the earth beneath or in the waters below. You shall not bow down to them or worship them; for I, the Lord

> your God, am a jealous God, punishing the children for the sin of the fathers to the third and fourth generation of those who hate me, but showing love to a thousand generations of those who love me and keep my commandments (Exod. 20:4).

Nowhere is this more dramatically fulfilled than in the lives of Ahab and Jezebel and their male descendants:

> There was never a man like Ahab, who sold himself to do evil in the eyes of the Lord, urged on by Jezebel his wife. He behaved in the vilest manner by going after idols, like the Amorites the Lord drove out before Israel (1 Kings 21:25).

The Lord prophesied through Elijah that every male descendant of Ahab would be destroyed and Jezebel would be eaten by dogs (see 21:17-24). The prophet Jehu said, "How can there be peace as long as all the idolatry and witchcraft of your mother Jezebel abound?" (2 Kings 9:22).

There can be no peace when the covenant people of God are idolatrous and practicing witchcraft. As prophesied, Ahab and 70 of his sons were beheaded and Jezebel was run over by a horse and eaten by dogs. After that evil bloodline had been purged from existence, the result on the kingdom of Judah was amazing. The next four kings were godly and ruled for 137 years:

> In the seventh year of Jehu, Joash became king, and he reigned in Jerusalem forty years. *His mother's name was* Zibiah (12:1,2, italics added).

> In the second year of Jehoash son of Jehoahaz king of Israel, Amaziah son of Joash king of Judah began to reign. He was twenty-five years old when he became king, and he reigned in Jerusalem twenty-nine years. *His mother's name was* Jehoaddin (14:1,2, italics added).

> In the twenty-seventh year of Jeroboam king of Israel, Azariah son of Amaziah king of Judah began

> to reign. He was sixteen years old when he became king, and he reigned in Jerusalem fifty-two years. *His mother's name was* Jecoliah (15:1,2, italics added).
>
> In the second year of Pekah son of Remaliah king of Israel, Jotham son of Uzziah king of Judah began to reign. He was twenty-five years old when be became king, and he reigned in Jerusalem sixteen years. *His mother's name was* Jerusha (vv. 32,33, italics added)

Notice that the mother was listed for each godly king. Ahaz was the next king in line, but he was godless and allowed the Temple to go to ruin. No mention is made of his mother. The next king was Hezekiah who led the way for one of the greatest revivals in the Old Testament:

> Hezekiah son of Ahaz king of Judah began to reign. He was twenty-five years old when he became king, and he reigned in Jerusalem twenty-nine years. *His mother's name was* Abijah (18:1,2, italics added).

What a testimony to godly mothers who raise their children to be spiritual leaders. Their faithful labors will be acknowledged, and their names will be recorded in history.

Matthew records the genealogy of Jesus through Joseph, His legal father. That ancestry established His claim and right to the throne of David. However, a curse was pronounced on Coniah (Jeconiah) that none of his descendants would prosper on the throne of David. Yet because He was not the natural son of Joseph, the curse did not affect Him. That is why Luke traces the physical lineage through Mary. Despite the fact that she was a virgin at His conception, it could be said that *His mother's name was Mary.*

GENERATIONAL SINS

So how do all these Old Testament accounts of godly bloodlines and godless bloodlines (which had to be purged out), or passionate love and demonic love (which had to be purged out), affect our freedom in marriage? We did not marry Adam or Eve before the Fall; we married one of their descendants after the Fall. The iniquities of our ancestors have been passed on for three and perhaps four generations. We did not have perfect parents who raised us in a sinless atmosphere using only godly principles. Our genetic code left us a little too short, or too tall, or slightly effeminate or masculine.

ALL OF CREATION HAS BEEN AFFECTED BY THE FALL. MARRIAGE IS NOT UNRELATED TO THIS COSMIC STRUGGLE; IT IS AT THE HEART OF IT.

It may be a sign of God's grace that Jezebel's iniquities were totally eradicated so no more damage was done. Had the iniquities of Abraham, Isaac and Jacob run their course so Joseph didn't have to follow in the same patterns, or did he repent? All of creation has been affected by the Fall. Marriage is not unrelated to this cosmic struggle; it is at the heart of it. How did the saints deal with this generational problem in the Old Testament? They repented of their sins and the sins of their fathers, both personally and corporately.

> The Lord said: I will not keep silent, but I will repay; I will even repay into their bosom, both their own iniquities and the iniquities of their fathers together (Isa. 65:6,7, *NASB*).

Jeremiah said:

> [God] showest lovingkindness to thousands, but repayest the iniquity of fathers into the bosom of

> their children after them (Jer. 32:18, *NASB*).

In the Old Testament they were to confess their sins *and* iniquities. The latter relates more to a rebellious spirit or strong self-will. Somehow these iniquities are passed on from one generation to another. Old Testament scholars note this:

> An important consideration is the distinction between corporate and individual responsibility for sin. In its early development Israel was very much influenced by a dynamic concept of corporate sin....The family group was a much more significant entity than the individual person. When the head of such a group transgressed, he transmitted guilt to every member of it....Thus, according to the Decalogue (see Exod. 20:5; Deut. 5;9; cf. Exod. 34:7; Num. 14:18), the iniquity of the father is to be visited upon the children, but only "to the third and fourth generation."[2]

In the context of idolatry, Hosea mentions demonic spirits affecting children, which are related to parents' sins:

> They consult a wooden idol and are answered by a stick of wood. A spirit of prostitution leads them astray; they are unfaithful to their God. They sacrifice on the mountaintops and burn offerings on the hills, under oak, poplar and terebinth, where the shade is pleasant. Therefore your daughters turn to prostitution and your daughters-in-law to adultery (Hos. 4:12,13).

The cause of the children's sin of adultery and prostitution is not only the parents' sin of idolatry, but also the demonic "spirit of prostitution." Notice how they were instructed to deal with this in the Old Testament:

> Those of you who are left will waste away in the lands of their enemies because of their sins; also because of their fathers' sins they will waste away.

> But if they will confess their sins and the sins of their fathers—their treachery against me and their hostility toward me (Lev. 26:39,40).

> Those of Israelite descent had separated themselves from all foreigners. They stood in their places and confessed their sins and the wickedness of their fathers (Neh. 9:2).

Nehemiah prayed:

> I confess the sins we Israelites, including myself and my father's house, have committed against you (1:6).

Jeremiah prayed:

> O Lord we acknowledge our wickedness and the guilt of our fathers; we have indeed sinned against you (Jer. 14:20).

Daniel prayed:

> We have not obeyed the Lord our God or kept the laws he gave us through his servants the prophets. All Israel transgressed your law and turned away, refusing to obey you. Therefore the curses and sworn judgments written in the law of Moses, the servant of God, have been poured out on us, because we have sinned against you (Dan. 9:10,11).

God had spoken and the prophets had warned the people about generational sins. In the early sixth century B.C., the prophet Ezekiel had to correct an abuse of this generational curse:

> The word of the Lord came to me: "What do you people mean by quoting this proverb about the land of Israel: 'The fathers eat sour grapes, and

> the children's teeth are set on edge'? As surely as I live, declares the Sovereign Lord, you will no longer quote this proverb in Israel" (Ezek. 18:1-3).

The popular proverb was not from the book of Proverbs nor from the mouth of God. The problem Ezekiel was trying to correct was a fatalistic response to the law and the abdication of personal responsibility. Children are not guilty for their parents' sins and they will not be punished for their parents' iniquities, which are visited upon them, if they are diligent to turn away from the sins of their parents. Scholars have clearly shown this to be the case:

> The corporate involvement of sin deeply impressed itself upon the people, however. The prophets proclaimed that it was not only a few wicked individuals, but the whole nation, that was laden with sin (see Isa. 1:4). Generation after generation treasured up wrath. Thus it was easy for those who were finally forced to bear the painful consequences to protest that all the effects of corporate guilt were being visited upon them. The exiles lamented: "Our fathers sinned, and are no more; it is we who have borne their iniquities" (Lam. 5:7, *NASB*). They even had a proverb: "The fathers have eaten sour grapes, and the children's teeth are set on edge." Against this both Jeremiah and Ezekiel protested (see Jer. 31;29,30; Ezek. 18:10-20). No son was to be held accountable for his father's crimes. "The soul who sins will die" (Ezek. 18:4, *NASB*). In saying this, they did not mean to deny corporate sin: this was beyond dispute. Their purpose was to accentuate individual responsibility, which was in danger of becoming submerged in a consciousness of overpowering national calamity. Even though the nation was now suffering a bitter corporate punishment, there was hope for the individual if he would repent.[3]

Under the old covenant, all of God's chosen people were

called to repent of their sins and iniquities regardless of whether the scope of their offenses was personal or national. National or corporate repentance cannot happen without personal repentance. We have seen in the Old Testament the transmission of sin from one generation to the next, and how the prophets called the people to confess their sins and the sins of their fathers. This is not just an Old Testament concept. Paul said, "Just as sin entered the world through one man, and death through sin, and in this way death came to all men. because all sinned" (Rom. 5:12).

The good news is that Christ died as an atonement for all our sins. "The death He died, He died to sin once for all" (Rom. 6:10). We receive that wonderful gift of eternal life and forgiveness of sins by faith and faith alone, but that doesn't mean we don't have to repent to mature in our relationship with Him and enjoy the fruit of His crucifixion and resurrection. John the Baptist preached, "Repent and believe the good news" (Mark 1:15). Listen to the words of Luke 24:45-47: "Then he opened their minds so they could understand the Scriptures. He told them, 'This is what is written: The Christ will suffer and rise from the dead on the third day, and repentance and forgiveness of sins will be preached in his name to all nations, beginning at Jerusalem."

The Greek word for repentance is *metanoeo*. *Meta* means "after," which implies change. *Noeo* means to perceive. It is derived from the root word, *nous* which is usually translated "mind." Repentance literally means a change of mind, but it is far more reaching in its application. When the Pharisees and the Sadducees came to be baptized by John, "He said to them, 'You brood of vipers, who warned you to flee from the wrath to come? Therefore bring forth fruit keeping with repentance'" (Matt. 3:7,8, *NASB*). He discerned their repentance was incomplete. They wanted the blessing of God without giving up their habits, traditions, customs and religious practices.

The Early Church would stand, face the west and make the following public declaration: "I renounce you Satan and all your works and all your ways." Every work of Satan and every way of Satan had to be renounced for repentance to be complete. Then they would face the east and declare their faith in God. They understood it was necessary to renounce all the evil practices that had gone on in their synagogues, families and their own personal lives.

The Early Church preached, "Repent, then, and turn to God, so that your sins may be wiped out, that times of refreshing may come from the Lord" (Acts 3:19). Paul said to King Agrippa, "I preached that they should repent and turn to God and prove their repentance by their deeds" (Acts 26:20). The Lord doesn't want "anyone to perish, but everyone to come to repentance" (2 Pet. 3:9).

Our churches and marriages will experience tremendous turmoil if we enter into those relationships with a saving knowledge of our Lord Jesus Christ, but without any evidence of repentance. Many people choose to believe in Christ, but they still hold on to their old ways of doing things which they learned from their families and cultures. Coming to Christ is not just one more thing to believe which we add to all the other world philosophies we learned. He is the way, the truth, and the life (see John 14:6). Jesus is not a way, He is the way. There is no other way and there is no other truth. Repentance means we renounce what we no longer believe to be true, choose the truth and then demonstrate this change by living godly lives. Paul says, "Do not conform any longer to the pattern of this world, but be transformed by the renewing of your mind. Then you will be able to test and approve what God's will is—his good, pleasing and perfect will" (Rom. 12:2).

The Lord said, "A student is not above his teacher, but everyone who is fully trained will be like his teacher" (Luke 6:40). The primary teachers in children's lives are their parents. Even in the best of Christian homes that training will be something less than perfect. We ought to thank God for the good things we have learned from our parents, but be willing to face the fact that there are no perfect parents. There is no reason to defend or blame our parents. Neither will help us resolve our personal or marital conflicts.

A committed couple talked with me at a marriage retreat. They were responsible members of their church and society. Both held key positions of spiritual leadership. For some reason they could not understand, they were not clicking as a couple. Marriage counseling had not resolved anything.

I asked them about their parents and grandparents. We

finally learned that her mother was a Religious Science practitioner, as was her grandmother. I asked her if I could take her through the "Steps to Freedom." There wasn't much to resolve because she was committed to living a righteous life. When she reached the last step, which renounced the sins of her ancestors, she suddenly came under attack.

"I have a spiritual problem," she cried. "How could that be? What do I do about it?"

"You just took care of it," I said. The change was immediate and lasting.

We will help you resolve this in our last chapter, which leads you through the process of setting your marriage free. We may very well be like all those who have gone before us unless we assume our responsibilities to repent and put our trust in God. Nobody can fix the past, but we can be free from it by the grace of God and the wonderful work of Christ on the Cross.

So am I a chip off the old block? Is my basic problem due to the environment in which I was raised, or can it be explained by hormones and genetic codes, or is my problem essentially spiritual? We believe the answer is yes. All three—social, physical and spiritual—have been affected by the Fall. The good news is that "Christ redeemed us from the curse of the law by becoming a curse for us" (Gal. 3:13). The remainder of this book explains how we can appropriate this sacrificial gift for ourselves and for our marriages.

Notes

1. Richard J. Banckham, *Word Biblical Commentary*, Vol. 50 on Jude and 2 Peter (Waco, Texas: Word Books, 1983), p. 51.
2. S.J. De Vries, "Sin, sinners," ed., G. Buttrick et al, *Interpreters Dictionary of the Bible* (Nashville, Tenn.: Abingdon, 1962), p. 365.
3. Brown, Driver, Briggs, *Hebrew and English Lexicon*.

Chapter Three

Christ First

Do not suppose that I have come to bring peace to the earth. I did not come to bring peace, but a sword. For I have come to turn "A man against his father, a daughter against her mother, a daughter-in-law against her mother-in-law—a man's enemies will be the members of his own household." Anyone who loves his father or mother more than me is not worthy of me; anyone who loves his son or daughter more than me is not worthy of me; and anyone who does not take his cross and follow me is not worthy of me. Whoever finds his life will lose it, and whoever loses his life for my sake will find it.

—MATTHEW 10:34-39

Chapter Three

A House Divided

When I (Neil) pastored a church, an elderly couple periodically sought my advice about their daughter. She had made a decision for Christ, and was active in church during her youth. Then she met a man who was not a Christian, and married him without her parents' consent. About every six months I would see her in church alone. Estranged from her parents and struggling in her marriage, she would stop by my office or give me a call to ask for prayer or advice. Finally the marriage ended in divorce.

The parents' uncompromising commitment to Christ, the daughter's half-hearted commitment to Christ and her husband's non-commitment to Christ became the sword that cut them apart. After the divorce she shared with me how she had planned to save the marriage. She had believed that if she went along with him to the bars and did whatever he wanted her to do, eventually she could win him over.

"I thought it was the only way to keep the peace," she said.

Wrong! In all my years of ministry I have never heard a testimony where that approach worked. I have heard many testimonies where non-Christian spouses were won over by their marriage partners who would not compromise their commitment to Christ, while faithfully assuming the responsibility in their marriages to love, accept and respect their partners. How can non-Christian spouses respect their Christian mates if they are not living what they profess to believe?

Did you notice in our opening text that no mention is made of bringing a sword between the husband and the wife? The conflict is between family members. The truth being driven home early in the gospels is that the family is not the primary focus of God's salvation. He came to save individuals, not marriages. Helping a couple get along at the expense of either spouse's salvation is not God's plan.

When I worked as an engineer, I knew a coworker who was separated from his spouse. All attempts at reconciliation proved futile. Finally they divorced. Both started searching for something in life that would give them meaning. Unbeknownst to each other, and in totally unrelated experiences, they both found the Lord. Six months later she mysteriously died at a young age. Could the Lord have used their separation, knowing that she had a terminal illness, to bring her to salvation before she died?

God places neither family nor even marriage first; rather it is God first and foremost. Why? Doesn't God care about our marriages and our families? Of course He does. The home is the first institution He created. But the whole can be no greater than the sum of its parts. A chain is no stronger than its weakest link. The measure of a marriage is the maturity of both the husband and the wife. What would a pair of synchronized swimmers look like if one listened to the coach, and the other didn't? The order of Scripture is to first present every person complete in Christ (see Col. 1:28), so our marriages and our families can be whole and functional again.

FALLEN NATURE

The Old Testament era ended on a sour note, and the New Testament begins no better. The Lord's chosen people were in political bondage to Rome and in spiritual bondage to an apostate Sanhedrin and the god of this world. The glory had departed from the nation of Israel, but the seed of Abraham (see Gal. 3:16) was about to make His entrance. "The Word became flesh and made his dwelling among us. We have seen his glory, the glory of the One and Only, who came from the Father, full of grace and truth" (John 1:14). The blessing of Abraham was about to be extended to all nations of the world (see Gen. 12:3).

Throughout the Old Testament nothing had changed about the basic nature of fallen humanity. As noted earlier, "The intent of man's heart is evil from his youth" (Gen. 8:21, *NASB*). Jeremiah says, "The heart is deceitful above all things and beyond cure" (17:9). The law had done nothing to change this. "For if a law had been given that could impart life, then righteousness would certainly have come by the law. But the Scripture declares that the whole world is a prisoner of sin" (Gal. 3:21,22). Telling people that what they are doing is wrong does not give them the power to stop doing it. The law is powerless to give life (Rom. 8:3,13).

Even more discouraging is the statement by Paul that "the

sinful passions aroused by the law were at work in our bodies" (Rom. 7:5). The law actually has the capacity to stimulate what it is trying to prohibit. If you don't believe that is true, try telling your children that they can go "here," but they can't go "there." The moment you say that, where do they want to go? They want to go "there." They probably didn't even want to go there until you said they couldn't.

I don't know why the forbidden fruit is more desirable, but it certainly seems to be. That is why portions of Romans 7 and Galatians 3 are written to correct the wrong conclusion that the law is sinful. Laying down the law, however, will not resolve sinful passions. The core problem is the basic nature of humankind, not its behavior. That is why marriage counseling that attempts to shape only the behavior of either spouse is so unfruitful.

The Pharisees were the moral perfectionists (legalists) of their day. But Jesus said, "For I tell you that unless your righteousness surpasses that of the Pharisees and the teachers of the law, you will certainly not enter the kingdom of heaven" (Matt. 5:20). The Sermon on the Mount confronts the issue of genuine righteousness, which is determined by the condition of the heart. For instance, "You have heard that it was said, 'Do not commit adultery.' But I tell you that anyone who looks at a woman lustfully has already committed adultery with her in his heart" (vv. 27,28). It isn't committing adultery to look, but looking is the evidence that adultery has already been committed in the heart.

The text goes on to say, "If your right eye causes you to sin, gouge it out" or "If your right hand causes you to sin, cut it off and throw it away" (vv. 29,30). Does your eye or hand cause you to sin? I don't think so. If we kept cutting off body parts to keep us from sinning, we would end up being nothing more than dismembered torsos rolling down the street.

I realize that many see this passage as an admonition to take whatever drastic means are required to stop sinning, thus emphasizing the hideousness of sin. In actuality it would be better to be dismembered than to spend eternity apart from Christ, but I don't think that is the point Jesus is trying to make. Taking cold showers to put out the fires of passion and walking blindfolded on a sunbathers' beach may bring temporary relief, but it does not deal with the condition of the heart. Such behavior would be necessary if the only option we had was to live under the law.

To further illustrate, Jesus continues: "It has been said, 'Anyone who divorces his wife must give her a certificate of divorce.' But I tell you that anyone who divorces his wife, except for marital unfaithfulness, causes her to become an adulteress, and anyone who marries the divorced woman commits adultery" (vv. 31,32). Apparently the religious leaders had

ONLY GOD CAN CHANGE WHO WE ARE; IT IS OUR RESPONSIBILITY TO BELIEVE THE TRUTH AND CHANGE HOW WE WALK.

adulterous hearts; therefore, to get around the law they simply gave their wives a certificate of divorce. The certificates supposedly freed them to marry the ones they desired in their hearts, without breaking the law. Jesus said they didn't have legitimate grounds for divorce, so instead of avoiding adultery they were actually propagating it.

Trying to live a righteous life externally when we are not righteous internally will only result in being "whitewashed tombs, which look beautiful on the outside but on the inside are full of dead men's bones and everything unclean" (Matt. 23:27). It is not what goes into a man that defiles him, it is what comes out. "For from within, out of men's hearts, come evil thoughts, sexual immorality, theft, murder, adultery, greed, malice, deceit, lewdness, envy, slander, arrogance and folly. All these evils come from inside and make a man unclean" (Mark 7:21-23).

A NEW NATURE

"The reason the Son of God appeared was to destroy the

devil's work. No one who is born of God will continue to sin, because God's seed remains in him" (1 John 3:8,9). No two verses in the Bible capture more succinctly what must happen for us to live a righteous life in Christ. Our basic nature has to be changed and we have to have a means by which we can overcome the evil one. We "were by nature children of wrath" (Eph. 2:3, *NASB*). "You were once darkness, but now you are light in the Lord. Live as children of light" (5:8). Only God can change who we are; it is our responsibility to believe the truth and change how we walk.

Look at the last chapter of the Old Testament. "He will turn the hearts of the fathers to their children, and the hearts of the children to their fathers" (Mal. 4:6). Malachi prophesied that the hearts of the fathers and the hearts of the children would be turned. Arranging programs and special events where the two will be together without changing their hearts will probably not accomplish much. Being alive in Christ is the only means by which our hearts can truly be changed.

We were born dead (spiritually) in our trespasses and sins (see Eph. 2:1). Jesus came to give us life, the same life that Adam and Eve lost when they sinned. I believe many of us are laboring under half a gospel. We have presented Jesus as the Messiah who came to die for our sins, and if we believe in Him, we will go to heaven when we die. What's wrong with that?

First, it gives the impression that eternal life is something we get when we die, which isn't true. "He who has the Son has life; he who does not have the Son of God does not have life" (1 John 5:12). Every child of God is alive in Christ right now. "For He has rescued us from the dominion of darkness and brought us into the kingdom of the Son he loves, in whom we have redemption, the forgiveness of sins" (Col. 1:13,14).

Second, it is only half the gospel. If you wanted to save a dead person what would you do? Give him life? If you did that, he would only die again. To truly solve the problem, you would have to do two things. First, you would have to cure the disease that caused him to die, and "the wages of sin is death" (Rom. 6:23). So Jesus went to the Cross to die for our sins. Is that all? Absolutely not! He was also resurrected so we may have life. Now finish the verse: "But the gift of God is eternal life in Christ Jesus our Lord" (v. 23). The fact that we are "in Christ" is our only hope. It is "Christ in you, the hope of glory" (Col. 1:27). Our position in Christ guarantees our victory over sin.

Because we are in Christ, we have the Spirit of God within us. Consequently, if we "walk by the Spirit, [we] will not carry out the desire of the flesh" (Gal. 5:16, *NASB*). We have to live our lives in total dependence upon God. All temptation is an attempt by the evil one to get us to live our lives independently from God. Remember, apart from Christ we can do nothing (see John 15:5).

In addition, because we are in Christ we have the assurance He will meet all our needs (see Phil. 4:19). Trying to resolve our marital conflicts without our essential needs being met in Christ will eventually prove counterproductive. We turn to our spouses and expect them to meet needs in our lives that only Christ can meet. In *Living Free in Christ* (Regal Books), I try to explain how Christ meets the most critical needs in our lives, which are the "being" needs. Let me encourage you to read aloud the outline of the book as follows:

WHO I AM IN CHRIST

I Am Accepted in Christ:

John 1:12	I am God's child
John 15:15	I am Christ's friend
Romans 5:1	I have been justified
1 Corinthians 6:17	I am united with the Lord and one with Him in spirit
1 Corinthians 6:20	I have been bought with a price—I belong to God
1 Corinthians 12:27	I am a member of Christ's body
Ephesians 1:1	I am a saint
Ephesians 1:5	I have been adopted as God's child
Ephesians 2:18	I have direct access to God through the Holy Spirit
Colossians 1:14	I have been redeemed and forgiven of all my sins
Colossians 2:10	I am complete in Christ

I Am Secure in Christ:

Romans 8:1,2	I am free from condemnation
Romans 8:28	I am assured that all things work together for good
Romans 8:33,34	I am free from any condemning charges against me
Romans 8:35	I cannot be separated from the love of God
2 Corinthians 1:21	I have been established, anointed and sealed by God
Colossians 3:3	I am hidden with Christ in God
Philippians 1:6	I am confident that the good work that God has begun in me will be perfected
Philippians 3:20	I am a citizen of heaven
2 Timothy 1:7	I have not been given a spirit of fear, but of power, love and a sound mind
Hebrews 4:16	I can find grace and mercy in time of need
1 John 5:18	I am born of God and the evil one cannot touch me

I Am Significant in Christ:

Matthew 5:13,14	I am the salt and light of the earth
John 15:1,5	I am a branch of the true vine, a channel of His life
John 15:16	I have been chosen and appointed to bear fruit
Acts 1:8	I am a personal witness of Christ's
1 Corinthians 3:16	I am God's temple
2 Corinthians 5:17-20	I am a minister of reconciliation
2 Corinthians 6:1	I am God's coworker
Ephesians 2:6	I am seated with Christ in the heavenly realm
Ephesians 2:10	I am God's workmanship
Ephesians 3:12	I may approach God with freedom and confidence
Philippians 4:13	I can do all things through Christ who strengthens me

No wonder Paul prayed, "I pray also that the eyes of your heart may be enlightened in order that you may know the hope to which he has called you, the riches of his glorious inheritance in the saints, and his incomparably great power for us who believe" (Eph. 1:18,19). The problem is *not* that every child of God doesn't share in His rich inheritance nor have the power to live victoriously in Christ; the problem is that we just don't see it. "You have been given fullness in Christ, who is the head over every power and authority" (Col. 2:10). We also have authority over the evil one as long as we are strong in the Lord, because we are seated with Christ in the heavenlies (see Eph. 2:4-6). Our responsibility is to submit to God and resist the devil (see Jas. 4:7).

GOD'S PLAN FOR MARRIAGE

We began this book with God's plan for marriage in the Garden of Eden in the absence of sin. What would be God's plan for Christian marriage in the context of a world darkened with sin? I believe the answer is found in 1 Thessalonians 4:3-8 (*NASB*):

> For this is the will of God, your sanctification; that is, that you abstain from sexual immorality [fornication]; that each of you know how to possess his own vessel in sanctification and honor, not in lustful passion, like the Gentiles who do not know God; and that no man transgress and defraud his brother in the matter because the Lord is the avenger in all these things, just as we also told you before and solemnly warned you. For God has not called us for the purpose of impurity, but in sanctification. Consequently, he who rejects this is not rejecting man but the God who gives His Holy Spirit to you.

The word "possess" in this passage of Scripture means to acquire. It is found in the Septuagint and other contemporary literature written at the time of Christ regarding marrying a wife. The word vessel is never used anywhere else in the Bible to mean body, but it is used in 1 Peter 3:7 (*NASB*) in reference to a man's wife. The Hebrew equivalent (*keli*) of vessel (*skeuos*) is used in Rabbinical writings concerning the wife. Thus the passage could be translated, "That each of you know how to take a wife for himself in sanctification and honor." Even if you translated vessel as your own body, as the *New International Version* does, the following application would still apply:

> Pre-marital sex is forbidden because it is counterproductive to the sanctifying process. We are to abstain from sexual immorality because that is not the means by which we should seek a life partner. Outward appearance and sexual appeal may be what attracts us to each other, but neither has any power to sustain the relationship. That kind of attraction is like perfume. Your senses will smell it when you are putting it on, but within minutes you will not be aware of the scent.

A young couple came to see me years ago because they were having marital problems. In an angry moment he had told her that she didn't satisfy him sexually as a previous girlfriend had. In tears she told me how hard she tried to be like that other girl, but in reality she couldn't.

One day he found her sitting on a couch with a pillow on her lap. She asked him if he loved her. He said he did, but her reply was, "Then I'm going to make you pay for it for the rest of your life." She removed his handgun from under the pillow and shot herself in front of him.

I realize that illustration is extreme, but if we keep ourselves pure until marriage, the problem of comparison will not be present. Freedom from sexual comparisons is just one of many reasons why God would have us wait.

Abstaining from immorality is not the primary focus of this passage, however. God views marriage in the context of sanctification, i.e., the process of conforming to the image of God. Nothing can be more important to us. We will do damage to our marriages and our families if we place greater prominence on them than on our relationship to God. When I make my relationship with God first in my life, then I can become the husband and father that He wants me to be.

Christian marriages become richer as all three relationships between God and each other become more intimate. I am not talking about external service for God without an accompanying internal change of heart. Pharisaic Christianity can kill a marriage. Service for God could become the greatest enemy of your devotion to Him.

THERE IS ONLY ONE CROSS, AND THAT IS THE CROSS OF CHRIST. WE PICK UP THAT CROSS WHEN WE ARE WILLING TO TOTALLY IDENTIFY WITH CHRIST AND SAY NO TO SIN AND SELF-RULE.

THE WORK OF THE CROSS

The synoptic Gospels all end with the Great Commission, to go into the world and make disciples. The central teaching of all the Gospels may be summarized with the following verse: "Anyone who does not take his cross and follow me is not worthy of me. Whoever finds his life will lose it, and whoever loses his life for my sake will find it" (Matt. 10:38,39). When the truth of that passage is understood and appropriated, then the fulfillment of the great commandment is possible: "Love the Lord your God with all your heart and with all your soul and with all your mind. This is the first and greatest commandment. And the second is like it: Love your neighbor as yourself. All the Law and the Prophets hang on these two commandments" (22:37-40).

The cross Jesus referred to in Matthew 10 is not our trials and tribulations. There is only one Cross, and that is the cross of Christ. We pick up that Cross when we are willing to totally identify with Christ and say no to sin and self-rule.

What follows next in the verse is a play on words. Anybody who builds his life around the natural order of things will lose it. In other words, if you try to find your identity and purpose in this present natural world without God, you will lose it some day. You can't take it with you. But when you give up your self-centered, self-seeking, self-sufficient living and find your identity and freedom in Christ, you will keep it for all eternity.

Paul put it in another way: "For physical training is of some value, but godliness has value for all things, holding promise for both the present life and the life to come" (1 Tim. 4:8). It seems to be the great ambition of man to be happy as animals instead of being blessed as children of God. The verse doesn't say that physical discipline has no value, but it has little value compared to what can be gained by putting Christ first and living a godly life.

Being alive in Christ is the essential foundation for all that we do. Nowhere is this more important than in gaining an understanding of who we are. John says, "Yet to all who received him, to those who believed in his name, he gave the right to become children of God—children born not of natural descent, nor human decision or a husband's will, but born of God" (John 1:12,13).

This is what breaks the curse of the Fall. We are no longer just products of our pasts. We are primarily products of the work of Christ on the Cross. "Therefore, if anyone is in Christ, he is a new creation; the old has gone, the new has come" (2 Cor. 5:17). We appropriate this new life by a sincere faith in the finished work of Christ and genuine repentance. We do this first as individuals and then as couples, so the two of us can become one in Christ.

KNOWING WHO WE ARE

"The Spirit himself testifies with our spirit that we are God's children" (Rom. 8:16). Why is this so critical? Because people cannot consistently behave in ways that are inconsistent with how they perceive themselves. It is not what we do that determines who we are, it is who we are that determines what we do. My role as a husband does not determine who I am. I am a child of God who has the responsibility to love my wife as Christ loved the Church. Nothing has a greater impact on how we live our lives than our understanding of God and a true knowledge of who we are in Christ.

Similarly, how we perceive others will have the greatest impact on how we relate to them. Peter admonished, "Husbands, in the same way be considerate as you live with your wives, and treat them with respect as the weaker partner and as heirs with you of the gracious gift of life, so that nothing will hinder your prayers" (1 Pet. 3:7).

Peter must have meant weaker in physical strength, because any Christian woman can be as spiritually strong in Christ as any man. Every husband should honor and respect his Christian wife as the child of God she really is, and vice versa. Not to do so would hinder their relationships with God. With two redeemed people married to each other, the two sides of the triangle that were broken by sin in the Fall are back in place, and the marriage is complete again.

The hard message recorded by Matthew (10:34-39), which I cited at the beginning of this chapter, raises another critical question. What happens if we try to seek self-verification in the world and in our families as opposed to finding it in Christ? Ironically, the family may become our biggest threat to really becoming somebody and amounting to something. To be somebody in this world without Christ, you have to:

1. Look good enough so others will admire you or what you wear, or
2. Perform well enough so others will applaud your accomplishments, or
3. Have enough social status so others will recognize you.

The world says you are lucky if you have all three, and it is tragic if you have no looks, abilities or status—so you had better try for at least one of them!

If you are more concerned about what the world says than what God says, you will be better off to remain single. What will happen to your public appearance if you get married and have children?

First, the house will never look as good again. You will

have to baby-proof everything three feet and below. Having a clean house will only be a temporary illusion. Forget about having a botanical garden out back. The backyard will be nature's playpen until it rains, then it will become a pigpen. Bikinis will be out, because they will show your stretch marks. The sports car the swinger owns will get traded in for a minivan with finger marks on every window and gum in the seats.

How will having a family affect your performance at work, Dad, if Danny has a little league game every Saturday? Your competition for promotion at work is often single people or "dinks" (double income and no kids). They can work on weekends when you should be with your family or attending church.

By the way, Mom, the world says you need to get out of the house to find yourself, to discover who you really are. The only way people can recognize your performance is through your own career. Children will only inhibit your opportunities.

Consider the poor father who is having a mid-life crisis. He simply cannot perform like he used to, so he starts thinking, *Maybe I need to buy a sports car that really performs, like the one that just passed my minivan.*

What will happen to your public status when you're saddled with a kid who won't do what he or she is told, and the wife who won't participate at the office party?

Do we ever feel publicly ashamed to be identified with our families?

Jesus healed a man who was born blind. He wanted to tell everyone about Christ, but the Pharisees claimed Jesus couldn't be of God because He healed the man on the Sabbath. The man wouldn't recant his testimony so they questioned his parents. Would they stand behind the testimony of their son? No! Why not? Because the Pharisees had agreed that if anybody professed Jesus to be the Messiah they would be thrown out of the synagogue (see John 9:22). We can't lose our social status because of our family, can we?

When we look to our marriages and families to find our sense of identity and worth, they become potential enemies. When we look to God to discover who we are and why we are here, then our marriages and families become the primary instruments God uses to conform us to His image. We will see how in the next chapter.

CHAPTER FOUR

Conforming to His Image

Put on the new self, which is being renewed in knowledge in the image of its Creator. Here there is no Greek or Jew, circumcised or uncircumcised, barbarian, Scythian, slave or free, but Christ is all, and is in all. Therefore, as God's chosen people, holy and dearly loved, clothe yourselves with compassion, kindness, humility, gentleness and patience. Bear with each other and forgive whatever grievances you may have against one another. Forgive as the Lord forgave you. And over all these virtues put on love, which binds them all together in perfect unity. Wives, submit to your husbands, as is fitting in the Lord. Husbands, love your wives and do not be harsh with them. Children, obey your parents in everything, for this pleases the Lord. Fathers, do not embitter your children, or they will become discouraged.

—COLOSSIANS 3:10-14; 18-21

When I (Neil) was a pastor, I got an emergency phone call from a young couple. Their plea was, "You better get over here; we are about to kill each other." I remember thinking on the way to their house, *This is the type of call that policeman don't like to respond to.* The number one cause of homicide is domestic violence, and more people are injured at home than anywhere else. It can be a dangerous place to live. So I was praying that the Lord would give me wisdom.

We decided to move the battle to the kitchen table. As they hurled verbal missiles at each other, I felt like the referee at a boxing match. I wanted to shout, "Keep your guard up, and do a little better at counter punching."

After about two hours, they ran out of breath and the fight stalled. I suggested they come up for air and go to their respective corners. She fixed a cup of coffee, and he found a pad of paper and a pencil for me to use. When they sat down again, I drew the following diagram:

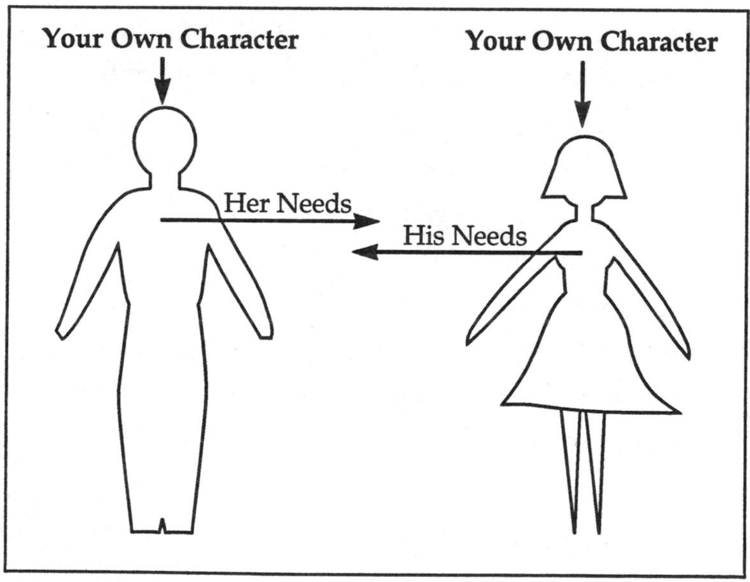

DIAGRAM 4.1

WRONG FOCUS

I explained that the entire focus of their relationship was

wrong. Before God, individuals are responsible for their own character and the other person's needs. They were doing just the opposite. They were ripping the other person's character, while looking out for their own needs. No relationship can withstand that orientation. What would our marriages, families and churches look like if every one of us assumed the responsibility to conform to the image of God (which is God's great goal for our lives), and committed ourselves to meet the needs of those around us (which is to love one another)? Surely that is what God has called us to be and then do. Why aren't we doing it? If everybody did, we would be living in paradise.

I gave them each a piece of paper and asked them to draw a line across the middle. On the top half they were to write down what they believed their three greatest needs were. On the bottom half they were to write down what they thought the other person's three greatest needs were. They struggled trying to identify their own needs, but when it came to listing the needs of their spouse, neither had a clue. They probably had never given it any thought.

Selfishness will kill any marriage! Selflessness by both spouses makes for a good marriage, and both husband and wife will be satisfied.

I suspect both the husband and the wife felt so deprived of their own basic needs that they couldn't see beyond them. When people are hurting, their overwhelming thought is, *Stop the pain!* That is why we are so insistent upon helping individuals resolve their personal and spiritual conflicts first, before we attempt to help their marriages. Being married does not resolve the core personal needs that can only be met in Christ. In fact, marriage has a tendency to expose our character deficiencies and reveal raw needs.

I talked with a husband who was destroying everything important to him. From his perspective, everybody else was wrong: his pastor, his boss and his wife. Finally his wife left him. Six months later I got a call from him. He had just been released from a three-month jail sentence. He said, "This is the first time I have been clean from drugs in 10 years."

I didn't even know he had a drug problem! I asked him, "Knowing that you were losing your church, your job and your marriage, why did you continue using?"

I will never forget his answer: "That was the only time I ever felt good about myself."

I explained that he didn't have to take drugs to feel good about himself. I also told him I believed he would feel very good about himself if he were free in Christ, and in the center of God's will.

COMMON MISPERCEPTIONS

Let me mention four personal and cultural perceptions that run counter to this simple principle.

Individual Rights

The first is our preoccupation about individual rights. Don't get me wrong. I believe in our inalienable rights. All people should be accepted and respected for who they are regardless of race, sex, social or economic status. But we have tipped the balance too far if individual rights are emphasized over personal responsibilities.

Witness the pro-choice pregnant mother who publicly demands her rights over her own body, and at the same time demonstrates her irresponsible use of it. We don't have an abortion problem; we have an irresponsible sex problem. We have the right to bear arms, and the right to free speech, but both are deadly when misused by those who are irresponsible. We legislate laws that deal with the effect, but not the cause. When our courts start to hold people accountable for what are clearly their own responsibilities, we will see justice return to our country.

Let's apply this to marriage. Do I have a right as a husband to expect my wife to be submissive, or do I have a responsibility to love my wife as Christ loved the Church? Do I have a right as a parent to expect my children to obey me, or do I have a responsibility to train them in the Lord and discipline them if they are disobedient? Nations, churches, families, marriages or individuals are weakened when they start demanding their rights without assuming their responsibilities.

What right do we have to expect anything from anybody

else? I have no right to demand that my wife and children fulfill my expectations. I have great hopes for them. I believe in their potentialities, and I will do what I can to help them be all God wants them to be. But if they should fall short or deviate from the expectations I have for them, I am not disappointed. Only God has that right, and only He has the grace to make it happen.

I help my wife and family most by assuming my responsibility to be the husband and father God wants me to be. The

NATIONS, CHURCHES, FAMILIES, MARRIAGES OR INDIVIDUALS ARE WEAKENED WHEN THEY START DEMANDING THEIR RIGHTS WITHOUT ASSUMING THEIR RESPONSIBILITIES.

same is true for my wife. Her primary responsibility is to be the wife and mother God wants her to be, and nobody can keep either of us from being that.

The hurting parent may say, "You don't understand; my child is rebelling." A rebellious child cannot keep us from being the mother or father God wants us to be. It will seriously test our characters, but if our rebellious children ever needed us to be the parents God wants us to be, it is right now.

Our Role in Others' Lives

A second misperception is the role we play in another person's life. When our mates are not living up to our expectations or fulfilling their commitments, we are tempted to act as their consciences. The moment we attempt to play the role of the Holy Spirit in their lives, we misdirect their battle with God onto ourselves. We are simply inadequate for the task of playing God in someone else's life. We are supposed to "accept one another...just as Christ accepted you [us], in order to bring praise to God" (Rom. 15:7).

How did Christ accept us? "God demonstrates His own love for us in this: While we were still sinners, Christ died for us" (Rom. 5:8). No other human factor is more important in helping others conform to the image of God than our unconditional love and acceptance of them.

The Difference Between Discipline and Judgment

Love and acceptance is consistent with the responsibility to discipline, but inconsistent with judging one another. Discipline is proof of our love, but at the same time we are commanded not to judge (see Matt. 7:1). Not knowing the difference between discipline and judgment is a third misperception.

Discipline is related to behavior, whereas judgment is related to character. We discipline those we love purely on the basis of observed behavior. We have to see him do it, or hear her say it. We cannot discipline someone on hunches, guesses or intuition. Discipline is not punishment. We don't punish somebody for doing something wrong out of revenge. We discipline them for the purpose of superintending future choices, so they don't do it again. It is a training in righteousness. Notice how Hebrews 12:10,11 supports this:

> Our fathers disciplined us for a little while as they thought best; but God disciplines us for our good, that we may share in His holiness. No discipline seems pleasant at the time, but painful. Later on, however, it produces a harvest of righteousness and peace for those who have been trained by it.

If I catch my son telling a lie, I have a responsibility to confront him. Suppose I say, "Son, what you just said is not true!" His response is, "You're judging me!" Am I judging him? No! I confronted him because of what he said, not because of who he is.

Now suppose I say, "Son, you're a liar!" What's that? That's judgment. I just attacked his character.

When discipline is appropriately administered, the whole situation can be resolved at the time. The offenders can confess, make retribution if called for and be reconciled. They may have to live with the consequences of their sins, but their characters have not been impugned.

If someone attacks our characters, what can we do? We can change our behaviors, but we cannot instantly change our characters. We can choose to change what we do, but we can't instantly change who we are. Attacking a person's character is one of the worst forms of rejection.

Much of what we do in the name of discipline is nothing more than character assassination. Stinging rebukes upon our character such as *stupid, clumsy, dumb, moron, jerk* and *nitwit* do lasting damage to a person's sense of well-being. Name calling and labeling build walls that only forgiveness can break down.

I have seen older adults weep while forgiving their deceased parents for such verbal abuse. Any time we attack another person's character—especially our spouse's or our children's—we should confess it and ask them for their forgiveness. If demeaning name calling has been occurring in your family, be sure to deal with it when you get to chapter 14.

We would eliminate at least half of our marriage, family and church problems if we would consistently practice just one verse in the Bible: "Do not let any unwholesome talk come out of your mouths, but only what is helpful for building others up according to their needs, that it may benefit those who listen" (Eph. 4:29). The next verse says, "Do not grieve the Holy Spirit of God" (v. 30). It grieves God to see His children using their words to tear each other down. The Holy Spirit is leading us to build up one another, not put down one another.

What if our spouses (or others) attack our characters? Should we be defensive? I believe the answer is no. Listen to what Peter said about Jesus: "When they hurled their insults at him, he did not retaliate; when he suffered, he made no threats. Instead, he entrusted himself to him who judges justly" (1 Pet. 2:23).

People who attack others' characters are wrong, and those who do so are hurting people. Mature, healthy people don't attack other people's characters. I have learned the hard way that defending myself only invites more verbal attacks. We can't let the unrighteous judgments of others determine who we are. We should entrust ourselves to Him who judges justly.

When people have unloaded their verbal guns, the last thing we want them to do is reload. If we respond in kind or try to defend ourselves, we hand them more ammunition. They will become even more adamant in their character assassinations. But what happens next if when they have emptied their guns, we don't retaliate or defend ourselves? The Holy Spirit brings conviction on the offender, and we may have a wonderful opportunity to minister to a hurting person.

Sharing Needs Appropriately

Is it appropriate to share needs with our spouses? It certainly is, but the fourth misperception is related to how we do it. Suppose a wife doesn't feel loved by her husband, so she says to him, "You don't love me anymore, do you?" Chances are she will hear back, "Yeah I do." And that will probably be the end of the conversation.

The problem is that she critiqued his responsibility instead of sharing her need. Some refer to that as a "you" judgment instead of an "I" reaction. It would be better if she said something like: "I just don't feel loved anymore." Because the husband and the wife are commanded by God to love one another and the spouse isn't playing the role of the Holy Spirit, God is free to bring conviction.

Paul says, "Let our people also learn to engage in good deeds to meet pressing needs, that they may not be unfruitful" (Titus 3:14, *NASB*). The most critical needs of life—identity, acceptance, security and significance—can only be met in Christ, but God intends to meet many other needs through marriage and family relationships. The need to depend upon God creates a tension that we often experience in our families, because the home is where most of our character is developed.

The capacity to meet others' needs is directly proportional to our growth in character. The more we become like Christ, the more we are able to love one another. All this is torpedoed when we stop growing and selfishly focus on our own needs at the expense of others.

FULFILLING COMMITMENTS AND RESPONSIBILITIES

God works in our lives primarily through committed relationships for two reasons. First, we cannot (or should not) run away from our commitments and responsibilities in our marriage and family relationships. Many relationships in life we can, and in some cases should, walk away from. For instance, Scripture warns, "Do not be misled: Bad company corrupts good character" (1 Cor. 15:33).

Homes are like pressure cookers: all kinds of trials and tribulations result from living together in the confinement of four walls. But that is precisely the point as Paul so clearly articulated in Romans 5:3-5 (*NASB*):

> We also exult in our tribulations, knowing that tribulation brings about perseverance; and perseverance, proven character; and proven character, hope; and hope does not disappoint, because the love of God has been poured out within our hearts through the Holy Spirit who was given to us.

Our fallen human nature wants to say, "This job is hopeless; I better change jobs," or "This marriage is hopeless; I better get a divorce." Paul said we should stay true to our commitments, honor our obligations, remain faithful to our vows and grow up.

There may be some legitimate times to search for another job and seek legal separation for our own protection, but what is our reason for leaving? Are we running away from the pressures of life instead of working through them? If so, we will be missing the primary means by which God intends to produce Christian character in us. Trials and tribulations reveal wrong goals in our lives, but they make possible the greatest goal of proven character.

What hope can we legitimately give to a wife who has just learned that her husband left her? We would give false hope by saying that she will win him back. We can't promise that, because it is beyond our right or ability to control. The fruit of the Spirit is not spouse control, it is not child control, it is self-control. The subtle implication by some who are separated is, *How can I manipulate the other person or the circumstances so they will have to come back?* That kind of attitude is probably why the other person left in the first place.

We offer a lot more hope if we say something like this: "If you haven't previously committed yourself to be the best possible wife and mother God wants you to be, then would you now?" The best way to change a situation is to change our-

---

THE BEST WAY TO CHANGE A SITUATION IS TO CHANGE OURSELVES, BECAUSE THAT IS THE ONLY THING WE HAVE THE RIGHT OR ABILITY TO CONTROL.

---

selves, because that is the only thing we have the right or ability to control. Changing ourselves is also the best way to win back the other person. Even if that person does not respond, we can come through the crisis of separation as better people than we were before it happened. This course gives us a win-win situation, because our hope lies in our own proven characters.

STRIPPING AWAY PRETENSES

Consider the second reason why God works primarily in committed relationships. Most of us can put on a public face and con our neighbors and casual friends, but we can't be a phony at home. Our children and spouses will see right through us.

When we tell our children to behave in public is it for their good or for us to look good? Our children know the difference. When we keep something from our spouses, they may not know what is wrong, but they definitely know something is wrong.

Our homes are fishbowls disguised as houses. When the spiritual tide is out, all the little tadpoles want to swim in their own little tidepools. But when the spiritual tide is in, they all swim harmoniously together as though somebody other than themselves were orchestrating every move. Such moments may be rare, but when they happen they are wonderful.

FROM DEATH TO LIFE

We can see how God intends to bring us from death to spiritual life and harmony by understanding the progressive flow of the apostle's message. Let me show this by highlighting the book of Colossians:

Chapter 1:

Verse 9	We are to be filled with the knowledge of His will in all spiritual wisdom and understanding.
Verse 13	We have been delivered out of the kingdom of darkness and transferred into the kingdom of Christ.
Verse 27	Christ in us is our hope of glory.
Verse 28	We are to present every person perfect in Christ.

Chapter 2:

Verses 6, 7, 10	We have been made complete *in Christ,* and are now being built up *in Him,* in order that we may walk *in Him.*
Verse 14	He canceled out our certificate of debt, and nailed it to the Cross.
Verse 15	Jesus disarmed the rulers and authorities, having triumphed over them.
Verses 20-23	Legalism and personal asceticism cannot accomplish what Jesus has already accomplished.

Chapter 3:

Verse 3	We have died to who we were in Adam and are now alive in Christ.
Verses 5-9	We have put off the old man (self),
Verse 10	And have put on the new self who is being renewed to a true knowledge according to the image of the One who created us.

What incredible truth! The Lord transferred us out of the kingdom of darkness into His Kingdom, and made us new creations in Christ. He forgave our sins and defeated the devil. We are to put off the old self and put on the new self. After salvation, God's will for our lives is to conform us to His image. Now let's refer to the text at the beginning of the chapter (Col. 3:10-14; 18-21), and see the necessary order of identity, character, marriage, family and career.

KNOWING WHO WE ARE

Knowing who we are is the foundation for what we do. The barriers that separated us because of our natural heritage no longer exist: "Here there is no Greek or Jew, circumcised or uncircumcised, barbarian, Scythian, slave, or free, but Christ is all, and is in all" (v. 11). In other words, for those who are in Christ there are no racial, religious, cultural or social distinctions; Galatians 3:28 adds neither "male nor female for you are all one in Christ Jesus." Every Christian is a child of God: "The Spirit himself testifies with our spirit that we are God's children" (Rom. 8:16). That is how we are to perceive ourselves, because it is the core of our identities according to God.

The Lord has not eradicated social order, sexual gender or lines of authority. Why did Paul refer to slaves in Colossians 3:22 when he said in verse 11 that there are no slaves? Verse 11 is referring to the identity of every child of God, and verse 22 is referring to the social situation in which someone may be called to live. All Christian men, women, fathers, mothers, masters, slaves and children should live like the children of God they really are. It is not what we do that determines who we are. We are all under authority. The employee must still be submissive to the employer, the wife to her husband and the child to his or her parents.

> Therefore, as God's chosen people, holy and dearly loved, clothe yourselves with compassion, kindness, humility, gentleness and patience. Bear with each other and forgive whatever grievances

> you may have against one another. Forgive as the Lord forgave you. And over all these virtues put on love, which binds them all together in perfect unity (vv. 12-14).

Where are we going to learn those character traits? If we grow together in the grace of God, we can potentially have perfect harmony. One overwhelming act of love we will repeatedly need is the grace to forgive as we have been forgiven.

FORGIVENESS THROUGH AGAPE LOVE

I have had the privilege of helping thousands work through the process of forgiving others. When they make lists of who they need to forgive, their own parents top the lists 95 percent of the time.

I mentioned in an earlier chapter that love is the glue that binds a family together. Bitterness or unresolved anger rooted in unforgiveness is the dynamite that blows it apart. Unforgiveness is Satan's greatest access to believers (see Matt. 18:21-35; 2 Cor. 2:10,11). We must forgive, because we don't live with perfect people. If we don't, Satan will destroy us. In helping others find their freedom in Christ, I have discovered that unforgiveness is the number one reason people are in bondage. In many cases it has been the only unresolved issue blocking their freedom.

Forgiving one another is the first step in loving one another. Jesus said, "A new command I give you: Love [agape] one another. As I have loved you, so you must love one another" (John 13:34). Why was that a new command? Weren't we always supposed to have loved one another? We were supposed to get along under the law, but we were not able to love one another the way God could because of our depraved natures.

Agape love is the love of God. We can be commanded to love others because we have become partakers of His divine nature (see 2 Pet. 1:4). God loves us, not because we are lovable, but because God is love. It is His nature to love us. That is why God's love for us is unconditional. God's love is not dependent upon the object of love: "If you love those who love you, what credit is that to you? Even 'sinners' love those who love them" (Luke 6:32).

If Christian husbands or wives say they don't love their spouses anymore, they have said more about their own characters than they have about their life partners' characters. Only the grace of God enables us to love the unlovely.

My understanding of the meaning of agape developed when I realized that the word is used in the New Testament as a verb *and* as a noun. When agape is used as a noun, it refers to God's character. It is the highest of all character attainments. For instance, "Love is patient, love is kind, etc." (1 Cor. 13:4f.). Paul said, "The goal of our instruction is love from a pure heart and a good conscience and a sincere faith" (1 Tim. 1:5, *NASB*). Proven character, which reveals itself in the love of God, should be the goal of every Christian ministry. "By this all men will know that you are my disciples, if you love one another" (John 13:35).

Agape can also be expressed as a verb. The love of God would compel us to meet the needs of others. It has to be given away. "For God *so loved* the world that he *gave* his one and only Son, that whoever believes in him shall not perish but have eternal life" (John 3:16, italics added). He saw our greatest need, and then because of His love, made the ultimate sacrifice to meet it.

The deep meaning of John 3:16 is captured in 1 John 3:16-18:

> This is how we know what love is: Jesus Christ laid down his life for us. And we ought to lay down our lives for our brothers. If anyone has material possessions and sees his brother in need but has no pity on him, how can the love of God be in him? Dear children, let us not love with words or tongue but with actions and in truth.

Those who are mature in Christ will be moved by the love of God to reach out and meet the needs of their spouses.

THE RULING VOICE

Listen to Paul's words tucked between his challenge for godly character and family instruction:

> Let the peace of Christ rule in your hearts, since as members of one body you were called to peace. And be thankful. Let the word of Christ dwell in you richly as you teach and admonish one another with all wisdom, and as you sing psalms, hymns and spiritual songs with gratitude in your hearts to God (Col. 3:15,16).

The peace of Christ can rule in our hearts only if the Word of Christ richly dwells within us.

I cannot overemphasize the need for the Word of God to be the ruling voice in your marriage and home. Marriages and families that pray and read their Bibles together still stay together. Movies, music and magazines that are counterproductive to your Christian growth should be eliminated from the house. There are too many voices inspired by the prince of power of the air (Satan) that will turn you against God and each other. "The Spirit clearly says that in later times some will abandon the faith and follow deceiving spirits and things taught by demons" (1 Tim. 4:1).

The ruler of this world, the father of lies, will seek to destroy your life, testimony and marriage. In the high priestly prayer, Jesus says, "My prayer is not that you take them out of the world but that you protect them from the evil one. Sanctify them by the truth; your word is truth" (John 17:15,17).

The Holy Spirit is the Spirit of truth and He will lead us into all truth, and that truth will set us free. Then we can be the husbands and fathers, wives and mothers He has called us to be; and we will sharpen each other's characters and meet one another's needs.

CHAPTER FIVE

Disappointment with Marriage

To keep me from becoming conceited because of these surpassingly great revelations, there was given me a thorn in my flesh, a messenger of Satan, to torment me. Three times I pleaded with the Lord to take it away from me. But he said to me, "My grace is sufficient for you, for my power is made perfect in weakness." Therefore I will boast all the more gladly about my weaknesses, so that Christ's power may rest on me. That is why, for Christ's sake, I delight in weaknesses, in insults, in hardships, in persecutions, in difficulties. For when I am weak, then I am strong.

—2 CORINTHIANS 12:7-10

No one is perfect. Everyone has strengths and weaknesses. The best marriages hurt some of the time; the worst marriages hurt all of the time. Weaknesses lead to disappointments.

"It was a major disappointment."
"I'm really disappointed."
"It's so disappointing."

One wag put a finger on the problem. "If a child of God marries a child of the devil, said child of God is sure to have some trouble with his father-in-law."[1] Marriage partners sometimes let us down. Our spouses blow it big time. Adultery, financial pressures or tragedies put us under extreme stresses. We feel deflated, hurt or betrayed—our plans failed, our dreams shattered, our hopes dashed.

We explode with anger, frustration and resentment. Or we withdraw, medicate our pain and hide from reality. Or we give up, get out or go away. None of these coping mechanisms work well. Hurting people hurt others. If we refuse to turn the other cheek, we continue the cycle of abuse. Spreading hurt around only intensifies and multiplies disappointment.

Because disappointments, great or small, come to every marriage, how can we handle them better? How can the stumbling blocks of family life become stepping stones for God's glory and others' good? How can they become a march toward a mature marriage?

> Disappointment calls for us to purify our spirits (see 2 Cor. 7:1). We must remove the barriers to God's grace, truth, love, power and righteousness. Our wrong reactions and self-protective behaviors must go. Let the anger cool, come out of hiding, face up to reality, get back on course, bear the unavoidable pain.
>
> Disappointment calls for our forgiveness. Forgiving partners who shortchanged us builds our characters.
>
> Disappointment calls for reevaluation. Why were we so hurt? What can be improved? Is communication a problem? Is an attitude out of

whack? How can we avoid it next time?

Disappointment calls for loving confrontation. Our marriage partners need to hear from our own lips, in private, how we feel grieved. We need to reconcile, start over or at the very least lodge a loving complaint.

THE BIGGEST DISAPPOINTMENTS OF MARRIAGE SOMETIMES HIDE THE FINEST BENEFITS.

When all else fails, we must remember that disappointment will not last forever. This too will pass. We need to put it into perspective. Things could be worse. If it's totally beyond our control, we can learn the grace of perseverance and the discipline of endurance.

Every marriage goes through cycles of pain and disappointment. Popular author and psychologist David Augsburger describes four stages of marriage:

The Dream of the 20s
The Disillusionment of the 30s
The Discovery of the 40s
The Depth of the 50s[2]

The biggest disappointments of marriage sometimes hide the finest benefits. Turbulence leads to transition. Out of the worst often come the best. God uses evil for good (see Gen. 50:20; Rom. 8:28). When you can't trace God's hand, trust His heart.

In this chapter we will look at a few typical marriage sins and weaknesses, major causes of disappointment—anger, rebellion and manipulation. Some marriages dissolve not only because of circumstances, but also because of damaging attitudes. Other marriages survive infidelity, death of a child, even abuse. These marriage partners find freedom in Christ, get help, make changes and become better people in the process.

Abraham Lincoln had a disappointing marriage. He was hardly the ideal husband. For years his judicial circuit kept him away from his Springfield home four months of every year. When he was home he worked until late at night at his law office or the State House. What little time was left, he spent in emotional withdrawal.

After his death, his wife, Mary Todd Lincoln, said that when he felt the most deeply, he expressed it the least. What a fun guy! He was enough to drive any wife crazy. When it came to being a father, he indulged his children, but seldom if ever disciplined them!

His wife, Mary, was a disappointment to him, too. She was an angry woman, at times flying into a violent rage. Physically abusive, she threw such things as firewood and potatoes at him. It is reported that once she chased him with a knife through their backyard in Springfield. She complained constantly about poverty, but overspent the budget (both before and within the White House) with gleeful abandon. Intensely jealous of any attention Lincoln gave to the opposite sex, she herself would flirt constantly and dress seductively. She nagged Abraham continually about seeking high public office, but after he became President she abused the White House domestic staff with no apology or remorse.

To put it bluntly, the Lincolns' marriage was a mess—a dysfunctional, hopeless disappointment to both of them. But that's not the end of the story. In the most famous presidency in our country's history, Lincoln worked effectively with rampant egos in his administration. The long years of living with his tempestuous wife taught him character qualities such as patience, tolerance, humor, forbearance and forgiveness. He turned the disappointment of a miserable marriage into the "University of Character" that made him the most celebrated of all our Presidents.[3]

ANGER

Human weakness easily leads to anger, and anger can either foul up a marriage, or protect it. There is a time to be angry, and a time not to be angry. The time to be angry is when God is angry, when His wrath burns against an attitude or behavior. The time not to be angry is when our own selfishness or sin is exposed. The time not to be angry is when we feel out of control. The time not to be angry is when we don't yet fully understand the other person's feelings. Our most explosive emotions can destroy or safeguard. Most often they destroy.

Our culture has overrated anger as a helpful emotion. It is excused as normal, natural and human. We are reminded that Jesus was angry—for the right reasons. In fact, we are told that anger is good. And sometimes it is.

"Go ahead and be angry. You do well to be angry—but don't use your anger as fuel for revenge. And don't stay angry. Don't go to bed angry. Don't give the Devil that kind of foothold in your life" (Eph. 4:26-27, *The Message*). It's that last part about giving the devil a place to grab hold that is scary.

Few outbursts cause worse damage than a display of destructive anger. The author of Proverbs wisely observed, "A fool gives full vent to his anger, but a wise man keeps himself under control" (Prov. 29:11). Rage and hostility not only beat down family members, they eat away at the one who vents them. If you live with an angry spouse, listen to Proverbs 15:1: "A gentle answer turns away wrath, but a harsh word stirs up anger."

To cool anger, the Bible gives wise counsel: "Lead with your ears, follow up with your tongue, and let anger straggle along in the rear. God's righteousness doesn't grow from human anger" (Jas. 1:19-20, *The Message*). Merle and Helen McCoy, veterans of over 50 years of marriage, gave similar counsel to a newspaper reporter.

"You and your husband should do a lot of listening and not much talking," Merle said. "Sometimes you need to hold your hand over your mouth."

"One hundred percent true!" Helen said.[4]

Think of destructive anger as a swamp. When we wade in—or even if we are thrown in—we get muddy and filthy. Yuk! The best thing we can do is take a bath or shower as soon as possible. But if we're smart, we will also look for leeches. In a swamp we may or may not get leeches, blood suckers or parasites. Our only safe course of action is to inspect ourselves, and have someone else look where we cannot see! (By the way, if we decide to stay in the swamp, we can expect the leeches to attack our bodies!)

Similarly, the Bible says that anger gives the devil a foothold, literally a "place." He or one of his parasite demons can attack and suck the lifeblood out of us. No fun! But God's Word isn't joking. If we fail to resolve anger, we are swimming in a swamp. The devil and his henchmen will attack. They have no mercy. Like leeches, they stay hidden while they do their dirty work. We must get out of the swamp—get out of the anger. We must give ourselves a daily deadline—sundown or bedtime: no pouting or sulking, no hiding or not speaking, no buried hostility or big blowouts after the deadline.

If our anger has spilled its swampy filth onto others in our families, then we must do our part in cleaning up the mess. Warm the bath water for them. Turn on the shower for them. Pull off a leech or two—with great tenderness. After a display of anger it's time to humble ourselves, go back to the person we hurt and ask for forgiveness. It's time to talk things out, or take a time-out, or agree to solve the problem later. Neil is right when he says that the sun can go down on your problem night after night—just don't let it go down on your anger.

All who are reading this and still defending anger as a helpful emotion, please relax. Of course anger is real, natural and not something to be suppressed. It is, however, best expressed in constructive ways. Sometimes it helps to sublimate it into recreation, hard physical labor or some creative outlet. Sometimes it is useful to express it in "I" statements. Other times it's best just to give it to God. But we all know that anger often produces more heat than light. One of the purposes of Christ's death on the Cross was to abolish the hostility between Jew and Gentile, and between all other human divisions, including male and female (see Gal. 3:28; Eph. 2:13-18).

Husbands are especially warned by God: "Husbands, love your wives and do not be harsh with them" (Col. 3:19). It's easy for men to become embittered against their wives, and nurture resentment. They quit taking deposits in their personal love banks and issue non-requested withdrawals instead. Even pastors' families suffer. A *Leadership Journal* survey revealed 41 percent of pastors report "anger toward spouse" as one of their marriage problems.[5] If pastors struggle with anger, so do their people. At its worst, harshness, bitterness, malice, rage and anger can end up in either of two extremes. One is the wife beater, the other is the "punkin' eater."

Wife battering is anger turned violent and ugly. It calls for a report to authorities, temporary separation and the help of caring people. It is a time for intercessors to pray, encouragers to support and interveners to act. I (Chuck) recall meeting with a man who had just been arrested for the second time for hitting his wife. He was scared. Already he had been through court-mandated counseling, and he was afraid this time he might go to jail. Together the man and I looked at a list of words that might describe the downward spiral of abusers—anger, rage, malice, intimidation, violence, incest, rape, molestation and murder.

He studied the list and said, "Anger, rage, intimidation," and halfway through violence, "that's me. Yes, I got mad and hit my wife. But the rest of that list is not me. In the court-mandated counseling, one other man and I were not like the others. We lost our tempers, but we were *not* proud of it. Those other guys were saying, 'I should have beat up on her more while I had the chance. She had it coming.' They were animals." His honesty and firsthand account show every man (and any woman who struggles with anger) the danger of riding the downward spiral.

Our visit concluded with a walk through the "Steps to Freedom in Christ." (See appendix A for these personal Steps). He left with fresh hope.

Do you recall this old nursery rhyme?

> Peter, Peter, punkin' eater,
> Had a wife and couldn't keep her,
> So he put her in a punkin' shell,
> And there he kept her very well.

A "punkin' eater" is a husband who smothers, pampers and isolates his wife. He treats her like a breakable China doll. At times he idolizes her, but he refuses to see where she is capable and competent. He is blind to her great potential.

I knew such a man. His wife seldom left the house. He spoke well of her, but let her do almost nothing for herself. How did I recognize his anger under his seemingly caring behavior? On rare occasions he would go on a rampage, throwing and breaking things all through the house. He never touched his wife, but he intimidated her beyond belief. He was a punkin' eater!

The Bible interestingly couples teaching about anger and forgiveness together in Ephesians 4:31,32: "Get rid of all bitterness, rage and anger, brawling and slander, along with every form of malice. Be kind and compassionate to one another, forgiving each other, just as in Christ God forgave you." Angry people often find that forgiving those who caused pain in the past relieves much of their rage. Spouses of angry people discover that forgiveness works much better than defense mechanisms and self-protective behaviors. Those who learn to let the flaming arrows of rage fly by, or use the shield of faith for the ones that hit, become strong in the Lord and the power of His might (see Eph. 6:10-20).

SUBMISSION

Anger, of course, is not limited to husbands. It can easily plague the strong-willed wife who hates to submit to anyone, especially her husband. One of the really distasteful words in the Bible is *submit*. It goes against our rugged individualism. It sounds un-American. It feels nasty, uncomfortable and binding. Submit to God, maybe. After all, He deserves all our trust. He has all authority, and He uses it with our best interests in mind. But when the Bible says, "Submit to one another" (Eph. 5:21), that's pushing it. And when it goes on to say, "Wives, submit to your husbands" (v. 22), that's way too far!

Some wives picture themselves turning into dominated doormats. *He's going to be this big alley cat and I'm going to be this little meek and mild mouse who gets eaten alive. He's going to give all the orders and I'm going to march to his tune. He's going to do the stepping and I'm going to get stepped on. Who wants to knuckle under all the time? Who wants to just fold, bury real feelings and comply to his every wish?*

Wait a minute! A big misunderstanding is going on here. Before we proceed, we need to understand what the Bible is really saying. It's not talking about becoming wimps, losing our personalities, and burying our feelings. Biblical submission does not mean refusing to express our opinions or letting sick controllers ruin our lives.

When the Bible speaks of submitting, it always does so in the context of authority:

- Submit to God (see Jas. 4:7).
- Submit to the civil government (see Rom. 13:1-7; 1 Tim. 2:1-4; 1 Pet. 2:13-17).
- Submit to church leaders (see Heb. 13:17).
- Submit to parents (see Eph. 6:1-3).
- Submit to husbands (see 1 Pet. 3:1-4).

One great value of submission is that it causes us to avoid rebellion (see Dan. 9:5,9). Rebels move out from under authority and expose themselves to the worst attacks from the devil, the world and the flesh. Rebels throw off God's controls and try to fly their own bombers (without flying lessons) until they crash and burn. Notice what happens to rebels. They go down in smoke—depression, disease or disgrace.

Husbands, please note a key verse: "Submit *to one another* out of reverence for Christ" (Eph. 5:21, italics added). We all need to submit to one another's needs in love. In the original Greek, the New Testament grammatically links this verse to the next one about wives submitting to husbands. We cannot separate these two verses without losing the Bible's context. If we rob a verse of its context, we steal a vital part of its meaning. The Bible commands husbands to sacrifice their selfish desires by loving their wives as Christ loved the Church. When the Bible says submit, it means *voluntarily yielding our rights to one another in love.*

Voluntarily means it's my choice.
Yielding means I defer on purpose.
My rights means that it involves something precious to me.
To one another means I give it and receive it as a gift.

In love means that I have a motive—my
reverence for Christ.

Simply stated, submit means to always put the other person first. In plain English, it means that in Christ we don't always have to have our own way. It means we can give up our rights because we love each other as Christ loved us. We can communicate. We can negotiate. We can compromise. Sometimes we can argue. But the time will come again and again when we will have to yield. We can do this because we belong to Jesus Christ who yielded His rights and His life on calvary's Cross for us.

The Bible explicitly says, "Wives, submit to your husbands *as is fitting in the Lord*" (Col. 3:18, italics added). Sometimes a wife should *not* do everything her husband demands. The term "as is fitting" means what is proper, what is one's duty. Some activities require holy disobedience. Wives must obey God rather than men (see Acts 4:19). This means:

No child abuse
No wife swapping or adultery
No brutality or battering
No refusing to let her worship
No illegal or immoral activity

Do you want to understand submission in its biblical sense? Then see the word *submit* for what it really means, it is like the Lord Jesus in His "reverent submission" (see Heb. 5:7,8; Phil. 2:1-11). The rewards of building a marriage God's way are deep satisfaction and lasting peace. And that is what we all want in our marriages, isn't it?

MANIPULATION

Those who buy into this world's values, and refuse to submit to God, try to get their own way by devious schemes. That is nothing less than manipulation. Isaac bitterly disappointed Rebekah by passing her off as his sister, right into the harem of Abimelech (see Gen. 26:7-9). Reading between the lines, it appears that love died in Rebekah's heart. From that moment on we see a different Rebekah. Instead of forgiving and rebuilding trust, she became a manipulator. My guess is that she made an inner vow to herself: "I will live *with* Isaac, but I will no longer live *for* him."

What Rebekah forgot, or chose to ignore, was that God had already promised to give her her heart's desire (see Gen. 25:23). All she needed to do was sit back, relax and trust God's promises. Instead she gave way to panic and took everything into her own hands. At the heart of manipulation lies a refusal to trust God.

Webster defines manipulation: "To control or play upon by unfair or insidious means; to manage by shrewd use of influence, especially in an unfair or fraudulent way for one's own purposes." Manipulation also hides behind other masks—blowing up, sulking, beguiling, deceiving, jockeying, maneuvering, pouting, withholding and scheming.

The list fits Rebekah, tricking Isaac to give his final blessing to her favorite son, Jacob, instead of their firstborn, Esau (see Gen. 27:1-40). (A father's last blessing in those days was legally binding in court, similar to a last will and testament today. Once spoken, it could never be changed).

Manipulation always rebounds with disastrous consequences. For Rebekah, it meant sending away her beloved son, Jacob, until Esau's rage cooled down (see Gen. 27:41-45). What she must have supposed might take a few months turned into 20 years. Rebekah was left with her unfavorite son and his idol-worshipping wives. They made life miserable for her (see Gen. 27:46; 28:8). Sadly, Rebekah never saw her son Jacob again. How much better it might have been if Rebekah had finished well, living out a life of respect for her husband.

RESPECT

My dad was wise. He said things I will never forget. Although death took him to be with the Lord sometime ago, his words still linger in my memory. Over and over I heard him say, "Marriage is built on respect."

He was the kind of father who always insisted we three boys respect our mother. We could dislike some of her decisions and say so—politely. We could complain to him, and sometimes he would understand, or so it seemed to us. But he would never, never tolerate any disrespect for her. Any "sassing," to use his word, resulted in severe punishment.

Mom deserved our respect. She was the greatest. She had been a school teacher, but chose not to teach after her family came along. She stayed home to "raise the boys." She poured her life into her family, and did a great job of it. Whatever grievances we had were most often based on the fact we didn't get our own way every time we wanted it. So what's new about kids!

I will never forget how Dad always treated Mom with respect—genuine respect. They had their normal differences. I remember seeing Mom in tears a time or two. But I never recall a single disrespectful act or word for her from Dad. He believed, and practiced, respect in marriage.

After I grew up, I was privileged to do some pastoral marriage counseling. The most common pattern to surface in marital tension was loss of respect. I observed that respect built a foundation for resolving marriage conflicts. Disrespect led to co-dependency or dissolution. But there was a problem. It seemed most people based their respect on behavior. Using behavior alone as a reason to respect someone is a trap. No one is perfect, so no one qualifies for perfect respect. Everyone has sinned and is born with the flesh, including its weaknesses and bent toward evil. Without major effort, every marriage will end in disrespect.

Some wives we talked with (and some husbands, too) saw their spouses as dirty, rotten, no-good, double-crossing, lowdown jerks. Based on behavior, sometimes we had to agree.

Please note a big difference between respect and trust. Respect is something everyone deserves. Trust is something that must be earned. We can respect people even when we do not trust their behavior. We respect their personhood and their positions in our lives, even after they may have shattered our trust. Everyone deserves respect, but only those who earn it gain trust.

In Christ, we can learn to respect our mate's person and position (see Eph. 5:33). Every husband or wife was created in the image of God. Everyone is so valuable that Christ died on the Cross for each person's sins. Everyone has a soul that will one day be joined to a resurrected body and live forever in

RESPECT IS A GIFT EVERY CHRISTIAN CAN GIVE, WHETHER OR NOT THE OTHER PERSON DESERVES IT.

either heaven or hell. We all, no matter how bad our behavior is, deserve respect for who we are. In addition, every true Christian deserves special respect as the temple of the Holy Spirit.

We can also respect another person's position, even if we do not approve of his or her performance (see Col. 3:13-15). Husband, wife, mother, father—each of these are God-given positions in the family. These positions deserve respect. If we dishonor the position, we dishonor God who created family life for His glory.

Respecting a spouse's person and position does not mean liking his or her behavior. It does not mean we should cover up abuse. It does not mean we should avoid seeking help for our marriage. *It does mean, however, that we attack the problem, not the person.* Focusing on the problem keeps husbands and wives respecting each other, even in the worst of times. It builds love on the biblical basis of sacrifice instead of the cultural basis of romance and blood chemistry. Respect is a gift every Christian can give, whether or not the other person deserves it.

David Augsburger writes about "dirty fighting strategies for getting your own way" in his book *When Caring Is Not Enough*[6]:

The Art of Manipulation

Dirty fighting strategies for getting your own way

1. Timing	Catch them off guard rather than choose a good time.
2. Turf	Pick your best turf rather than choose a neutral place.
3. Anxiety	Step up the anxiety rather than set a caring atmosphere.
4. Fogging	Filibuster, fog and fume instead of communicating equally.
5. Mystifying	Ramble, chain react, confuse rather than be clear and honest.
6. Generalizing	Universalize and exaggerate instead of simplify and focus.
7. Analyze	Intellectualize, theorize, advise instead of admitting pain.
8. Gunnysacking	Save up grievances rather than deal with here and now.
9. Neutrality	Be silent, superior, detached rather than open and present.
10. Temper	Hide anger then ventilate rage rather than clean anger.
11. Blaming	Find who is at fault rather than practice no-fault fights.
12. Righteousness	Find who is right instead of find what's right.
13. Exit	Walk out, clam up, shut off instead of working through.
14. Questioning	Use clever or concealed questions instead of statements.
15. Triangling	Pit people against people instead of dealing firsthand.
16. Put-downs	Use sarcasm, jibes, digs rather than share humor.
17. Undermining	Undermine self-esteem rather than enrich self-respect.
18. Guilt	Play either judge or martyr to hook guilt not responsibility.

19. Mind-reading	Read or rape the other's mind rather than listen, wait, learn.
20. Delaying	Ignore, forget, postpone rather than honor commitments.

WHERE IS GOD WHEN IT COUNTS?

Suppose we've tried everything and our marriages are still not working. Where is Christ when we really need Him? Why doesn't He answer prayer for our marriages? Where is God when it counts?

Sometimes science tells us lies. We expect it from evolutionists who tell us we descended from apes or that human beings are only animals with better brains. But a scientific false teaching can subtly sneak up on us, and we believe the lie. Or we half believe it in ways that make us function as if we believed it wholeheartedly.

One of those scientific lies is empty space. We are taught that vast light years of space exist with absolutely nothing in it. It is said to be void of an atmosphere (true); has only occasional stars, asteroids or any other material scattered apart by enormous distances (true); and has no inhabitants (false).

That is the lie! God inhabits every part of His universe, including space. It is not empty. It is full of His glory. It is full of His presence. "The heavens declare the glory of God; the skies proclaim the work of his hands. Day after day they pour forth speech; night after night they display knowledge" (Ps. 19:1,2).

If we believe the lie, then we think of heaven as somewhere far beyond the vast reaches of space. Because God is in heaven, where does that lie put Him? Far away from us, too! But God is omnipresent—everywhere present, always present.

Far from empty space, the kingdom of heaven (literally "the heavens" in Matthew) begins at our toes. God's presence is as close as the air we breathe. People ask, "Where was God?" when something terrible happens. The answer is that He was right there at our shoulder—and He's right here right now!

Sin, Satan and the curse upon creation (as well as deceived and evil people) may have their day, but their actions do not remove God's presence. He still reigns. He still rules. The great Judgment Day is coming! Everyone will get their due. In the meantime, He is up close and personal.

This truth has vast implications for daily living. In our marriages, God is always present. He watches everything that is done, feels every emotion, records every word spoken. He knows when we are loving and submissive, and when we are preoccupied and self-seeking.

In our parenting, He's there to help us. He cares for every child and gives each one a guardian angel (see Matt. 18:10). He knows when we are trying hard and trusting Him, and when we are ignoring or over-reacting. Always remember that God is revealed in Jesus Christ—and Jesus had an incredible love for children.

Our personal lives matter to Him. God the Holy Spirit keeps urging, nudging us toward Himself. He understands us better than anyone else does. He cares about our weaknesses. He even knows the thoughts we think and the motives within our souls. None of the complexities and perplexities of our lives catch Him by surprise, or even puzzle Him.

God rules! His reign, His kingdom surrounds us. Yet it fills all the universe, including every part of space. Nothing is empty, not even a vacuum! So how do we pray when we're disappointed, when our sins rear their ugly heads, when our weaknesses are exposed? For starters, we can remember that we have the treasure of "the light of the knowledge of the glory of God in the face of Christ" (2 Cor. 4:6) in these weak jars of clay in which we live. Despite our strengths we still have weaknesses. We are clay pots that hold glistening treasures!

CLAY POT'S PRAYER
2 CORINTHIANS 4:5-10; 12:7-10

Heavenly Father,

You know the disappointments that grieve my spirit and club me to my knees. When I reach the end of my rope, move in with Your power and rescue me to safety. When I hit the wall, pick me up with Your energy and keep me going. When

I just can't take it anymore, move in with Your strength and give me a fresh start. Let me die with Jesus in the middle of my disappointments so I can rise with Jesus to His destiny appointments.

O Lord, You also know my weaknesses, my disabilities, my limitations that just will not go away. Thank You that in the mystery of Your sovereign grace, You use this clay pot of my humanity as storage for Your glistening treasures. Let the light of the knowledge of the glory of God shine through the cracks of my clay pot.

Teach me to face up to my weaknesses, to work on improving them and to find people whose strengths compensate for them. Most of all use my weaknesses for Your glory. Your power is sufficient for me. Make Your strength perfect in my weaknesses—the chains that I cannot escape.

I know I am a child of God, united with Christ in an organic union. I believe with bedrock conviction that God's power is really within me. So let this imperfect container of mine spill out the riches of God's surpassing power.

I give You the pain of my past, the times I was hurt, misled, insulted, cheated, betrayed, abused, victimized or grieved. As Paul said, "I delight in weaknesses, in insults, in hardships, in persecutions, in difficulties. For when I am weak, then I am strong" (2 Cor. 12:10).

I release my present to You. I am content in Christ with the assurance that because of Your surpassing power I am not crushed, not in despair, not abandoned, not destroyed. Instead, the life of Jesus is revealed in my mortal body.

I place my confidence in Your future for me. I trust Christ's power as I forgive, and thank You for the release of the torture that unforgiveness inflicts upon me. In union with Christ I claim Your power to keep going, to release negative attitudes, to overcome trouble, to build character and to minister to others.

In Jesus' powerful name, Amen.

Fork in the Road

Are you really in touch with your deep feelings? Some of us protect ourselves from unpleasantness by separating our conscious thoughts from our emotional pain. It is a self-protective behavior. We may have faced a past trauma far more devastating—incest, rape, child abuse or some major shock to our systems. In God's mercy He allows our brains to block these painful memories. He protects us from the devastation that might otherwise lead to insanity, or even death.

Years later, often in the safer environment of a good marriage, fine church or support group, the memories come flooding back. Like a volcano building up pressure, they one day erupt. The damaged emotions that come with them disrupt our lives. Once the painful memories surface, something must be done. But what? At this time it is vital to pick the right counselor, pastor or friend, because Christian and non-Christian counselors point in different directions at this crucial fork in the road.

Non-Christian counselors and therapists emphasize restoring a healthy self-image, building self-esteem and enhancing self-worth. This sounds good on the surface. Closer examination, however, reveals that the secular mindset sometimes produces a person who is self-satisfied, self-indulgent sexually and self-reliant apart from God. Too often the "self" is built up with non-biblical tactics. The counsel given is to blame, accuse, fight back, become independent or divorce.

Biblical counselors know the danger of that easy road. They also realize that it is impossible to dress up the flesh or make the selfish self pleasing to God (see Rom. 8:6-8). Instead they point people down the right road. Wise Christians call for death to the flesh and new life in Jesus Christ. They teach us to find our true identities in dying with Christ and rising with Him to newness of life. Their counsel is to give genuine forgiveness from the heart, the kind that faces up to the emotional core of pain. They point to the justice of the Cross.

The crucial fork in the road leads those wanting help to travel toward totally different destinations. One road leads to self-sufficiency, the other to Christ-sufficiency. One leads to hell, the other to heaven. Which fork of the road are you on? Check your road signs and correct your course if necessary.

Notes

1. Anonymous, Frank S. Mead, Ed., *The Encyclopedia of Religious Quotations* (Westwood, N.J.: Fleming H. Revell Co., 1965), p. 296.
2. David Augsburger, *Sustaining Love, Healing and Growth in the Passages of Marriage* (Ventura, Calif: Regal Books, 1988), p. 12.
3. Mark Noll, "The Struggle for Lincoln's Soul," *Books and Culture, A Christian Review* 1, no. 1, (September/October 1995). Noll reviews the excellent research by historian Michael Burlingame in *The Inner World of Abraham Lincoln* (University of Illinois Press).
4. Melissa Balmain, "Golden Tips on Marriage from Real Pros," *The Orange County Register*, Wednesday, 31 May, 1995, Metro, p. 1.
5. David Goetz, "Is the Pastor's Family Safe at Home," *Leadership Journal* (fall 1992): 39.
6. David Augsburger, *When Caring Is Not Enough* (Ventura, Calif: Regal Books, 1983), pp. 5-7.

CHAPTER SIX

Created Male, Created Female

So God created man in his own image, in the image of God he created him; male and female he created them.

—GENESIS 1:27

There is neither Jew nor Greek, slave nor free, male nor female, for you are all one in Christ Jesus.

—GALATIANS 3:28

My wife, Nancy, and I (Chuck) were on vacation in Maui, Hawaii, celebrating our 13th wedding anniversary. Morning after morning we sat on the second-story deck of our condo reading, praying, sipping tea, soaking up the sun while watching two small birds build their nest in a tree just a few feet away.

It's amazing how God builds the principles of cooperation and teamwork into His creation. The male (identified by his markings) was the supplier, bringing in the resources, strands of plants about six inches to a foot long. The female was the architect and builder, working steadily inside a covered nest that kept her hidden from view most of the time. But the shaking, pulling and weaving were obvious.

A couple of times intruders threatened. The male flew into action—diving, harassing and attacking. He made life so miserable for any bird, no matter how large, that came near his nest that it simply chose to go elsewhere. Call it protective or possessive or jealous if you like, but this little male was defending his home and his family.

Watching how this industrious male handled failure and success was interesting. When he dropped a strand to the ground below, an obvious failure, he looked and looked for it but never recovered it. Then he rested for awhile. He didn't work more frantically to try to make up for it. Instead he rested and recovered his senses. After success, however (sticking a strand into the nest where the female would pull it inside and weave it into a beautiful place), he quickly flew off for another strand. It was success upon success, resource upon resource. Every success led quickly to another, and another.

Meanwhile the skillful female was designing and building a home for her future young. It took shape strand by strand, day by day. When finished, it had a neat entrance in a fully enclosed nest. It provided shelter, protection and privacy. It was well anchored so the high winds would not blow it down

The pair of nest builders provided a living parable before our watching eyes. It is a picture of what happens in a good marriage. Think of some of the lessons God teaches through this pair of little birds:

TEAMWORK

- Efficiency through division of labor
- Resting after failure
- Working hard until success comes
- Defending home and family
- Providing resources hour after hour, day after day
- Creating design and beauty
- Furnishing shelter, protection and privacy
- Preparing diligently for the future

Building a great marriage and family requires nest-building principles in action. Genesis, the first book of the Bible, gives the role of "suitable helper" to Eve, and by implication to all wives (see Gen 2:18, 20-24). It literally means one corresponding to her husband. She complements and completes him. The New Testament gives the husband the same role in the family as Christ has in the Church, namely "head" (see Eph. 5:23). He is to think ahead on her behalf, to protect and direct the marriage for her good. He is to love his wife and sacrifice himself for her just as Christ did for the Church. Both the husband's role of loving, sacrificing head of his wife and the wife's role of suitable helper who corresponds to her husband are biblical—and practical. Let's learn from the Creator. He knows how marriage is supposed to be done!

Christ not only loves the Church, He also understands it completely. With the human limitations of maleness and femaleness, we find understanding each other in marriage rather difficult at times. How can any husband serve as the Christlike head of his wife without growing in his understanding of her? How can any wife give godly submission to her husband without growing in her understanding of him? It is so easy to act like our spouses are just like us, even though we know better. When we grasp the hidden differences between men and women, we just might gain new insights into our biblical roles as wives and husbands.

HIDDEN DIFFERENCES

Everyone knows men and women are not the same. Although both share the image of God, they are created *male* and *female* (see Gen. 1:27). I recall teaching a small child to identify men and women. He was at the age when recognizing the difference was just beginning. Daddy was a man, Mommy was a woman. His brother was a man, his sister was a woman. (We're keeping it simple here!) In about 10 minutes he understood how to identify every person he met as male or female. That lesson, one we all learned as small children, stays with us for a lifetime.

MEN AND WOMEN VARY IN HOW THEY SEE THE WORLD AND THEIR ROLES IN IT.

The hidden differences that extend far beyond physical characteristics are not so obvious. Men and women hold within their souls different ways of seeing the world, different dialects in communicating, different ways of coping with stress, etc. Whole books have been written about this subject. A few examples and insights in this chapter may help us appreciate what God intended by designing men and women as He created them.

Before we explore that issue, however, a disclaimer is needed. Please understand that individuals vary more among themselves because of personality and character differences than because of their sexes. Your spouse may not be at all like the men or women described in this chapter. These generalities are given as clues to help you understand your mate. But the real task is to get a grip on how your spouse is different from you, and vice versa.

WORLDVIEW

Men and women vary in how they see the world and their roles in it. Men see the world as a race, a war, a hunt. Their job is to achieve, to produce and to succeed. Like the male nest builder, men see themselves as runners, warriors and providers. Men feel driven to generate, fabricate and procreate. Ask most men who they are, and they will usually respond in terms of their occupations: "I am a teacher, an electrician, an engineer." They may care deeply for their families, as intensely as their wives do, but in their souls men long to achieve, to succeed, to win. God created them male.

Women see the world as a family, a nest, a place of beauty. Their job is to nurture, to care and to shelter. Like the female nest builder, women see themselves as settlers, peacemakers and designers. They feel driven to relate, associate and cultivate. Ask most women who they are and they will often respond in terms of their relationships: "I'm a friend of...the wife of...the mother of...." Women may succeed in their careers, and outdo their male competitors, but in their souls they long for friendships, family, children and home. God created them female.

My caring wife, Nancy, brought home a moving description of this passion for family and relationship. It's called "What Motherhood Really Means."

> Time is running out for my friend. While we are sitting at lunch, she casually mentions that she and her husband are thinking of "starting a family." What she means is that her biological clock has begun its countdown, and she is being forced to consider the prospect of motherhood.
>
> "We're taking a survey," she says, half joking. "Do you think I should have a baby?"
>
> "It will change your life," I say carefully, keeping my tone neutral.
>
> "I know," she says. "No more sleeping in on Saturdays, no more spontaneous vacations...."
>
> But that is not what I mean at all. I try to decide what to tell her.
>
> I want her to know what she will never learn in childbirth classes. I want to tell her that the physical wounds of childbearing heal, but that becoming a mother will leave an emotional wound so raw that she will be forever vulnerable.

I consider warning her that she will never read a newspaper again without asking, "What if that had been my child?" That every plane crash, every fire will haunt her. That when she sees pictures of starving children, she will look at the mothers and wonder if anything could be worse than watching your child die.

I look at her carefully manicured nails and stylish suit and think that no matter how sophisticated she is, becoming a mother will reduce her to the primitive level of a she-bear protecting her cub. That an urgent call of "Mom!" will cause her to drop her best crystal without a moment's hesitation.

I feel I should warn her that no matter how many years she has invested in her career, she will be professionally derailed by motherhood. She might arrange for childcare, but one day she will be going into an important business meeting, and she will think about her baby's sweet smell. She will have to use every ounce of discipline to keep from running home, just to make sure her child is all right.

I want my friend to know that everyday decisions will no longer be routine. That a five-year-old boy's desire to go to the men's room rather than the women's at a restaurant will become a major dilemma. That issues of independence and gender identity will be weighed against the prospect that a child molester may be lurking in the restroom. However decisive she may be at the office, she will second-guess herself constantly as a mother.

Looking at my attractive friend, I want to assure her that eventually she will shed the pounds of pregnancy, but she will never feel the same about herself. That her life, now so important, will be of less value to her once she has a child. That she would give it up in a moment to save her offspring, but will also begin to hope for more years—not to accomplish her own dreams, but to watch her child accomplish his.

My friend's relationship with her husband will change, but not in the ways she thinks. I wish she could understand how much more you can love a man who is always careful to powder the baby or who never hesitates to play with his son or daughter. I think she should know that she will fall in love with her husband again for reasons she would now find very unromantic.

I wish my modern friend could sense the bond she will feel with women throughout history who have tried desperately to stop war and prejudice and drunk driving. I hope she will understand why I can think rationally about most issues, but become temporarily insane when I discuss the threat of nuclear war to my children's future.

I want to describe to my friend the exhilaration of seeing your child learn to hit a baseball. I want to capture for her the belly laugh of a baby who is touching the soft fur of a dog for the first time. I want her to taste the joy that is so real it hurts.

My friend's quizzical look makes me realize that tears have formed in my eyes. "You'll never regret it," I say finally. Then, squeezing my friend's hand, I offer a prayer for her and me and all of the mere mortal women who stumble their way into this holiest of callings.[1]

Thank you, Dale Hanson Bourke, for a mother's view of what it means to be created female.

DIALECTS

Women and men vary in how they talk, in their dialects. Watch small children and you will see that girls are more verbal and have larger vocabularies than boys. Boys make more action noises—brmmm, eeeoow, whoooow—and have smaller vocabularies than girls. As adults women tend to share feelings with a bent toward drama. Men tend to share information with a bent toward problem solving. Women thrive on communication; men thrive on action (even watching it on TV). In marriage women desire to maintain verbal relationships with their husbands, no matter how much time it takes. In marriage men desire companionship in recreation, social activities and church functions, no matter how inconvenient the timing.

Men prefer facts; women prefer feelings. I was waiting in the Portland, Oregon, airport when I overheard a couple talking with a friend. I noticed with interest that they were both talking at the same time! The man was giving information about the letter he would write tomorrow. The woman was sharing her complaint about the postal service. She was telling about a friend who had mailed two letters at the same time. One had arrived in a single day; the other had arrived a week later. Both kept talking non-stop. He spoke a male dialect and she spoke a female counterpart. Their poor friend couldn't get a word in edgewise.

Women and men also vary in their choice of topics for conversation. Simply contrast women's magazines with men's magazines. A humorous example came from the first Promise Keepers Conference in Anaheim, California, in May, 1994. It was an awesome experience to be gathered together with over 50,000 men. (Neil and I wholeheartedly affirm the seven promises of a Promise Keeper). A delightful moment in the conference occurred when a PK staff member's wife sent a note to be read from the platform. She suggested (tongue in cheek) that the topics these men were considering were far too inadequate. Instead, she made some creative suggestions.

- PMS—How to Keep Your Mouth Shut
- Why a Vacuum Cleaner Is Not a Good Birthday Present
- Parenting Does Not End at Conception
- The Male Ego—God's Little Joke

I laughed with her, but please note something. A quick look at her topics will show that all of them are relationship oriented. God created her female.

Sexuality

Men and women vary in understanding their sexuality. Men see sex primarily as gender and a physical act. Women see sex primarily as gender and an emotional relationship. Sexual attraction for men begins with the eye gate. A beautiful woman raises his physical voltage. Sexual attraction for women begins with the ear gate. A man with a gift for tender talk raises her emotional voltage.

A man's sexual desire is often impulsive. He responds to an attractive woman—or picture or image of one—and his desire is aroused. It makes no difference at first whether or not he even knows her. A woman's sexual desire is often selective. She responds to a particular man, to his caring, his attentiveness, his personality, his words and especially the awareness that he finds her attractive. These qualities make the difference in whether she knows him, or would like to know him.

Take a look at male lust and female lust after the Fall and sin's entrance into the world. The differences highlight the evil ways men and women pervert sexual desire. In our culture the epitome of male lust is pornography. It is full of nudity, exploitation, copulation and rape. Seldom is a woman addicted to pornography, but men often are. In our culture the epitome of female lust is the TV soap opera. It is full of drama, romance, intrigue and adultery. Seldom is a man addicted to soap operas, but women often are. Male lust is impersonal. Female lust is intensely personal. Male lust tends to conquer and exploit. Female lust tends to captivate and control.

Men need sex in order to feel love.[2] The act of sex itself puts them in touch with their feelings of emotional love for a woman. For years as a pastor I counseled wives in troubled marriages to increase the frequency of intercourse, and to take the initiative in doing so. It was a shortcut to opening their husbands up to feelings, conversation and sometimes even church attendance. When men's sexual needs are satisfied they become more open, tender and ready to deal with communication problems and marriage hassles. Their interest in the marital relationship increases.

Women need to feel in order to have sex. They need communication and understanding first. They need relaxation and a great relationship to enjoy sex fully. They need commitment, love and understanding to release their sensual side to their husbands, and the passion that accompanies it. It took Neil and me far too long to discover these basic realities about our own wives. Taking time to listen, to empathize and to understand was a big part of loving our wives in the way they wanted to be loved. When the Bible says, "Husbands, love your wives, just as Christ loved the church and gave himself up for her" (Eph. 5:25), it certainly includes sacrificing our own preferences for their good. That includes restraining our passions so our total relationship can benefit in the long run.

STRESS

Men and women vary in the way they handle stress. Men will take time out to be alone, no matter who they may hurt in the process. They will fight for their freedom. Women will find time to share their feelings, whether or not their husbands will listen. They will fight for some understanding of their emotional ups and downs. Take a look at each:

Almost all men go away into their own private caves at times. They simply walk out on the women (and men) in their lives and hibernate for an hour or two, or even a day or two. It's typical of men...and women seldom understand it.[3]

Men and Caves

What frustrates wives is that men seldom if ever explain what they are doing or why. They just disappear, walk out, leave the room or the house. When they come back, usually in a good mood and ready to talk, they have no idea why the women in their lives seem upset.

When men enter their caves they are anchoring their souls. They isolate to find the solutions to their problems, or fresh views of a situation or new perspectives on life. When men spend all their spare time with their wives or with other men, they lose a valuable part of themselves. They can't explain it, but it's gone. Troubles begin to bother them; they feel irritable; little things don't make sense. Men need time to sort things out, think things over and pray to the Lord.

Not all caves are the same. Some men (the famous "couch potatoes") use the TV. Some go hunting or fishing, often alone. Some become engrossed in a hobby or working overtime. Some just go for a drive, or for a walk or somewhere to be

MEN FIGHT FOR THE FREEDOM TO BE ALONE; WOMEN CARE INTENSELY ABOUT THEIR FEELINGS. THEY ALSO WANT THEIR MEN TO UNDERSTAND AND CARE.

alone. Some go to their offices, or their computers or their places of prayer. But all walk away, and their wives are usually left feeling rejected and misunderstood.

Two helpful tips for understanding caves can make all the difference in marriage. One is for husbands, the other is for wives. For husbands, the magic words are, "I'll be back" or "I'll be right back." Men don't have a clue how much reassurance these words provide for their wives when they walk out. She feels valued because he acknowledges her; she feels secure because he commits himself to her again; she feels safe because he reassures her that he is not leaving for good.

For women, the helpful tip is to do something enjoyable while he is hibernating. Wives, never, never, ever follow a man into his cave. A man goes into his cave like a frustrated bear seeking hibernation or a dragon spitting fire. Following a man into his cave is a sure way to get clawed or burned. Leave him alone, and he will come home wagging his tail behind him, usually happy and at peace with himself and you! Meanwhile, phone a woman friend, go shopping, enjoy a hobby, read a good book or magazine. Do something you want to do, and thoroughly enjoy it.

Men are almost always ready to talk, communicate and be decent human beings when they come out of their caves. If they are Christians, they may have met with God during this time, or at least relaxed and rested. If they are not, they are still men and will have found something within themselves that makes them more whole, more fun, more decent to live with.

These simple insights can help your marriage. Wives, give men the freedom they desire at moments when they desperately need it. Then capitalize on the communication time when they come out of their caves. Husbands, give women the reassurance that the cave is normal, that it's not their fault and that you will be back. Putting these insights into practice can help you both, and make your marriage happier.

Women and Waves

Men fight for the freedom to be alone; women care intensely about their feelings. They also want their men to understand and care.

Like waves in the ocean, women's feelings about themselves, and about life in general, reach high tide and low tide. The wave builds to a peak, then subsides. The cascading of the wave gains momentum, then tumbles toward shore.

Because God pronounced His creation of women as very good, He has a wonderful purpose in the waves of their experiences. God created the ebb and flow as cleansing for the inner stains and wrinkles in their souls. But like waves, the cleansing process requires emotional descent and ascent.

As each new wave rises, women feel better, renewed, reinvigorated. Christian women feel closer to the Lord Jesus and to their families than before. Even non-Christian women feel emotionally released and recharged. It's all part of being created female, and few men (especially husbands) understand it.

Men in general, and particularly husbands, often foul up this God-given rhythm in women's lives. Because men don't understand waves, they often react incorrectly. They try to stop the cascading by fixing the problem, denying women's feelings or taking it all personally. Many husbands try to change their wives when they begin an emotional descent, or simply give up and walk away. Both reactions leave wives feeling unsafe to share their deepest feelings.

Disaster upon disaster occurs when women stifle their God-given feelings; they remain uncleansed, plagued with inner wrinkles and blemishes. The sad result is that they can neither love as freely nor feel as good about themselves as God intended.

In cases of clinical depression (for either women or men), intense treatment is needed. The personal Steps to Freedom often make a dramatic change for the better. A support group, caring counselor and a medical exam by a competent physician may all help.

Sometimes men feel like they've failed as husbands when wives express their tumbling feelings. More often, they think their wives are crazy, or at least a little irrational. Men tend to react by putting up (fighting, blaming, accusing) or shutting up (running, quitting, giving up). Husbands need to train themselves to simply listen, accept and understand their wives. When they do, women can descend and ascend in their waves more easily and rapidly.

Women and waves are God-created and inevitable. When men simply love, accept and understand this, they validate their wives' feelings. Wise husbands are not personally affected by their wives' negative feelings. Nor do they run for their caves, unless staying out only makes matters worse. Nor do they try to solve their problems for them. Wise men simply admit they don't have the answers, and try to understand their wives' feelings. They stand by, listen attentively and give no explanations. As a result, they create a sheltered beach where waves can ebb and flow without harm.

Then, oh then, a man sacrifices himself for his wife just as Christ does for the Church (see Eph. 5:23-28). He goes all out in his love for her, letting God release her inner radiance. It's beauty treatment for the soul. (Women, when we men fail miserably, as we often do, turn to your women friends and to the Lord Himself. They understand!)

The list of male and female differences could go on and on. The point is we need to understand that our spouses see life, approach life and handle life differently than we do. God knows what He is doing by making us different, yet one in Christ (see Gal. 3:26-28). The differences make up much of the magnetism that draws men and women together in marriage. What we all have in common is being made in the image of God.

We must never use our maleness or femaleness as an excuse for taking advantage of the other. Instead we use our uniqueness to meet one another's needs, help each other and encourage each other. The better we understand our differences, the more we will appreciate each others' strengths. Rejoice that you are created male or created female, and your spouse complements you.

Notes

1. Adapted from Dale Hanson Bourke, *Everyday Miracles, Holy Moments in a Mother's Day* (Dallas: Word Publishing, 1989), pp. 1-4. Used by permission.
2. John Gray, *Mars and Venus in the Bedroom, A Guide to Lasting Romance and Passion* (New York: Harper Collins Publishers, 1995), pp. 1-6.
3. John Gray, *Men Are from Mars, Women Are from Venus, A Practical Guide for Improving Communication and Getting What You Want in Your Relationships* (New York: Harper Collins Publishers, 1992), pp. 30-35.

CHAPTER SEVEN

Resolving Conflicts

Wives, in the same way be submissive to your husbands so that, if any of them do not believe the word, they may be won over without words by the behavior of their wives, when they see the purity and reverence of your lives. Your beauty should not come from outward adornment, such as braided hair and the wearing of gold jewelry and fine clothes. Instead, it should be that of your inner self, the unfading beauty of a gentle and quiet spirit, which is of great worth in God's sight. Husbands, in the same way be considerate as you live with your wives, and treat them with respect as the weaker partner and as heirs with you of the gracious gift of life, so that nothing will hinder your prayers. Finally, all of you, live in harmony with one another; be sympathetic, love as brothers, be compassionate and humble. Do not repay evil for evil or insult with insult, but with blessing, because to this you were called so that you may inherit a blessing.

—1 PETER 3:1-4; 7-9

Troubled wife: "Pastor, I don't think our marriage is going to last."

Pastor: "Why do you feel that way?"

Troubled husband: "Well, we're so different!"

Pastor: "Do you see that as a weakness or a strength in your relationship?"

DIFFERENCES CAN BE STRENGTHS

Too many couples perceive their differences as weaknesses and retreat to their personal caves and holes rather than try to understand and complement each other with those differences. I (Neil) believe God intended our differences to be the strength of our marriages. When I taught a young married's Sunday School class, I often used a teaching technique that required the class to either agree or disagree with several statements. Occasionally I would have them gather in *agree* or *disagree* groups to find biblical support for their positions, and to allow them to prepare for sharing their insights and perspectives with the others.

Two men from the class took me out for lunch one day. They were good Christian friends of mine, but they were having a problem with my teaching techniques.

"What's your concern?" I asked.

"We don't believe you should use the agree or disagree statements in Sunday School."

"Why is that?"

"Well, sometimes our wives don't agree with us!"

I really don't know how I kept a straight face! I can't even restrain myself from laughing as I write this.

They remind me of the old farmer when he first got married. He had always been taught the husband was supposed to be the head of the home. As such, he had to make sure the right perspective was brought to bear on all issues, which of course was his own perspective. Then he grew up a little, and began to tolerate his wife's perspective. Then he grew up a little bit more, and began to appreciate his wife's perspective. Then he grew up a little bit more, and he began to seek it out. Her perspective was just as valid as his, albeit quite different.

Being an intelligent man, he finally figured it out: His wife was a helpmate, not a farmhand.

Our differences imply conflict. In fact marriages can potentially thrive on conflict in a constructive sense. No husband and wife will see life from the same perspective, nor perfectly agree about how it should be lived. When our son was only two years old, he fell and scratched his knee. Given the way my father raised me, I was inclined to say, "Get up, son, and be a man." Joanne was more likely to say, "Oh! Poor baby." After 30 years of marriage, I respond to my grandchild when he falls by saying, "Get up, poor baby!" Then I hug him, throw him up in the air and tickle him until he stops crying. Joanne now says, "Poor baby, get up!" Then she holds him until he stops crying. We have had that kind of effect on each other. Little boys need both their mothers and their fathers, and we need each other.

I was raised on the farm in Minnesota; Joanne was raised in Minneapolis. I was an outgoing kind of person; Joanne liked to read and study. I liked contemporary music; Joanne liked classical music. I liked the outdoors; Joanne liked the indoors. I liked roast beef, mashed potatoes and gravy; Joanne liked gourmet food. I came from an intellectually competitive family; Joanne watched in horror as we "played" family games. I came from a family of five; she is an only child. God couldn't have picked a better helpmate. We are like a hunk of red and green clay, all rolled together in one ball. Traces of both the red and the green are visible, but the overall appearance is a combination of both. Opposites have a tendency to attract.

We had one other major difference when we were first married. I enjoyed getting up early in the morning. I used to sing in the shower. That was the best I was going to feel all day, and I wanted to tell the world about it. Joanne was a night person. One day she approached me with Bible in hand and said, "Buster, I have a verse for you." Then she read Proverbs 27:14: "If a man loudly blesses his neighbor early in the morning, it will be taken as a curse."

"Let me see that," I said. Sure enough, that's what it said! I was speechless, until I saw the next verses: "A quarrelsome wife is like a constant dripping on a rainy day; restraining her is like restraining the wind or grasping oil with the hand" (27:15,16).

"Look, Joanne," I said, "there is your verse!" Isn't God great?

DIFFERENT ROLES

Have you ever tried to restrain the wind or grasp oil with your hand? You can't. So what does the passage mean? It doesn't make much sense unless you understand that wind and oil represent the Spirit. It is my contention that a natural man cannot contend with a woman's spirit.

What do most men do when they know they can't win? They don't play the game. They lose themselves in their careers, sit in front of their television sets, play sports or work on their hobbies in the garage. Consequently, the functional head in most homes is the wife. Men, however, are physically stronger. Throughout most of recorded history they ruled by brute force. They fought the wars, plowed the fields and shot the game. Women in many cultures are subjected to demeaning roles because of male physical dominance.

Christianity elevated the status of women wherever the gospel was shared. Men should not use their physical advantage to dominate, but to provide and protect. Men should not manhandle their wives—physically beating them is totally against Christian principles. If men voluntarily surrender their physical advantage, what happens if women don't do the same with their spiritual advantage? The question will no longer be, who rules the roost? It will be, who rules the rooster? What should women do? According to 1 Peter 3:1-4, they should voluntarily choose to be submissive and adopt a quiet and gentle spirit, which has great worth in God's sight. Men should not dominate physically, but should strive to be strong in God's Spirit.

After I shared that truth from 1 Peter 3 at a church conference, a young lady said, "Now I understand what happened last night." She explained how she had been nagging her husband while driving to a function. She wouldn't stop, no matter what he did. Finally he got so angry, he pulled the car over, got out and walked home. He just left her sitting there and retreated to his cave. What he did was probably better than the alternative in his mind.

Being in a submissive role is like riding in the passenger seat of a car. Nobody has a problem riding shotgun provided two things are true about the driver.

First, the driver needs to know where he is going, or at least be willing to ask for directions. If I as a passenger know where we should be going and the driver doesn't, my natural instinct is to say, "Slide over, buster, and let me drive or let me out."

I DON'T BELIEVE THE PRIMARY PROBLEM IS WOMEN'S LIBERATION; I BELIEVE THE PRIMARY PROBLEM IS A LACK OF SPIRITUAL LEADERSHIP.

Second, the driver needs to obey the rules of the road. When the driver is running red lights, going the wrong way down one-way streets and turning corners on two wheels, the survival instinct of any rider is to get out of the car or say, "Slide over, buster, and let me drive!"

THE RESPONSIBILITY OF LEADERSHIP

I don't believe the primary problem is women's liberation; I believe the primary problem is a lack of spiritual leadership. Many men would bolt or rebel under the same circumstances in which many ladies find themselves. To be submissive to a leader who seems unable or unwilling to lead creates a great deal of anxiety for anyone, male or female. Being the head of the home is not a right to be demanded, it is an awesome responsibility. Husbands will have to stand before God some day and give an account for what has been entrusted to them.

When the sons of Zebedee were striving for positions of honor with Jesus, the Lord used the opportunity to teach a critical lesson about leadership. He said we should not be like the rulers of the Gentiles, who lord it over others. "Instead, whoever wants to become great among you must be your servant, and whoever wants to be first must be your slave—just as the Son of Man did not come to be served, but to serve, and to give his life as a ransom for many" (Matt. 20:26-28). Nobody is lower in position than a servant or a slave. So how does this apply to being the head of the home? It doesn't take away position, but it does describe responsibility. Every husband is subject to the needs of his wife and children, as the provider and the protector.

A husband simply cannot meet all of his wife's needs. Only Christ can meet every essential need. That is why every husband should be the spiritual leader, and take whatever steps are necessary to ensure that Christ is the center of his life, his marriage and his family. The best way to ensure that his wife and children become all that God wants them to be is by being all that God wants him to be as a husband and a father.

One woman said, "My husband is like Moses—he can wander around in the wilderness for 40 years and never once ask for directions!" Her friend one-upped her by saying, "My husband is like God—seldom seen; and when he does anything, it's a miracle!"

Paul lays it on the line concerning what we must teach regarding these matters in Titus 2:1-8:

> You must teach what is in accord with sound doctrine. Teach the older men to be temperate, worthy of respect, self-controlled, and sound in faith, in love and in endurance. Likewise, teach the older women to be reverent in the way they live, not to be slanderers or addicted to much wine, but to teach what is good. Then they can train the younger women to love their husbands and children, to be self-controlled and pure, to be busy at home, to be kind, and to be subject to their husbands, so that no one will malign the word of God. Similarly, encourage the young men to be self-controlled. In everything set them an example by doing what is good. In your teaching show integrity, seriousness and soundness of speech that cannot be condemned, so that those who

oppose you may be ashamed because they have nothing bad to say about us.

SUBMITTING TO AUTHORITY

Self-control is a fruit of the Spirit, and the primary instruction to both the husband and the wife is for godly character. It is not hard for a woman to be subject to a man of character who is in subjection to God. Being under authority is for our own protection. "Everyone must submit himself to the governing authorities, for there is no authority except that which God has established. The authorities that exist have been established by God. Consequently, he who rebels against the authority is rebelling against what God has instituted, and those who do so will bring judgment on themselves" (Rom. 13:1-3).

I knew a Christian leader who was verbally critical of everybody he was supposed to be submissive to—his pastor, his employer, his governor and his president. He couldn't understand why all of his children were rebellious. Ironically, I'm sure he never even considered himself to be rebellious. Like many, he would go to church and critique the message and criticize the music. We don't sit in judgment of the message, the message sits in judgment of us. We should enter into the experience of worship rather than sit outside acting like critics. Scripture requires us to submit to and pray for all those who are in authority over us.

I have also known wives who believe they were born to rule. They marry some spineless mouse who wouldn't dare stand in their way. One such woman brought her pathetic husband to see me about their college-aged daughter. The mother didn't like her daughter's boyfriend. I didn't either for that matter. I listened politely for an hour as she described her marriage and her family. Several times she made a point of saying she didn't want to be the head of her home. Finally she ran out of steam and, to my surprise, asked, "We have been together for an hour now; what do you think of me?"

I said, "Mrs. Apple Blossom, you have said you don't want to be the head of your home 3 times, but you have spoken 1000 words to your husband's 1. What do you want me to believe?"

The daughter's choice for a boyfriend was not good, but why did she choose him? If her parents got rid of that boy, chances are she would look for another just like him. Her choices were deeply affected by the conflict she had to live with at home, and the role reversal she had witnessed in her parent's relationship. Her boyfriend was the exact opposite of her father. He took charge and ran the show, but not in a godly way. After her parent's visit, I asked their daughter how it was going at home.

"Nothing has changed," she said. "Whenever I ask for something, Mom says, 'Go ask your father; he is the head of the home.' She's still directing traffic!"

Trusting God to work in our lives through less than perfect government officials, employers, husbands and parents requires great faith. Yet every biblical instruction to submit to governing officials accompanies a promise for us. Sometimes, however, we must obey God rather than man. First, people issuing commands or directives outside the realm of their authority do not have to be obeyed. Second, authority figures who issue commands morally contradictive to God's Word do not have to be obeyed. Third, authority figures who violate their responsibilities through abusive behavior should be reported to the governing authorities of the land, which have been established to protect the innocent.

Refusing to be submissive simply because we don't like our less-than-perfect authorities is also contrary to Scripture. It is rebellion, and rebellion leads to social anarchy. "Pick and choose" submission violates God's command to obey our parents. Every child could refuse to obey their parents, because there are no perfect parents.

IRON SHARPENS IRON

After mentioning the quarrelsome wife, King Solomon then said, "As iron sharpens iron, so one man sharpens another" (Prov. 27:17). Consider how iron sharpens iron. It generates a lot of heat, smoke and sparks. How can friction be avoided when a man and a woman from two different backgrounds make a commitment to live together? Conflict is inevitable.

The question is, how can we handle it? Let's look at the following ways of dealing with conflict as it relates to achievement in relationships:

CONFLICT STYLES

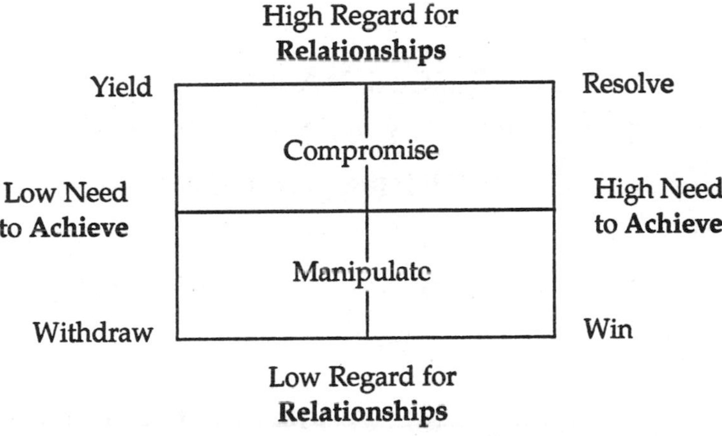

DIAGRAM 7.1

The diagram indicates that people with a high need to achieve and little regard for relationships are likely to approach conflict with the goal of winning. If they don't care about either, they usually withdraw from any conflict. Manipulators have little or no regard for honest relationships, so they avoid the battles necessary to win. Compromisers seek the middle ground.

Those who have a high regard for relationships seek to resolve conflicts when they believe something can be accomplished by confrontation. If it isn't worth the effort to seek resolution, they yield to keep the peace. No single right way to approach every conflict exists. If I went to a diner where a fight was about to erupt and nobody obviously wanted to establish any meaningful relationships, I think I would withdraw. Other situations call for us to win, such as standing for righteousness' sake. However, I can't think of any situation when we would be called to be manipulators.

Conflict is an inevitable part of life, and we have all adopted styles for dealing with it. Paul and Peter would have sought winning before their conversions. They were both high achievers. Before they could become reconcilers, God had to strike Paul down, and Peter had to be humbled by denying Christ. Judas was a manipulator. Barnabas would yield and John

---

CONFLICTS HANDLED INCORRECTLY CAN LEAD TO STALEMATES RATHER THAN DECISIONS, AND ULTIMATELY DAMAGE OUR RELATIONSHIPS.

---

would probably compromise to keep the peace. Compromise is not a dirty word when it is related to living with others. It only becomes wrong when we compromise our identities as His children and our beliefs in the truth of His Word.

Who are the most insecure? Those who routinely withdraw, manipulate or strive to win. Why do certain people always have to win, get their way or run away? Is it because the basis for a sense of security is deep meaningful relationships? People who have meaningful relationships are far more secure than those who have to win or be right, including high achievers. Howard Hughes lived a highly accomplished life by worldly standards, but he died a lonely, insecure man.

How many verses in the Bible can you find that say you have to be right or win in every circumstance? How many verses in the Bible require us to be loving, kind, merciful, patient, forgiving, accepting and gentle? When the price for winning costs us meaningful relationships, the price is too high. Yielding or compromising to keep the peace when something can be resolved will also be costly in the long run. We can sweep issues under the carpet for a time, but eventually we will trip over them. The goal is to resolve conflicts, not just manage them.

Dealing with Conflicts

How did we learn to deal with our conflicts? Our primary teachers have been our parents. Their modeling was more caught than taught. Comment on the following questions:

1. Which conflict style typified your father and how has it affected you?
2. Which conflict style typified your mother and how has it affected you?
3. Which conflict style best typifies you?
4. Which parent are you most like?
5. How well did you relate to this parent as opposed to your other parent?
6. Which conflict style best typifies your spouse?
7. How does knowing this about yourself and your spouse affect your relationship?

Husbands and wives have different experiences, interests, concerns and perspectives about resolving conflicts. The best opportunity for resolving the conflict will emerge when both perspectives are heard and appreciated. By entertaining diverse ideas and perspectives, we have the potential to unearth more alternatives.

Conflicts handled incorrectly can lead to stalemates rather than decisions, and ultimately damage our relationships. Whether the conflict is constructive or destructive will be determined as follows:

Destructive when:	**Constructive when:**
spouses do not understand the value of conflict that naturally comes when other opinions and perspectives are shared.	spouses understand the need to hear the other side so responsible decisions can be made.
there is a competitive climate that implies a win-lose situation.	there is a cooperative spirit and commitment to the marriage that searches for a win-win situation.

"getting my own way" is all important.	doing it God's way is all important.
spouses employ all kinds of defense mechanisms including: projection, suppression, blame, withdrawal and aggression.	spouses aren't defensive and assume that disagreements evolve from the other person's sincere concern for the marriage.
spouses are locked into their own viewpoints, unwilling to consider the perspective and ideas of their mates.	spouses believe they will eventually come to an agreement that is better than any one individual's suggestion.
spouses resort to personal attacks instead of focusing on the issues.	disagreements are confined to issues rather than personalities.
personal ideas and opinions are valued over the marriage relationship.	the marriage relationship is more important than the need to win or be right.

COMMUNICATION STYLES

Destructive relationships perpetuate cliques, subgrouping, deadlocks, stalemates and tension. Couples within these settings live with many unresolved personal conflicts. Those personal conflicts must be resolved before healthy decisions can be made. Constructive conflict resolution results in unity and a high level of trust; sharing between spouses is open and honest.

When couples or families attempt to resolve their conflicts, it is not necessary to agree with everything everyone else says. Instead, it is important for all parties to have an equal opportunity to express their views and share their feelings. Fathers or husbands will ultimately be responsible for the final decision. Wise fathers make decisions only after they have heard all the facts and humbled themselves before God. Often the final decision will be, "You're right, honey, let's do it the way you suggested." Sometimes the decision is, "You were right, son, and I was wrong."

The three criteria for successful conflict resolution are (1) the grace of God, (2) care and concern for one another and (3) the ability to mutually communicate. Let's look at possible styles of communication as they relate to relationships and achievement:

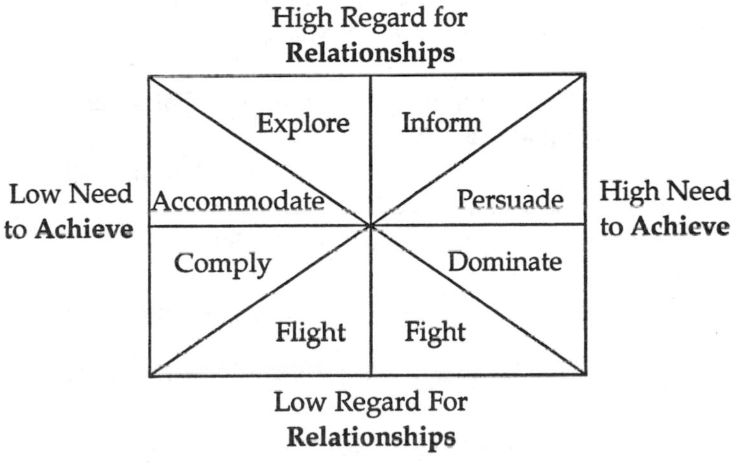

Diagram 7.2

People with high needs to achieve tend to control the conversation. If they have a higher regard for relationships, they will try to persuade the other person. If they don't care or value relationships, they tend to dominate. In controlling styles, one person assumes the primary role. The conversation is usually one-way. On the other extreme, people who have a low need to achieve tend to relinquish control of the conversation to the other person. Their styles are to accommodate and comply. They are usually quite receptive to others. They prefer to stay in the background and shift the responsibility for conversation to others.

People who have little regard for relationships tend to withdraw. They tend to fight when they want to achieve something, or flee if they don't. People with these styles of communication avoid contact with others. They block communication by neither soliciting nor contributing to the conversation. On the other extreme, people who have a high regard for relationships seek to develop the relationship by adapting to the styles of informing and exploring. These styles involve mutual sharing among equals. Communication is two-way, and flows back and forth between two people. Both attempt to contribute to the conversation and to understand each other.

How did we learn to communicate? The same way we learned to deal with conflict. Our primary teachers have been our parents. Comment on the following questions:

1. Which communication style typified your father and how has that affected you?
2. Which communication style typified your mother and how has that affected you?
3. Which communication style best typifies you?
4. Which parent are you most like?
5. How well did you relate to this parent as opposed to the other parent?
6. Which communication style best typifies your spouse?
7. How does knowing this about yourself and your spouse affect your relationship?

Now compare your answers with those of your spouse to the following statements:

	Agree	Disagree
1. Some things are better left unsaid even if your spouse insists on knowing.	___	___
2. Quarreling is always wrong in a marriage relationship.	___	___
3. Spouses should be able to discuss their marital problems with their best friends.	___	___
4. Only positive feelings should be expressed in a marriage relationship.	___	___
5. The husband should always make the final decisions.	___	___
6. Speaking the truth in love doesn't mean you always have to tell the truth.	___	___

7. If you become very angry, the best thing to do is to walk away. ___ ___
8. A good fight now and then makes for a better marriage. ___ ___
9. The wife should tell her husband when she wants sex because he is always ready. ___ ___
10. The husband should have control of the finances in the home. ___ ___
11. You don't have to forgive each other if the other person won't admit to being wrong. ___ ___
12. Wives are actually in a better position to make decisions concerning the family. ___ ___
13. A husband and wife should always sleep in the same bed. ___ ___
14. There should be no secrets between the husband and the wife. ___ ___
15. The husband should stay out of the kitchen. ___ ___
16. The father should lead the family devotions. ___ ___
17. It is okay to go into debt if the family will benefit from it. ___ ___
18. A husband should trust his wife's discernment. ___ ___
19. A husband should always tell his wife where he is going and for how long. ___ ___
20. We (Chuck and I) should never have suggested we discuss these issues. ___ ___

Chapter Eight

Love Language

Gifts

Everyone is the friend of a man who gives gifts.

—PROVERBS 19:6

Service

Having loved his own who were in the world, he now showed them the full extent of his love...so he got up from the meal, took off his outer clothing, and wrapped a towel around his waist. After that, he poured water into a basin and began to wash his disciples' feet, drying them with the towel that was wrapped around him.

—JOHN 13:1,4,5

Time

Jacob was in love with Rachel and said, "I'll work seven years in return for your younger daughter Rachel."...So Jacob served seven years to get Rachel, but they seemed like only a few days to him because of his love for her.

—GENESIS 29:18,20

TOUCH

How beautiful you are and how pleasing,
O love, with your delights!
Your stature is like that of the palm,
and your breasts like clusters of fruit.
I said, "I will climb the palm tree;
I will take hold of its fruit."
May your breasts be like the clusters of the vine,
the fragrance of your breath like apples,
and your mouth like the best wine.

—SONG OF SONGS 7:6-9

WORDS

Pleasant words are a honeycomb,
sweet to the soul and healing to the bones.

—PROVERBS 16:24

Would I pique your interest if I (Chuck) promised to share one truth that, if practiced, will revolutionize your marriage? This one truth will nourish the souls of your children or grandchildren. If you are single, it will improve your skills in the closest of human relationships.

COMMUNICATING WITH POWER

One of the finest skills anyone can master is love language. Learn to speak the love language of others, and you will communicate with power, nourish your marriage partner and draw your children—even adult children—closer to you.

In his insightful book *The Five Love Languages*, Gary Chapman observes that people speak different love languages.[1] Everyone has a love language. We all have ways we especially like to give and receive love. Rivet these five love languages in your mind, and never forget them:

- Gifts
- Service
- Time
- Touch
- Words

Little children seem most open to all the love languages. They squeal with delight when someone gives them *gifts.*

ALTHOUGH WE MAY ENJOY ALL THE LANGUAGES OF LOVE, WE LIKE TO RECEIVE LOVE IN ONE OR TWO WAYS MUCH MORE THAN IN OTHERS.

They love Christmas and birthdays. Children naturally respond to people who *serve* them by doing special things for them. They crave *time,* constantly wanting adults to "Watch me" and take time to play with them. What about *touch*? Think about hugs! Who gives more spontaneous and innocent hugs than little children? They give them freely and receive them with joy. They love to sit on the laps of adults who will read their favorite stories to them. Warm *words* brighten their eyes. Grandparents are usually great at giving love in all these ways.

God has created even in children a primary love language. Most often young children cannot express their love verbally, but will show it instead. Do they constantly make you presents? Think gifts. Do they naturally help their brothers and sisters, or always want to help you? It's probably service.

Do they always want your attention and want it now? Try time. Do they climb into your lap, run to hug you often? It's touch. Do they tell you what a good mommy or daddy you are? Think about words. Next to the gift of a relationship with the Lord Jesus Christ, one of the finest gifts we can give our children is to enrich their lives with their unique love language.

PREFERRED LOVE LANGUAGE

Most adults have a preferred love language or two. Although we may enjoy all the languages of love, we like to receive love in one or two ways much more than in others.

We are not usually aware that our spouses' love languages are different from our own. So we tend to give love in our own languages, and miss our marriage partners'. The best way to discover our spouse's and our older children's love languages is simply to ask. When we learn their preferences, we should start using them often. Nancy and I tried it. We like the results, and you will too.

Nancy's love language is made up primarily of gifts and service. She frequently buys things for me. My inner response often was, "That's nice, but I really didn't need it all that much. Besides, we really can't afford it." She was not using my love language, and I wasn't doing well at receiving hers.

She is also an excellent housekeeper, well organized and constantly taking care of the little things that make life better for me. I did appreciate this one, but did not always think of it as love. I thought she was a little compulsive about the house and a well organized perfectionist. I envied her abilities, but I didn't feel the love message on an emotional level.

Later I learned that what really communicates love to Nancy is taking out the garbage or vacuuming the floor. To me that is slave labor, not love! But when I learned to give service freely and without grumbling, it became a love language that touched her soul. After a day off with lots of work around the house, we will pray together in bed at night. She will thank the Lord with great satisfaction for "all the things we got done today." Her tone of voice tells me she feels loved. (I'm just glad it's over and praying silently that we will have a better day tomorrow!)

My love language is made up primarily of words and touch. I like to write notes or send cards to Nancy. She always says, "Thank you. That was nice." But somehow it doesn't cause her to turn cartwheels.

Touch is a big one for me. I can never get enough, it seems, until she quietly communicates—usually not in words—"Back off. You're bugging me." Tender talk and lovemaking turn me on. Who cares if we're poor or what kind of house we live in as long as we have each other! Sorry, Charlie, but Nancy doesn't see it that way. Words and touch have their place, but real love gets practical. Oh my, sometimes opposites do attract!

When we asked Kirk and Lisa, our grown children, what each thought their love language was, they both responded, "Time." Maybe it's because their dad was so busy while they were growing up. Or maybe it is their generation with its high priority on friendships and time spent together. As I'm writing this, Kirk and his wife, Debbie, live in Connecticut; Lisa is working in South Korea; and we're in California. Kirk can easily spend a half-hour talking on the phone to us, even if there is not much to say. Lisa writes several times a week by e-mail. They are giving love in their language: time.

One Thanksgiving vacation we were at Kirk and Debbie's apartment. It was getting late, and Kirk had to work the next day. We urged him to go to bed and get some sleep. His response seemed strange to me, because I operate with a different primary love language. He said, "I want to stay up and talk with you. That's how much I love you."

Giving love in the other person's language has made an enormous difference in our lives. Nancy has received some gifts I knew she wanted. She lights up like a Christmas tree. I've seldom previously seen her so happy. And she's hugging me all the time—much to my delight! We spend all the time we can together in person, on the phone or writing to Kirk and Debbie and Lisa. They thrive on it. We think it's great, too.

More than 20 times in the New Testament we are instructed to give love. The command most often repeated in the New

Testament is to love each other (see John 13:34,35; 15:12,13,17; Rom. 13:8-10; 1 Cor. 13; Gal 5:13,14; 1 Thess. 3:12; 4:9,10; 2 Thess. 1:3; 1 Pet. 1:22; 3:8; 4:8; 1 John 2:10; 3:11,14,15; 4:7,11,21; 2 John 5). Husbands are specifically commanded to love their wives as Christ loved the Church (see Eph. 5:25,28,33; also see Col. 3:19).

Agape, the Greek word for love used in the passages to husbands, means sacrificing his life for his wife. A small part of his sacrifice might mean learning her love language and communicating to her in that language. Learning to love is not just for men, however. Older women are also encouraged to *train* younger women to love their husbands and children (see Titus 2:4). Becoming skillful in another love language takes training!

Consider a basic truth from what Scripture does *not* say. The Bible never says anyone can demand love. Love is a command, not a demand. Nowhere does Scripture indicate love is a right rather than a responsibility. Men who demand sex and women who demand affection usually create resentment, not love. The Holy Spirit must create the fruit of self-sacrificing love, the desire to give ourselves away (see Gal. 5:22).

GIFTS

Many cultures consider gift-giving an essential part of love and marriage. It's true in the United States, too. Every wedding Neil or I have conducted has included the exchange of rings as a meaningful symbol.

Gary Chapman, author of *The Five Love Languages*, explains that gifts need not always be expensive. They can be made, or sometimes even found. Pick a wildflower and put it in a vase. Pluck a paper sack out of the trash, fold it in two, cut out a heart, write "I love you," and sign your name. Ask your spouse what kinds of gifts he or she really likes most.[2]

For one of our anniversaries I used the letters of the alphabet to remind me of Nancy's outstanding character qualities. I put them in two columns, framed them and gave it to her. The frame was not expensive, but she still keeps it displayed (where I can see it). It reads as follows:

Nancy my sweetheart,

You are everything to me. You are:

Amazing
Beautiful
Compassionate
Desirable
Efficient
Fun
Gentle
Humble
Intimate
Just
Kind
Loving
Merciful
Neat
One and only
Pure
Quiet
Rewarding
Steady
Tender
Understanding
Virtuous
Wonderful
Xcellent
Youthful
Zealous

The whole alphabet can never exhaust what you mean to me!

Happy 28th Anniversary!
Your adoring husband,

Chuck

I admit that my love language of words crept in, but they were all true of her!

Most of us do tend to give love in the ways we most want to receive it. If we are blind to differences in our family members and friends, we will try to give love our ways instead of their ways. When we do, most people do not receive love as fully as they would if it came in their own preferred love language. So husbands and wives or parents and kids can miss genuine closeness, even while trying to give it. It is tragic to give love without connecting—it is also unnecessary.

It is possible to have the same love language and still miss one another's hearts. Shirley complained to her pastor that in more than 30 years her husband, David, had *never* given her a birthday, anniversary or even a Christmas present. When her pastor asked how that made her feel, her eyes filled with tears.

Then she broke down and wept for several minutes, releasing years of disappointment and disillusionment. But Shirley had not learned the freedom of forgiveness nor the wisdom of communicating her love language to others.

The pastor could hardly believe David was so insensitive. But when he later had an opportunity to talk with him, he understood David's reasons. He had grown up in a dysfunctional family where everyone was either fighting or in a cold truce, merely tolerating each other. But on Christmas and birthdays they went through a meaningless ritual (or so it seemed to him) of giving each other gifts. David made a foolish childhood vow that he would never give a gift just because it was expected. He would give gifts only when they really meant something. He lived by that vow.

So David brought home plenty of gifts throughout the years—gold certificates, stock options and practical presents that built financial security. Emotionally, he was a saver, not a spender, and he showed love by saving for Shirley. But David's gifts never came on birthdays, anniversaries or Christmas mornings. Worse yet, they were not the kind of gifts Shirley desired. She wanted ceramics, cards, romantic gifts—gifts that showed his tender feelings for her. She couldn't care less about money in the bank! David thought her gift ideas were only trinkets, and not that important.

Having grown up in a poor family, David believed he was building security in ways his parents had not provided for him, but the generational sin of insensitivity to his spouse's feelings still plagued him. He had never learned to honor and value his wife's preferences and tastes. Both Shirley and David understood gifts as love language, but they totally misunderstood the other's expectations. They were communicating on different wavelengths.[3]

When addressing another's love language, don't guess, don't assume; don't say, "I already know"—just ask. Mark it down as a rule. Ask, seek, find (see Matt. 7:7,8). To enjoy rich love relationships we must ask for input, observe what is valued, learn by trial and error and discover the secret wishes of others' hearts. Then we can speak the love dialects that penetrate their souls and cause them to fall deeply in love with us. The other love languages are worth trying, too. Some people like them all!

SERVICE

If I read the Gospels correctly, one of Jesus' primary love languages was service. He said of Himself, "For even the Son of Man did not come to be served, but to serve, and to give his life as a ransom for many" (Mark 10:45). Jesus dumbfounded His disciples at the last Passover by washing their feet, a task reserved for slaves. John the beloved saw the significance. He summed it up with this caption: "Having loved his own who were in the world, he now showed them the full extent of his love" (John 13:1). Even after His resurrection and while enjoying His immortal body, Jesus cooked breakfast for the disciples (see 21:9).

During dating and engagement most couples eagerly serve one another. But after a year or two of marriage, they soon revert to what they saw in their parents' homes. The generational blessings or curses are far more powerful than we realize. When we use our own love language (or our parents') instead of our marriage partners', we will probably be misunderstood.

Although Sue and Dan had been married for 15 years, misunderstanding occurred. At a marriage retreat they asked the guest speaker to talk to them for a few moments alone. After he asked how they showed love to each other, he received some surprising replies. Sue loved flowers, and sometimes at night would put a vase with a fresh cut flower from her garden on Dan's nightstand. It was her way of telling him she might like to make love that night. Because gifts were not his love language, he did not get the hint. He just thought she liked flowers!

When asked how he showed love to Sue, he told about his service on her behalf. He did the dishes, folded and put away the laundry, and tidied up the house. But as he continued talking, Sue was obviously hot under the collar, flushed in the face. The speaker asked why she was so upset about something most wives would love.

Sue shared her story of back surgery and time in traction, confined to bed for nearly a year. The doctors were unsure if she would ever walk again. She felt useless because her family had learned to get along without her. However, in the last

18 months she was making progress. The two things that made her feel most worthwhile were (you've got it) doing the dishes and folding the laundry. Dan's use of his own love language was actually robbing her of feeling that he cared.[4]

Anger and criticism don't win friends and influence people, including marriage partners. Just as in dating days, love must be won, not demanded. No one ever forced anyone to fall in love by criticizing them or demanding that they do so. Review your engagement days and ask your mate what made him or her fall in love with you. The only constructive thing criticism *can* do is help you discover your partner's love language. Both wives and husbands tend to be critical of whatever they perceive as the blockage to the love language they want to receive.

Mary criticized Mark's hunting trips with intense hostility. He couldn't understand her feelings because he had often hunted during their courtship. But in those days Mark also returned home early enough to wash his truck, go over to Mary's house for dinner and help her with projects. Now he went hunting, but did not help her. A friend exposed the missing ingredient. It was not the hunting, but the acts of service that expressed love to Mary. When the service was gone, she felt unloved and ferociously criticized hunting as the hated enemy. Once each understood the other's love language, and agreed to a short list of primary preferences, they found fresh hope.[5]

Dean and Kris were moving to another state. Before they left, they asked for some counsel from Patti, a respected friend. Patti shared the love language concept. Kris told Dean she really wanted him to hold her often and tell her he loved her. Because he had previously been involved in affairs, she needed his reassurance. Dean said he could do that. When asked what he wanted, Dean said he would appreciate having the house straightened up and the counters cleared and tidy.

Later Kris called Patti and complained. "He just didn't get it. He didn't tell me how to love him; he only wanted me to keep the house cleaner."

"Maybe service is his love language," Patti replied.

"Oh, I never thought of that."

So Kris began to serve Dean, doing little things to keep their place tidy and neat. Later she called Patti. "This really works! I can't believe how much better he is treating me just because I'm doing a few little things to please him."

Kris had discovered Dean's love language, and its power.

TIME

As a love language, *time* does not mean two bodies in the same room or the same car. It means tender talk and mutually enjoyed activities. It does not mean watching TV together, unless you both want to, but rather active listening to one

---

HUSBANDS AND WIVES DO NOT ALWAYS SHARE THE SAME DIALECT WHEN TIME IS THE LOVE LANGUAGE, NOR DO THEY ALWAYS UNDERSTAND EACH OTHER WHEN THEY SIMPLY TRY TO COMMUNICATE.

---

another. The emphasis is not on what is said—that is the love language of words. With time the emphasis is on quality and quantity: what you say or do and how much of yourself you put into it.

By the way, the time crunch is especially severe in the 30-something age group (and sometimes into the 40s). Careers are demanding and the children are time-consuming. During these years setting aside periods for tender talk or fun as a couple requires time management skills—the same discipline of time and energy usage that goes into career and children. It must have the same priority as eating or sleeping. We make time for what is most important to us. When the time simply is not currently available, it may mean making an appointment.

- "I can't talk right now, but I'll be free in just a few minutes."
- "Could we compare datebooks and find the best time for both of us?"
- "How about turning off the TV as soon as this program is over so we can talk?"
- "Have you thought about a weekly (or even monthly) date night?"
- "Let's go out for dinner and then do something we both enjoy."
- "Can you meet me for lunch?"
- "Let's make phone contact a couple times each day!"

WATCH THOSE DIALECTS

Husbands and wives do not always share the same dialect when time is the love language, nor do they always understand each other when they simply try to communicate. When men feel stressful they often need to go into their caves to be alone for awhile or, at the very least, to be silent. Men feel they lose something of themselves if they are always with their wives. When men are hurting, they honor each other by giving one another space. They seldom intrude into another man's private world unless they are asked or given specific permission. When men do talk they express information or find solutions to problems.[6]

When women feel stressful they often need to be with someone supportive, to explore their feelings by talking. Women feel as if they lose something of themselves if they are seldom engaged in sharing real feelings. When women are hurting they honor each other by giving one another support. They seldom withdraw their caring conversation unless the other person makes them feel unwanted or unwelcome. When women talk they not only express information but also explore feelings and thoughts, create intimacy or simply try to feel better.[7]

Many men and women may share the same love language of time, yet speak different dialects. When time is a man's love language, he may desire shared activity. He may want to go places, have fun, enjoy recreation, do the things they did together when they were dating. When a woman's love language is time, she may desire understanding and conversation. She may want to go out to dinner where they can talk uninterrupted, have some relaxed adult conversation (especially if she spends the day with toddlers and young children), enjoy the kind of in-depth communication they had while they were dating. Each desires time, but with an entirely different focus. He focuses on doing, she focuses on feeling. These gender stereotypes are occasionally reversed.

AVOIDING ARGUMENTS

A counselor taught my friends the technique of the blue stone. The goal was to talk through a touchy subject from their past without getting into an argument. They purchased a blue agate stone that was to be held by the person talking. The other had to remain quiet, except to summarize what the first person said. No distractions, interruptions or added comments were allowed unless permission was given by the one who held the stone. When the first one agreed that the second understood what was meant, the stone was passed.

Then the second person could respond, and seek the same understanding before giving up the stone. Or the one with the stone could bring up a new subject, explore another feeling or try to explain his or her own viewpoint. Whoever held the blue stone was in charge of the conversation until understanding was reached. Passing the stone back and forth stopped interruptions, accusations and stomping out in anger. It was an old technique with a new twist. The stone became the evidence of whose turn it was to control the conversation. Because they agreed to live by the rules, it worked!

TOUCH

During times of crisis or emotional trauma, people naturally tend to put their arms around one another. They sense the love that comes from a hug. Listen up, men. If your wife's love language is touch, always hold her close when she cries. (The only exception is when you made her cry and *she doesn't want you to touch her*).

If a tragedy or crisis has occurred, hold each other as long as the tears flow. In times of intense pain, we all need more of our primary love languages than ever before. This is the time to give love in the other person's language, even while we crave it in our own.

With touch, as in all of the love languages, understanding our spouses' preferences is vital. Some kinds of touching feel wonderful, others are irritating. Hugs and kisses, holding hands and sitting close are strictly private acts for some, more public for others. Using honesty and openness, we can learn the kinds of touching our partners enjoy most, and the circumstances in which they are preferred.

Many men and some women, both Christian and non-Christian, judge the happiness of their marriages by the frequency of intercourse. Those with another primary love language may find the romance and passion involved more satisfying than the physical act itself. The Bible clearly directs husbands and wives to submit to one another's sexual needs (see 1 Cor. 7:3-6). Meeting God-given sexual needs is not the same as trying to satisfy another's lust.

Our sex-saturated society with its pornography and quirky deviations causes many spouses to feel harassed and demeaned. Husbands are most likely to make unreasonable demands for weird sex. Usually their wives resent it and wonder whether the Bible demands that they submit to what has been learned through pornography. (It doesn't, and wives shouldn't!) This is not love language, it is lust language. This is not spiritual obligation, it is spiritual abuse. Sexual harassment, abuse, addictions and other bondages can be broken through Christ, and freedom is so refreshing.[8]

Spouses should aggressively meet each other's sexual needs with the variety and passion described in the Song of Solomon. Sexual intercourse freely given may fill the love bank; however, spouses who give grudgingly may actually cause emotional pain. Why not use the blue stone method to discuss what both of you might feel comfortable doing or trying?

WORDS

Do you recall this little ditty from grade school days?

> "Sticks and stones may break my bones, but words will never hurt me."

We chanted it defiantly to protect ourselves from the mean and nasty remarks others kids said to us. In childhood innocence we even may have believed it, but it was a lie.

- Words hurt or heal.
- Words tear down or build up.
- Words criticize or compliment.
- Words express harshness or kindness.
- Words speak truth or lies.

Words penetrate, especially when spoken by someone we love, someone in our families, someone close to us. Personal words touch our souls with extraordinary power.

Recently I wrote each of our grown children a love letter. I didn't call it that, of course. My message was tucked away in a paragraph or two among other more mundane matters. But the crucial paragraphs told them how much I loved them, and why. Their Mom, my wonderful wife, Nancy, added a simple note saying, "Ditto to everything Dad said," and "I couldn't agree more."

Their responses were heartening. Not only did these young adults appreciate their letters, but the seemingly feeble words empowered them with fresh strength. They appeared to give them confidence in their relationships with Christ, in their characters and in their abilities. The effect of a few loving words can be amazing!

The same principle works in marriage. A woman whose husband had recently died of cancer spoke at the 1994 Promise Keepers Conference at Anaheim Stadium in California. She told how her thoughtful man had brought her a cup of coffee each morning along with a note. He simply drew a little Valentine saying why or how he loved her that day. This grief-stricken wife was yet a radiant witness to thousands of men about the power of a husband who gave away loving words. Both husbands and wives need to hear "I love you," again and again daily. Combined with specific compliments about character, ability and intimacy, the words build up the marriage.

By the same token destructive words tear down all relationships, including marriages and families. Often the tone of our voices stirs up more trouble than the words we have spoken. Harshness, nagging, criticism, nit-picking and ridiculing—all these and more eat away at the souls of our marriages. Bridling our tongues requires God's grace and our utmost discipline, but it pays wonderful dividends. "A word out of your mouth may seem of no account, but it can accomplish nearly anything—or destroy it!" (Jas. 3:5, *The Message*).

Our friend Bob Ramsey is a gifted thinker and writer. He is currently pastor of Denair Friends Church in Denair, California. Listen to his colorful account and insightful wisdom.

Yogi Berra was one of the greatest baseball players of all time. He hit for power, and for average. He fielded his position without equal. Forty years after his prime, he continues to hold many of the hitting records for the World Series, and he was easily elected to the Hall of Fame.

Yogi is even more famous, however, for his grasp of the obvious, and for his personal twist on the English language. Fans and non-fans alike often collect what some call "Berra-isms," Yogi's unique perspectives on life and baseball. He was the first one to say, "It ain't over 'til it's over." When asked about his technique, he said, "90% of hitting is mental. The other half is physical." He once gave up going to a popular restaurant. His reason? "No one goes there anymore. It's too crowded."

Yogi's sayings were so famous, some believed they were being made up by witty sports writers with too much time on their hands. When asked about this, Yogi said, "I never said half the things I said."

"I never said half the things I said." How many of us wish we could say the same thing. We all have a backlog of things we wish we hadn't said. Maybe it was the tone of voice. Perhaps it was accidental, and you were mortified to find out the effect of what you had said. Maybe you even meant to be hurtful or spiteful, and only thought better of it later.

If I could be granted a super or magical power, I would want the ability to recall ill considered words. Perhaps even better though, would be the ability to say just the right words. I have seen the right words heal a long standing hurt. I have seen the wrong words almost destroy a person in just a few seconds.

The Bible tells us, in Proverbs 25:11, "A word aptly spoken is like apples of gold in settings of silver." The right word at the right time is a gift beyond any monetary value. It has a beauty which exceeds the finest craftsmanship.

Not many of us have the ability to create beauty with gold or silver. But the Lord is at work making us into masters of creating beauty and empowering others with our words. Let's give ourselves to learning this skill. And don't tell yourself it's too late to start or too hard to change. Remember, as Yogi said, "It ain't over 'til it's over."[9]

Why not ask your marriage partner, the members of your family and close friends what their emotional love languages are—gifts, service, time, touch, words? Then try giving yourself away. You'll love it—so will they!

Notes

1. Gary Chapman, *The Five Love Languages, How to Express Heartfelt Commitment to Your Mate* (Chicago: Northfield Publishing, 1992), p. 14.
2. Ibid., p. 76.
3. Rich Buhler, *LOVE No Strings Attached* (Nashville, Tenn.: Thomas Nelson Publishers, 1987), pp. 60-63.
4. Ibid, pp. 58-60.
5. Chapman, *The Five Love Languages*, pp. 89-96.
6. John Gray, *Men Are From Mars, Women Are From Venus, A Practical Guide for Improving Communication and Getting What You Want in Your Relationships* (New York: Harper Collins Publishers, 1988), pp. 59-91.
7. Ibid.
8. (We have each written on this subject earlier.) See Neil T. Anderson, *A Way of Escape* (Eugene, Oreg.: Harvest House Publishers, 1994); and Charles Mylander, *Running the Red Lights, Putting the Brakes on Sexual Temptation* (Ventura, Calif.: Regal Books, 1986).
9. Bob Ramsey, "Apt Words," The Encourager, News and Views from the headquarters of the Friends Church Southwest Yearly Meeting, 9 December, 1994, pp. 1-2.

CHAPTER NINE

The Lust for Money

You can't worship two gods at once. Loving one god, you'll end up hating the other. Adoration of one feeds contempt for the other. You can't worship God and Money both. If you decide for God, living a life of God-worship, it follows that you don't fuss about what's on the table at mealtimes or whether the clothes in your closet are in fashion. Instead of looking at the fashions, walk out into the fields and look at the wildflowers. They never primp or shop, but have you ever seen color and design quite like it? The ten best-dressed men and women in the country look shabby alongside them. If God gives such attention to the appearance of wild-flowers—most of which are never even seen—don't you think he'll attend to you, take pride in you, do his best for you? What I'm trying to do here is to get you to relax, to not be so preoccupied with getting, so you can respond to God's giving. People who don't know God and the way he works fuss over these things, but you know both God and how he works. Steep your life in God-reality, God-initiative, God-provisions. Don't worry about missing out. You'll find all your everyday human concerns will be met.

—MATTHEW 6:24,25; 28-33, THE MESSAGE

Once upon a time there lived a peanut vendor in South India. Every day he walked up and down the beach calling out, "Peanuts! Peanuts for sale! Peanuts!" The man was miserably poor. He barely earned half a living, hardly enough to feed his family. But at night he bragged to his wife and children, "I am the president and the vice president, the secretary and the treasurer of my own company!"

The grinding poverty wore his nerves paper thin. One day he snapped. He sold all his peanuts. He sold most of his meager belongings. He decided to go on a big fling. "For one day I am going to live like a rich man!" he vowed. So he stopped by the barber for a clean shave and a hairstyle trim. He visited a fine men's clothing store and purchased an expensive suit, white shirt and tie, and all the accessories needed to look rich. Then he checked himself into the finest luxury hotel for the night. He had just enough money left to pay for the gourmet breakfast buffet the next morning.

He enjoyed the night's accommodations in his luxury suite. When morning came he located the private, beachfront patio for the breakfast buffet. Although it was crowded with tourists he found a table by himself. He had just filled his plate when in walked a man who was elegantly dressed. By this time no more tables were available so the man moved toward him and asked, "May I join you?"

The peanut vendor replied, "Why, yes! Please sit down." To himself he was thinking, "This is my lucky day! Not only am I living like a rich man, I am going to eat with a rich man."

As the two began to talk the stranger asked, "What do you do?"

"I am the president and the vice president and the secretary and the treasurer of my own company," he replied. "And what do you do?"

The richly dressed man looked a bit sheepish. "I'm sorry. I should have introduced myself. I just supposed that with the coverage in the newspapers you might have recognized me. My name is John D. Rockefeller."

Although he had not recognized the face, the peanut vendor did know the name. He thought to himself, "This is wonderful! I am eating with one of the richest men in the whole world."

After talking for awhile Mr. Rockefeller said, "I like your style. We are starting a new company here in South India. Why don't you come to work for me? I will make you vice president of sales in my new firm."

The peanut vendor replied, "Why, thank you. What a generous offer! I would like a few minutes to think it over."

"Of course," said Mr. Rockefeller, "but I would like some indication of your interest before we part company."

The two leisurely enjoyed the rest of their meals. When they were finished, the peanut vendor stood up. He wanted to announce his decision with style. He took a step away from the table, and then turned and spoke in a voice loud enough that many could overhear.

"Thank you, Mr. Rockefeller, for offering me the position of vice president in your new company. But I must decline. I prefer to be the president and the vice president and the secretary and the treasurer of my own company." He turned on his heel and walked out.

Years later an old peanut vendor walked up and down the same resort beaches croaking in a broken voice, "Peanuts! Peanuts for sale! Peanuts!" But at night he boasted to his grandchildren that long ago, one of the richest men in the world offered to make him vice president of a huge firm.

"I turned it down," he bragged, "so I could be the president and the vice president and the secretary and the treasurer of my own company."[1]

We think to ourselves, What a fool! Yet by not committing all our finances to God, we may turn down partnership with the Lord of unlimited riches. In effect we want to be the president and the vice president and the secretary and the treasurer of our own enterprise. In light of eternity, we keep working for what amounts to peanuts!

FINDING SECURITY

Annual income greater than annual expenses equals a marriage at peace. Annual expenses greater than annual income equals a marriage in pain. Money and marriage always go together, but they do not always mix well. Deep within the human psyche is an inner longing for security. We want to know we will be safe and cared for. We desire protection from anything that threatens our cherished way of life.

What makes us feel secure? Money? House? Family? Circumstances under control? Law and order? In varying degrees, if we are honest, all of these may increase our feelings of human security. Yet in our heart of hearts we know that tangible and outward things are not enough.

- Money can vanish so quickly. Bankruptcies, lawsuits, and outright nonpayments are commonplace.
- Houses can be foreclosed or forced into sale. The number of homeless is on the increase.
- Family can be fractured by divorce and severe conflict. The shocking statistics about broken homes hardly phase us anymore.
- Circumstances so easily get out of control. Reversals, losses, disasters, radical changes, setbacks happen with frequency.
- Law and order cannot stop crime. Child abuse, wife battering, thefts, murders, rapes and other crimes abound.

So what is a person to do? Since God puts the longing for security in our hearts, He intends to fulfill it. He is our rock, a favorite Old Testament name that suggests protection, stability and security:

> May the words of my mouth and the meditation of my heart be pleasing in your sight, O Lord, *my Rock* and my Redeemer (Ps. 19:14).

Whenever the Bible uses the term "my rock" for God, we can accurately substitute "my security." (Check a good concordance for many more references). The best kind of security always comes from God. He is always there, always reliable, alway the same. Through the Cross and the Resurrection He provides eternal life that transcends death, character that triumphs over tragedy and peace that wins over anxiety. In Christ our security is as solid as a rock (see Rom. 8:35-39).

The apostle Paul taught that contentment was far better than loving money and trying to get rich (see 1 Tim. 6:3-10). James warned rich people that misery was coming upon them (see Jas. 5:1). Jesus taught that financial security was not something to worry about. Real security, He said, was found by seeking first God's kingdom (see Matt. 6:25-34). What is He talking about? What is this security that is better than money? What does Jesus mean by the kingdom of God?

WHAT IS UNDER GOD'S DAILY CONTROL AND CONFORMS TO HIS WILL IS IN HIS KINGDOM. WHAT IS NOT, IN ACTUAL PRACTICE, UNDER GOD'S CONTROL AND FAILS TO DO HIS WILL IS NOT IN HIS KINGDOM.

WHERE YOU HAVE SAY

The Kingdom is God's rule, God's reign, God's government. It is His kingship. Thus, the Kingdom is the King Himself and everything under His control. That is why the kingdom of God is embodied in Jesus Christ. He is King (Lord), and everything in heaven and on earth is under His ultimate authority (see Eph. 1:20-23). Even while on earth in a physical body, the love and power of the Kingdom flowed through Him. He had more influence and more say than anyone who ever lived.

Dallas Willard, professor of philosophy at the University of Southern California, described the Kingdom as the effective range of God's will. In other words, what is under God's daily control and what conforms to His will is in His Kingdom. What is not, in actual practice, under God's control and fails to do His will is not in His kingdom.

We like to think we are the king of our own kingdoms. Our kingdom is where "we have say." How fast we drive, what we eat, the money we spend—all may be under our say. Our kingdom includes what is under our own control, what we have the ability to decide. What furniture we decide to buy for our homes or offices, and how we arrange it in the rooms may be under our say. Our kingdom is where we have the power to choose, or at least to influence. One of the benefits—as well as dangers—of becoming adults is that we have more say, we have more choices to determine our destinies, we have more money to express our values. In short, we have larger kingdoms.

What Jesus desires is for God's Kingdom to take over our kingdoms. He wants us to bring our marriages and our daily lives, including our finances, into God's Kingdom. We first become children of God, subjects of the Kingdom, by accepting Jesus Christ as Lord and Savior—as our King! Yet it is possible, even likely, that not all of our financial habits are in His Kingdom; not all of our own rule is under His rule, and not all of our personal say is under His say (see Matt. 6:10,33).

Two parts of my own kingdom (Chuck), two places where I have say, came to my attention recently. One was my cluttered desk, and the other was how I drive. If these are to become part of God's Kingdom in my daily life, then I must change. I must exercise simple obedience to what I already know is His will. I have started bringing the effective range of my will under the effective range of God's will. For me this includes putting things away and driving better. (By the way, both of these bad habits drive my wife crazy.)

I let my desk get messy because I am lazy, or because I make some wrong choices or because I become too busy. I let my driving get lousy because I'm preoccupied, or because I'm in a hurry or because I leave too late. It is easy to think I will change, but I meet resistance. Laziness, poor choices, busyness, preoccupied thoughts and a habit of hurrying do not change easily. I will have to go into training, to keep practicing. It will take a trainload of God's grace *and* a carload of my discipline to pull these bad traits into God's Kingdom.

Other parts of life—attitudes, motives, desires—also meet resistance. What does it take to love more, to worship better and to think cleaner? What about marriage, family and finances? Will we invite Christ to put us together, set us right, complete us with joy? Submitting ourselves to the kingdom of God requires more than trying harder; it requires the power of God, the God of the Kingdom. Submission takes all the resources and riches Christ provides. It takes a heart relationship that wants to please Him.

One of the biggest struggles in many marriages is to bring the finances under God's control. The excuses in our minds might go something like this:

"The kingdom of God is fine for church, but *my money* is something I prefer to control."

"It's in style. Of course I need it."
"I really wanted a nicer car."
"I'm working all these hours so you can be well taken care of, sweetheart. It's all for you."
"If only you didn't spend so much on yourself..."
"If only you made more money..."

Craving Money

- "For the love of money is a root of all kinds of evil. Some people, eager for money, have wandered from the faith and pierced themselves with many griefs" (1 Tim. 6:10).
- One of the requirements for overseers and elders is that they not be "lovers of money" (1 Tim. 3:3).
- Christians are commanded to put to death whatever belongs to their earthly nature, including "greed, which is idolatry" (Col. 3:5).
- Jesus taught, "You cannot serve both God and money" (Matt. 6:24).
- The Bible specifically warns against a desire to get rich: "People who want to get rich fall into temptation and a trap and into many foolish and harmful desires that plunge men into ruin and destruction" (1 Tim. 6:9).

Take a few moments to make a fearless moral inventory. Go

through these Scriptures asking yourself, "Who do I really serve between Sundays? Is it the God who revealed Himself in Jesus Christ, or is it money? Does my money help me serve God, or do I expect God to help me make more money?" Serving God gives both present and eternal rewards. Serving money leads to a decaying character and a dying society. A little parable describes the relationship between God, us and our money.

THE TEN APPLES

Once upon a time God gave a prehistoric man 10 red apples. None of the people who lived near him had tasted apples before. They would give almost anything for an apple.

God told the man to trade three of the apples for a cave. It would shelter his family from the wind and rain. The man obeyed God and found a good cave. For three apples, the owner sold him the cave.

God told the man to trade three of the apples for clothing. It would cover his family's bodies and warm them during wet, chilly weather. The man obeyed God and found a trader with skin garments. He traded three apples for clothes for his whole family.

God told the man to trade three of the apples for food to eat. It would sustain and nourish his family. The man obeyed God and traded one apple each for fruit, grain and meat.

Then God told the man to give one apple back to Himself as a gift. It would serve as a symbol of thanksgiving, relationship and love. It would allow God to plant the last apple and produce many more apples in the years to come. The man had already traded three apples for a cave, three for clothes and three for food. He had only one apple left.

The man looked at his last apple. It looked bigger and shinier than any of the others. He could imagine its sweet taste. He could smell its sweet aroma as he held it near his mouth. He longed to sink his teeth into the delicious apple, to savor its juices.

The man reasoned that God could create an apple tree if He wanted to. God really didn't need this one last apple to plant as a blessing for his future. So he ate the last apple—and gave back to God the core!

Some people consume the money God trusts into their care. They spend most of it on necessities, some on little pleasures and then they finish off God's share. They only give God the leftovers. Tragedy of tragedies, they miss the blessings God promised.

Greed, avarice, cupidity—words for lusting after money not often used in our daily talk. Instead we admire the rich and belittle the poor. The bitter truth is that lust for money brings trouble and more trouble into our marriages and families. The problem with grabbing for whatever attracts our fancy is that it bypasses God. A lust for money is shaped by feelings and things, not by our Lord Jesus. Peterson's paraphrase in *The Message* warns us of how our cravings for money make God feel: "It's because of this kind of thing that God is about to explode in anger" (see Col. 3:5,6).

Why is God so angry?

- Because our lust for money replaces our love for God;
- Because it twists and warps our God-given desire to help the poor;
- Because it cripples our efforts to support His churches and ministries.

So what is a believer to do in this materialistic society?

- Admit that God is the owner of everything, including our money.
- Learn contentment, the kind that comes with godliness.
- Find delight in simple pleasures.
- Become a wise steward of all the resources God gives, including our finances.
- Give more, live on less.

Money has a good side and a bad side. Its good side is what it provides—daily needs for the family, support for ministry, even a few enjoyable luxuries in life. Its bad side is what loving money destroys—compassion, self-sacrifice, intense love for God.

The love of money, and what money can buy, creates havoc in many marriages. No surprise. We each want what we want, and find ways to buy it. Then the bills and monthly payments stack up until we are at our limit. A genuine emergency occurs—medical expenses, car breakdown, job loss—and we're overwhelmed. Tensions rise as we each blame the other for spending too much or not earning enough. Too often financial pressures contribute to divorce.

The good side of money becomes the bad side. What provided for our needs and pleasures has now turned into payments due and no way to pay. Resolving the conflict between husband and wife may bring temporary relief, but a lasting solution will not come until we submit our love for money to Christ, and bring our earning and spending into the kingdom of God.

We do not change our money habits permanently without changing who we are on the inside—our very being. We fail at changing our innermost being until we change our beliefs. Believing God's truth precedes living Christ's way. To put it simply, we must believe God's truth about money before we will change our spending habits. We must honor God with our finances before we can expect Him to honor us with inner contentment.

GOD OWNS EVERYTHING

The biggest difference between God's economy and man's economy is *God.* In man's economy, people own things. Governments, corporations, non-profit organizations, communities, families or individuals own things. In God's economy, God owns everything—absolutely everything. He created the heavens and the earth and all that is in it (see Gen. 1:1; Ps. 146:6; Isa. 44:24; Col. 1:15-17; Rev. 4:11). What's more, He still retains ownership of everything He created. Meditate on the following Scriptures (italics added):

> To the Lord your God belong the heavens, even the highest heavens, the earth *and everything in it* (Deut. 10:14).

> Yours, O Lord, is the greatness and the power and the glory and the majesty and the splendor, *for*

> *everything in heaven and earth is yours.* Yours, O Lord, is the kingdom; you are exalted as head over all (1 Chron. 29:11).
>
> *The earth is the Lord's and everything in it,* the world, and all who live in it (Ps. 24:1).
>
> For every animal of the forest is mine, and the cattle on a thousand hills. I know every bird in the mountains, and the creatures of the field are mine. If I were hungry I would not tell you, *for the world is mine, and all that is in it* (Ps. 50:10-12).

No truth in family finances is more important than this one: God owns everything! This truth is revolutionary because our culture teaches the opposite. Our culture teaches that God has nothing to do with money, except the use of "charitable giving." Everything else belongs to us—and the government! Because of the pressure of this world's system, we need to remind ourselves again and again of God's truth:

- More often will we acknowledge that all money and material things in our care belong to God.
- More often will we pursue good management of the Lord's money and resources.
- More often will we consult the Lord, and seek wise counsel in financial decisions.
- More often will we pray, "Give us today our daily bread."
- More often will we rejoice in knowing that God provides and blesses.
- More often will we learn contentment when God withdraws financial resources and teaches trust.
- More often will we actually act like God is in charge of our money!

GENEROUS PEOPLE

Did you see the Dennis the Menace cartoon? As Dennis and

his dad were walking out of church, he asked the pastor an embarrassing question. Dennis blurted out, "What are you going to do with my dad's quarter?"

OUR FINANCIAL GOAL IN MARRIAGE IS NOT TO BECOME RICH, BUT TO BECOME CONTENT IN CHRIST. CONTENTMENT COMES FROM SECURITY IN CHRIST AND FROM GOOD STEWARDSHIP OF OUR MONEY.

Some people are like Dennis' dad: They don't tithe, they tip. They disobey God and suffer the consequences. Worse yet, they miss the seed of generosity God wanted to plant in their hearts.

Generous people are fun to be around.
    They have so many friends.
Generous people can be trusted.
    They are givers, not takers.
Generous people are kind.
    They reach out to the poor and needy.
Generous people get outside of themselves.
    They care about the lost.
Generous people never go hungry.
    They find that God and their friends rush
to their aid.

Throughout the Bible, tithing is used as the standard guide for giving. Tithing means a tenth goes to God, right off the top. It is commanded in the Old Testament and commended in the New Testament (see Lev. 27:30-32; Mal. 3:10; Matt. 23:23). "God loves a cheerful giver" (2 Cor. 9:7).

THE JOY OF CONTENTMENT

Our financial goal in marriage is not to become rich, but to become content in Christ. Contentment comes from security in Christ and from good stewardship of our money. (Note that six of the seven references to contentment in the New Testament are in a context of money). Contentment comes from our attitudes and our actions. It comes from our being and our doing. We learn to *be* content and grateful for what we have. We also *do* what God commands us with our finances, and our marriage relationship related to finances. A few specifics may help:

1. Sign it all over to God. One of Satan's lies is that we own our money and property, rather than serve as God's trustees of material things. One way to rivet God's ownership in our minds is to make up a quitclaim deed, signing over to God all the possessions the Lord has given us. An excellent course on Christian discipleship and finances called Crown Ministries even provides the form![2] After taking this important step, my wife, Nancy, suggested changing our vocabulary from "my" to "the." We talk about "the car" and "the house" instead of "my car" and "my house." This is a small discipline to remind ourselves that it all belongs to God, not us.

2. Practice gratitude. Few things build contentment like thanking God. Praising God for everything He has given us changes greed to gratitude. Christians are the richest people on earth! We have everything money can't buy and thieves can't steal. We are rich toward God and have treasures in heaven! In the here and now we have all of God's resources and riches, plus many material benefits He showers upon us. What's more, God takes care of His children financially. King David wisely sang:

> I was young and now I am old, yet I have never seen the righteous forsaken or their children begging bread. They are always generous and lend freely; their children will be blessed (Ps. 37:25,26).

Have you ever noticed that although missionaries work for a mere pittance in foreign countries, their children always seem to prosper financially? A high percentage of their children graduate from private Christian colleges—in spite of the high costs. God provides when we respond to how God guides. He gives everything we need for doing His will—and bonuses as well. One of His incredible promises relates to eternal prosperity: "And everyone who has left houses or brothers or sisters or father or mother or children or fields for my sake will receive a hundred times as much and will inherit eternal life" (Matt. 19:29). No wonder we are grateful!

3. *Resolve differences.* In marriage, how we spend our money reflects our values. The husband wants to spend the money one way and the wife another. Of course! We are different people with differing values, desires and tastes. Even our view of what's an absolute need and what is a mere want differs drastically. The sooner a married couple agrees on basic principles and values for using their money, the better. This is why the process of budgeting may be as useful as the budget itself.

Conflict about money, even about being a good steward of it, cannot be avoided in marriage. Face the conflict, work it through and get the problem resolved. Then work out minor arguments as they arise. Couples who fight about money experience trouble, and seldom resolve their problems. They keep up their bad habits, and blame each other for the mess they're in.

It may help to think in percentages. What percentage will we give to the Lord's work? What percentage will we save? (The old adage "Give ten percent, save ten percent, and spend the rest with joy," isn't bad for starters! But stay alert to the Holy Spirit's guidance).

4. *Manage finances wisely.* Nowhere in the Bible are we commanded to make a budget, but a major theme of God's Word is the accountability we have for the use of money. One of the shockers in Jesus' teaching was that how we handle money is a training course for God trusting us with spiritual riches. Our Lord taught, "So if you have not been trustworthy in handling worldly wealth, who will trust you with true riches?" (Luke 16:11). A budget proves useful because it forces us to plan our giving and monitor our use of money. Financial crisis counselors report no incoming clients who regularly use a budget.

5. *Reduce debt.* The biggest trap for most consumers today is

debt. Credit card companies, finance companies and banks are getting rich from interest! Advertisers perfect the art of increasing our desires and decreasing our satisfaction. Then they dupe us into thinking in terms of monthly payments instead of total price. Before long the issue becomes, "Can we afford the payment?" rather than, "Do we have the cash to buy it?" The Bible says that debt is *slavery!*

> The rich rule over the poor, And the borrower is servant to the lender (Prov. 22:7).

If you don't believe this proverb, try skipping two or three car payments and see what happens! Debt is bondage. Worse yet, the Bible teaches that debt is one of the curses God sends if we disobey Him (see Deut. 28:15,43,44). Debt is a curse. Why would anyone want to live under slavery, bondage and a curse? Many Christian writers such as Ron Blue, Larry Burkett and Howard L. Dayton give fine counsel on becoming debt free. Dayton suggests 10 points as commonsense guidelines:

1. Pray.
2. Establish a written budget.
3. List your assets—everything you own.
4. List your liabilities—everything you owe.
5. Establish a debt repayment schedule for each creditor.
6. Consider earning additional income.
7. Accumulate no new debt.
8. Be content with what you have.
9. Consider a radical lifestyle change.
10. Do not give up![3]

6. Give generously. If debt is a curse, giving is a blessing. Love is the heart of giving. We are not to give reluctantly as we muse, "Just think what I could do with all this money." Nor are we to give under compulsion as we think, "Rats! To be a good Christian I have to tithe." Remember it all belongs to God. The good news is that givers prosper. People know they are generous, honest and kind, so they like to do business with them. In addition, God always keeps His promises, including the ones about rewarding us in proportion to our generosity (see Luke 6:38; 2 Cor. 9:6-8,11). When we give our money to Christ's work, our hearts follow our treasures (see Luke 12:32-34). Note three practical principles from God's Word:

- Give before we can afford it (see 2 Cor. 8:2).
- Give beyond our ability (see v.3).
- Give ourselves first to the Lord (see v.5).

7. *Invest wisely*. Consistent savings prepare for future difficulties—and those troubles are sure to come (Prov. 21:20). Worthy goals for saving and investing are to provide for family, operate a business or free up our time to serve God. Unworthy goals include a desire to get rich and to build a false sense of security in wealth (see Luke 12:13-21; 1 Tim. 6:9). Diligent planning leads to a profit, but rushing into an investment leads to loss (see Prov. 21:5). In business, in investments and in life, constant alertness is necessary (see 27:23,24). Wise investors do not put all their eggs in one basket; they diversify (see Eccles. 11:1,2).

FINANCIAL ETHICS

In a culture devoted to greed and built upon the false god of money, every Christian and every godly family needs a code of financial ethics. Although much could be added to what follows, not much can be subtracted. These 12 principles are based upon God's written Word, the Bible.

1. We will avoid greed and be honest in all our financial dealings. We will not lie, cheat, steal or beat people out of money (see Deut. 5:19-21; 25:15,16; Prov. 20:10,23; Luke 12:15; Eph. 4:28).
2. We will show God's love with the money He entrusts to us. We will put God first in our lives through giving tithes and offerings. We will give to the church, to missions, to the poor and especially to the needy among our own families, relatives and Christian

friends (see Deut. 14:22,23; 1 Chron. 29:11-14; Mal. 3:8-10; Matt. 23:23-25; Luke 6:38; 11:42; Acts 20:35; Rom. 13:9,10; 1 Tim. 5:8; 6:18,19).

3. We will pay our debts promptly and seek to stay out of debt (see Ps. 37:21; Prov. 3:27,28; 22:7; Matt. 5:25,26; Rom. 13:8). We will not co-sign for another's debts (Prov. 6:1-5; 17:18; 22:26,27).
4. We will save a portion of our incomes for future difficulties (see Prov. 13:11; 21:20; 30:24,25; note the cautions about over-saving taught by Jesus in Matt. 6:19,20,24-26; Luke 12:16-21).
5. We will avoid risky investments and get-rich-quick schemes (see Prov. 28:20-22; Eccles. 5:13-15; 1 Tim. 6:9,10).
6. We will look for investments that produce redemptive results, not destructive ones. We will use our investment money for God's glory (see Lev. 25:47-55; Ps. 49:20; 1 Cor. 10:31; Col. 3:17; 1 Tim. 6:17-19).
7. We will live by the highest standards of financial integrity in our families, our churches, our chosen work or professions (see Job 1:8; Ps. 112:1-10; Prov. 10:2; 11:3,18; Matt. 7:12; 2 Cor. 7:2).
8. We will neither oppress the poor, nor bribe the rich (see Exod. 23:8; Prov. 15:27; 22:16,22,23; Isa. 5:22,23; 33:15).
9. We will make restitution for any wrongs we have committed against the person or property of another (see Lev. 6:1-5; Num. 5:5-7; Prov. 6:30,31; Ezek. 33:14,15; Luke 19:8-10).
10. We will not use the courts for lawsuits against other believers, nor engage in any unethical legal proceedings designed to gain unjust money (see Exod. 23:1-3; Lev. 19:15; 25:17; Deut. 1:17; 2 Chron. 19:5-7; Prov. 24:23; Zech. 8:16,17; Luke 12:13-15; 1 Cor. 6:1-8).
11. We will work faithfully and diligently for our incomes as good stewards of the Lord (see Prov. 12:11; 13:4; 1 Cor. 4:2; Eph. 6:5-9; Col. 3:23,24; 4:1; 1 Thess. 2:9; 2 Thess. 3:6-13).
12. We will balance work and rest (see Exod. 20:8-11; Deut. 5:12-15; Ps. 127:1,2; Heb. 4:1-11).

Money and marriage can mix well if both are centered in God. Time and discipline are needed to master our money for God's glory, to bring it fully into His Kingdom. When King Jesus rules both our marriage and our money (what a glorious thought!), then we receive the rewards. Then we experience the benefits of the Kingdom—righteousness, peace and joy in the Holy Spirit. We become pleasing to God and respected by the people who matter most to us (see Rom. 14:17,18). The kingdom of God is good news—great news! It brings God's best—forgiveness, cleansing, gifts, fruit, character, virtue, joy, light, life—and much more! Happy marriages, good families, satisfying careers and healthy finances are often the by-products.

Money, used wisely for God's glory, helps build a happy marriage. Money misused foolishly for personal gain helps create an unhappy marriage.

Notes

1. Dr. Mylander first heard the peanut vendor story from Dr. Sam Kameleson, Vice President of World Vision International, at the 1987 International Friends Conference on Evangelism in Guatemala City, Guatemala.
2. For more information on this excellent Bible study, including *Small Group Financial Study* and *Practical Application Workbook,* write to: Crown Ministries, 530 Crown Oak Centre Drive, Longwood, FL 32750 (407)331-6000.
3. Crown Ministries, *Small Group Financial Study,* pp. 40-43.

Chapter Ten

Sexual Freedom

It is good for a man not to marry. But since there is so much immorality, each man should have his own wife, and each woman her own husband. The husband should fulfill his marital duty to his wife, and likewise the wife to her husband. The wife's body does not belong to her alone but also to her husband. In the same way, the husband's body does not belong to him alone but also to his wife. Do not deprive each other except by mutual consent and for a time, so that you may devote yourselves to prayer. Then come together again so Satan will not tempt you because of your lack of self-control.

—1 CORINTHIANS 7:1-5

A few years ago I (Neil) conducted a "For Women Only" seminar. Because I was the only male there, I felt a little vulnerable. After lunch the ladies suggested I would be more comfortable if I took off my coat. I said, "Okay, but that's all I'm taking off!" I told them I would honestly answer, to the best of my ability, any questions they asked. For those who didn't want to ask their questions in front of the others, they could write them out and leave them in a basket at the back of the room.

Did I get questions! To my surprise most of the written questions dealt with sex in marriage. If I could synthesize their questions into one, it would be, "Do I have to do whatever my husband wants me to do in bed?"

BIBLICAL GUIDELINES

To answer that question, refer to the Corinthian passage quoted at the beginning of this chapter (7:1-5). It may be noble that one not marry to serve the Lord, but I'm sure it's not normal. Sexual immorality was obviously a problem in those days, just as it is today. This passage seems to be the sexual corollary to Ephesians 5:21: "Submit to one another out of reverence for Christ." Notice the spiritual dimension of the marital relationship. If we are not going to have sex with our spouses, then it should be only because we have decided to abstain for the purpose of prayer for a mutually agreed upon time. We are not to withhold ourselves from our spouses because that would give Satan an opportunity to take advantage of our lack of self-control. We should never use sex as a weapon or a means to get even.

Okay, I still haven't directly answered the question, "Do I have to do whatever my spouse wants?" I suspect the heart of this question is the husband's problem with lust. His rationalization might sound something like this: "The Bible says her body belongs to me. My wife should submit to whatever turns me on. It is her responsibility to meet my sexual needs." Let's look at what the Bible says about this subject: "Marriage should be honored by all, and the marriage bed kept pure, for God will judge the adulterer and all the sexually immoral" (Heb. 13:4). So what does a wife (or husband) have to submit to?

First, a wife can and should meet the sexual needs of her husband, and vice versa. She is the only one who can do it without guilt or shame. But she cannot resolve his problem with lust. Men who struggle with lust somehow think their wives are responsible for resolving it. They falsely reason, "If my wife would only dress more sexy or participate in some kinky sex act, then I wouldn't have this problem." That view is degrading. Even if she tried to be the sex object of his fantasy, it would only increase the lust. Lust is a bondage only Christ can break.

Second, we never have the right to violate another person's conscience (see Rom. 14). If our spouses believe a certain sexual act is wrong, then it is wrong for both of us. If we violate the other person's conscience, we destroy the trust in the relationship and undermine the vulnerability that is crucial to real sexual fulfillment. Time and tenderness will overcome the inhibitions. Scripture says, "What is desirable in a man is his kindness" (Prov. 19:22, *NASB*), not his crudeness. God created a helpmate for Adam, not a playmate.

I have asked the ladies in my conferences throughout the world, "If you had to choose in your husband between strong masculinity or kindness, which would you choose?" Without hesitation, they all say, "Kindness."

My wife once asked me, "Do you know when you really turn me on?" I flexed my muscles a little and asked, "When?" She responded, "When you are kind to our children!"

SEXUAL BONDAGE

Sexual bondage destroys many marriages, and the origin of the problem can usually be traced to pornography, promiscuity, incest and rape *before* marriage. Getting married will not resolve it. In many cases the problem becomes accentuated. I have dealt extensively with the problem of sexual bondage and freedom in my book *A Way of Escape*. Let me highlight the essential issues, especially as they relate to marriage.

Wouldn't it be great if we all had perfect parents who taught us the truth about love and sex? But such is not the case. Most have been raised in pagan and/or broken homes, and many Christian homes are also dysfunctional. Consequently, our children are seldom afforded the opportunity to develop their sexuality as God intended. The effect can be felt in the succeeding generations. Let's examine King David's sexually dysfunctional family to understand the steps that led to his defilement and that of his sons.

"One evening David got up from his bed and walked around on the roof of the palace. From the roof he saw a woman bathing. The woman was very beautiful, and David sent someone to find out about her" (2 Sam. 11:2,3). Nothing is wrong with this woman, Bathsheba, being beautiful, and nothing is wrong with David seeing her. God made us with an attraction to the opposite sex. Bathsheba may have been wrong for bathing where others could see her, and David was definitely wrong for continuing to look at her. God provided a way of escape, but David did not take it. Instead he sent someone to find out about her. I wonder if this costly choice was the catalyst for God's inspiring Solomon (David's son) to write Proverbs 7:6-23:

> At the window of my house I looked out through the lattice. I saw among the simple, I noticed among the young men, a youth who lacked judgment. He was going down the street near her corner, walking along in the direction of her house at twilight, as the day was fading, as the dark of night set in. Then out came a woman to meet him, dressed like a prostitute and with crafty intent. (She is loud and defiant, her feet never stay at home; now in the street, now in the squares, at every corner she lurks.) She took hold of him and kissed him and with a brazen face she said:
>
> "I have fellowship offerings at home; today I fulfilled my vows. So I came out to meet you; I looked for you and have found you! I have covered my bed with colored linens from Egypt. I have perfumed my bed with myrrh, aloes and cinnamon. Come, let's drink deep of love till morning; let's enjoy ourselves with love! My husband is not at home; he has gone on a long journey. He took his purse filled with money and will not be home till full moon."

> With persuasive words she led him astray; she seduced him with her smooth talk. All at once he followed her like an ox going to slaughter, like a deer stepping into a noose till an arrow pierces his liver, like a bird darting into a snare, little knowing it will cost him his life.

This married and seductive woman claimed to be religious. She prepared her home and then planned the event to be carried out under the cover of darkness. Such is the nature of sexual temptation. If we yield, our minds see only the immediate gratification of sexual desires, never the consequences. The way of escape is only powerfully available the moment our minds register the first thoughts of temptation. Once we allow our minds to entertain thoughts contrary to God's Word, a whole chain of physiological responses are set in motion. The more we contemplate the sin, the more emotionally involved we become, and the less likely we will be to stand against it.

THE WAY OF ESCAPE

If we are going to take the way of escape God has provided for us, we must take the original thought captive to the obedience of Christ (see 2 Cor. 10:5). If we allow tempting thoughts to ruminate in our minds, we will eventually take paths that lead to destruction. For instance, suppose a man is struggling with lust. One night his wife asks him to go to the store for some milk. When he gets in his car, he pauses to decide which store he should go to. He decides on a local convenience store. He knows good and well the convenience store has a display of pornography. He does not have to go to that store. He could get the milk in a much safer environment, such as an all-night supermarket.

The battle for his mind has already been lost the moment he starts driving to the wrong store. Before he even leaves the garage, all kinds of compromising thoughts cross his mind. For instance, "If you don't want me to look at the pornography, Lord, have my pastor be at the store buying milk, or cause a wreck in the intersection." Since there is no wreck and the pastor isn't there, he reasons it must be okay to take a look.

The mind has an incredible propensity to rationalize, but the justifications don't last. Before he has even left the store, guilt and shame overwhelm him. The tempter (Satan) switches strategies and becomes the accuser. The choice to take the way of escape had to be made before the man got into his car. Rare is the person who can turn the car around once the plan has been set in motion.

That is why I am so disgusted with the public concept of "adults only." It implies there is a separate standard of morality for adults and for children. Adults should be mature enough to know that they should not allow their minds to be programmed with filth. Television programs say, "The content of the following movie is suitable for 'mature' audiences only. Viewer discretion is advised." It isn't suitable for anyone, and mature people should be the first to know that. We have already been advised by God, "Don't watch!"

When David sent messengers to get Bathsheba, he was too far down the trail of temptation to turn around. They slept together and she became pregnant. Here comes the cover up! David called for Uriah, her husband, to come home from the battlefield, but he wouldn't sleep with Bathsheba while his men on the field were being deprived. So David invited him to stay another day and tried to get him drunk. He still wouldn't sleep with her. Then David sent orders for him to be strategically placed in battle so he would be killed. Uriah died on the battlefield. Now David had become a murderer as well as an adulterer! Sin has a way of compounding itself. Living righteously is difficult, but living unrighteously is even more difficult. Cover up, denial and guilt make for a very complex life.

After a period of mourning, David married Bathsheba. He lived with his guilt and covered his shame for nine months. The Lord allowed plenty of time for David to come to terms with his own sin. He didn't, so God sent him the prophet Nathan. He told David a story about a rich man who ripped off the only lamb of a poor man for his own use. David responded in anger, "The man who did this deserves to die! He must pay for that lamb four times over, because he did such a thing and had no pity"(2 Sam. 12:5,6). Then Nathan informed David that he was the rich man. Gotcha!

A DUAL LIFE

How could David live such a dual life? He was an adulterous murderer on the inside while maintaining the facade of a righteous king on the outside. His inner torment is described in Psalm 32:

> Blessed is he whose transgressions are forgiven, whose sins are covered. Blessed is the man whose sin the Lord does not count against him and in whose spirit is no deceit. When I kept silent, my bones wasted away through my groaning all day long. For day and night your hand was heavy upon me; my strength was sapped as in the heat of summer. Then I acknowledged my sin to you and did not cover up my iniquity. I said, "I will confess my transgressions to the Lord" and you forgave the guilt of my sin (vv. 1-5).

Such is the inner world of those who live in bondage. "There is nothing concealed that will not be disclosed, or hidden that will not be made known" (Matt. 10:26). Secret sin on earth is open scandal in heaven. God won't let his children live in darkness for long because He knows it will eat them alive.

I heard of a pastor who had a pornography addiction. At a pastor's conference, some of his colleagues asked for some material he brought with him. As he opened the briefcase with a crowd around him, he suddenly realized he had brought the wrong one. This briefcase had his pornography collection in it! The sham was over.

When I was a pastor, a lady from a previous ministry called for an appointment. She thought her husband was having an affair, but there was no proof. I called her husband and he agreed to see me, but he denied being sexually involved with anyone.

Two weeks later the wife called again: "He says he has a business trip that will take him out of town for the weekend. I don't believe him; could I possibly come by and see you again?"

I discerned the husband was lying, but what could I do? There was no proof. All I could think of was the story of David. I related the story to her and suggested we ask God to send him a Nathan. So we prayed together and she left.

My wife called shortly thereafter and proposed we take our children out for dinner that evening. We went to a little seaport village that had some fine restaurants. I had no idea I was going to be "Nathan." There was the wayward husband with one woman on each arm. He tried to avoid eye contact, but it was too late; he was caught.

I didn't hear from them for two years. Then I got a Christmas card, thanking me for the time I spent with them. He asked for and received a transfer shortly after the embarrassing encounter. Apparently their marriage is now doing much better.

Sadly the public lives of many people are radically different from their private lives. As long as they believe the facade can continue, they will not deal with their own issues. Ironically, they are often most critical of others. People who haven't dealt with their own guilt often seek to balance their internal scales by projecting blame on others. But the Lord said in Matthew:

> Do not judge, or you too will be judged. For in the same way you judge others, you will be judged, and with the measure you use, it will be measured to you. Why do you look at the speck of sawdust in your brother's eye and pay no attention to the plank in your own eye? How can you say to your brother, "Let me take the speck out of your eye," when all the time there is a plank in your own eye? You hypocrite, first take the plank out of your own eye, and then you will see clearly to remove the speck from your brother's eye (7:1-5).

FORGIVENESS AND JUDGMENT

David acknowledged his sins, both of which were capital offenses under the law. Then Nathan said, "You are not going to die. But because by doing this you have made the enemies of the Lord [Satan and his angels] show utter contempt, the son born to you will die" (2 Sam. 12:13,14). I don't think we have any idea of the moral outrage our sexual sins cause in the spiritual realm. The accuser of the brethren throws them into God's face day and night (see Rev. 12:10). What we think we are doing privately is done openly before the god of this world and his fallen angelic hoard! Far worse, our sexual sins are an offense to God, who is grieved by our failure.

Judgment would come upon the household of David, however. "This is what the Lord says: 'Out of your own household I am going to bring calamity upon you. Before your very eyes I will take your wives and give them to one who is close to you, and he will lie with your wives in broad daylight. You did it in secret, but I will do this thing in broad daylight before all Israel'" (2 Sam. 12:11).

David told Nathan after hearing his story that the rich man who stole the sheep should pay fourfold. He didn't know he was speaking of himself. Four of his sons died prematurely. Bathsheba's son died and another son, Amnon, raped his sister. Then Amnon was killed by Absalom, another brother, for raping his sister. Absalom would then "lay with his father's concubines in the sight of all Israel" (16:22), and be killed because he wanted to take the throne from David. Finally Adonijah, another brother, was executed because he also wanted to become king (see 1 Kings 2:25).

The Lord spared David, but why did Bathsheba's child have to die? Recall that the law did say God would visit "the iniquity of the fathers on the children, on the third and the fourth generations of those who hate Me" (Exod. 20:5, *NASB*). Is it possible that God had to cut off the rebellious seed that was sown? The first male offspring of this adulterous relationship could not receive the birthright. Remember, this is the throne of David upon which the Messiah would someday reign. But God is merciful. He took the infant home to be with Him, and David had the assurance he would be with the child in eternity (see 2 Sam. 12:23).

WARNING AGAINST SEXUAL IMMORALITY

Paul offers the following instruction and warning against sexual immorality:

> The body is not meant for sexual immorality, but

> for the Lord, and the Lord for the body. By his power God raised the Lord from the dead, and he will raise us also. Do you not know that your bodies are members of Christ himself? Shall I then take the members of Christ and unite them with a prostitute? Never! Do you not know that he who unites himself with a prostitute is one with her in body? For it is said, "The two will become one flesh." But he who unites himself with the Lord is one with him in spirit.

OUR BODIES ARE TEMPLES OF GOD BECAUSE HIS SPIRIT DWELLS IN US. TO USE OUR BODIES FOR SEXUAL IMMORALITY IS TO DEFILE GOD'S TEMPLE.

> Flee from sexual immorality. All other sins a man commits are outside his body, but he who sins sexually sins against his own body. Do you not know that your body is a temple of the Holy Spirit, who is in you, whom you have received from God? You are not your own; you were bought at a price. Therefore honor God with your body (1 Cor. 6:13-20).

This passage teaches that we have more than a spiritual union with God. Our "bodies are members of Christ himself" (v. 15). Paul said, "If the Spirit of him who raised Jesus from the dead is living in you, he who raised Christ from the dead will also give life to your mortal bodies through his Spirit, who lives in you" (Rom. 8:11). Our bodies are actually temples of God, because His Spirit dwells in us. To use our bodies for sexual immorality is to defile God's temple.

It is difficult for us to fully appreciate the moral outrage of uniting a member of Christ with a prostitute. It would be like Antiochus Epiphanes slaughtering a pig on the altar after declaring Mosaic ceremonies illegal, and then erecting a statue of Zeus in the holy place of the Temple. Can you imagine how God's people must have felt when that very thing happened in the second century before Christ? Many were martyred as they attempted to stop the defilement of the Temple.

Christian, aren't you offended when people suggest that Jesus was sexually intimate with Mary Magdalene? I am! It also offends me when people suggest Jesus masturbated.

I believe Jesus was fully God and also fully man. I believe He was sexually a man and was tempted in all ways such as we are, but He never sinned. His earthly body was not meant for sexual immorality; neither is ours. If our eyes were fully open to the reality of the spiritual world and we understood the consequences of sinning against our own bodies, we would obey Scripture and flee from sexual immorality.

ALIVE IN CHRIST

The apostle Paul taught that we are alive in Christ, and therefore identified with Him in His death, burial and resurrection (see Rom. 6:1-11). Because Christ triumphed over sin and death, so have we, because we are in Christ. The law of life in Christ Jesus has set us free from the law of sin and the law of death (see 8:2). Therefore Paul said:

> In the same way, count yourselves dead to sin but alive to God in Christ Jesus. Therefore do not let sin reign in your mortal body so that you obey its evil desires. Do not offer the parts of your body to sin, as instruments of wickedness, but rather offer yourselves to God, as those who have been brought from death to life; and offer the parts of your body to him as instruments of righteousness (6:11-13).

Can you think of a way you could commit a sexual sin and not use your body as an instrument of wickedness? I can't. If we do commit sexual sins, we allow sin to reign in our mortal bodies. We also lose a degree of freedom and damage our relationships with God. "For you were called to freedom, brethren; only do not turn your freedom into an opportunity for the flesh, but through love serve one another" (Gal. 5:13, *NASB*). What happens when a child of God, who is one spirit with the Lord, unites himself with a prostitute and becomes one flesh with her? Let me illustrate.

How many times have you heard of a nice Christian girl getting involved with an immoral man, having sex with him and then continuing in a sick relationship for years? Her friends try to tell her, "He's no good for you." Mom and Dad abhor the idea that he could be a future son-in-law, but she won't listen to them. Even though he treats her badly, she won't leave him. Why doesn't she just get away from him? Because they've bonded. They have become one flesh.

A pastor asked for my help with a young lady in his congregation. He said, "If you can't help this girl, she is going to be admitted to a hospital. The voices in her head are so loud she's wondering why we cannot hear them." Being inexperienced with resolving spiritual conflicts, he didn't know whether he was supposed to nail down the chairs in his office or what! It was the classic scenario, a girl gets involved with an immoral man who sexually uses her. In this case he was also dealing drugs.

I remember asking the young lady, "If I said you had to leave that guy, what would you say?" She responded, "I'd probably leave right now." I didn't want to ask her to do that until we had a chance to work through the "Steps to Freedom in Christ" (see appendix A), so I said, "We are not going to deal with that relationship right now. Instead, because we have this time together, can we help you resolve some of your problems?"

After hearing her story, I asked her if she would be willing to walk through the Steps. During the process she asked God to reveal to her mind every sexual use of her body as an instrument of unrighteousness. As the Lord brought one experience after another to her mind, she renounced each one. Then she committed her body to the Lord as a living sacrifice.

I never brought up her boyfriend's name, but she did. "I'm

never going to see him again," she said. She left her pastor's office, free in Christ.

In helping others find their freedom in Christ, we have learned through much experience to have them ask the Lord to reveal every sexual use of their bodies as instruments of unrighteousness. Many will openly share one or two sexual experiences during a normal counseling process, but when they sincerely pray that prayer, all the other sexual experiences come to their minds. Why? Because God is the One who grants repentance, which leads us to a knowledge of the truth, which sets captives free (see 2 Tim. 2:24-26).

A hurting mother and father asked if I would talk with their daughter. Usually nothing good comes from appointments made by parents for their children who don't want to be helped. But I agreed to see their child under the condition their daughter wanted to see me. They assured me she did, but her opening statement was, "I don't want to get right with God or anything like that!"

Hiding my own frustration, I said to her, "That is certainly your choice, but now that we are together, maybe we could try to resolve some of the conflicts you are in." She said she thought that would be okay.

She told me her story of being date-raped by the campus "hero" while in high school. At the time she was too embarrassed to tell anyone about this supposedly wonderful boy who had used her body as an instrument of unrighteousness. She had no idea how to resolve it. This was a bad date from the beginning, and she knew it. But how does a starstruck underclassman say no to a superstar upperclassman?

Having lost her virginity, she became sexually promiscuous. Eventually she lived off and on with a real loser. It was tearing up her parents and their Christian home. She told me about the rape and a little about the last guy. Then I asked her if she would prayerfully ask the Lord to reveal to her mind every sexual use of her body as an instrument of unrighteousness.

"That would be embarrassing," she said.

"Would you feel better if I waited outside?" I asked.

She said yes, she thought she could work through it better if I were not there. So I stepped outside while my female prayer partner helped her through it. This young lady sang in church that night for the first time in years. She was free.

FAR-REACHING CONSEQUENCES

After years of helping people find their freedom in Christ we have observed several generalities. First, if people have had "unholy" sex, they don't seem to enjoy "holy" sex. I have counseled many wives who loathe being touched. In difficult cases they are actually repulsed by the idea until they break the bondages that come from sex outside God's will. Incredibly, their feelings toward their spouses change almost immediately after finding their freedom in Christ. One pastor hadn't had sex with his spouse for 10 years. To his surprise—and that of his wife—he asked for and had intimate relations with her after attending one of our conferences.

We have also noticed that promiscuity before marriage leads to a lack of fulfillment after marriage. The fun and excitement of sex outside the will of God leaves one in bondage. If sex was entered into with both partners' consent, the bondages only increase as they attempt to satisfy their lusts. If it was without consent (by that I mean sex was forced or the unwilling partner went along with it but didn't really want to), they shut down and remain in bondage to their pasts until resolution is achieved. They lack the freedom to enter into mutual expressions of love and trust. We help them by having them renounce those previous sexual uses of their bodies, commit their bodies to God as living sacrifices and reserve the sexual use of their bodies for their spouses only.

Imagine the consequences this will have on future generations and marriages, because most of our younger generation have been sexually active before marriage. Recall Paul's words, "This is the will of God, your sanctification; that is, that you abstain from sexual immorality; that each of you know how to possess his own vessel in sanctification and honor, not in lustful passion, like the gentiles who do not know God" (1 Thess. 4:3-5, *NASB*).

A former college student under my ministry was dating a lovely Christian lady. He shared with me a profound thought:

"I treat my girlfriend the way I think her future husband would want her to be treated." They are now happily married.

I was speaking about sex to a group of high schoolers at an outreach. A non-Christian was there with his girlfriend. He asked, "If I had sex with my girlfriend, would I later regret it?"

What a mature question! But I think there is an even more mature question: "Would my girlfriend later regret it?"

My first attempt at discipling a young college man resulted in nothing. He wrote me off after he heard me talk about sexual purity and freedom. At the time he was dating one of the nicest young ladies in our group. Two years later he shared with me that, during the time I was trying to disciple him, he was sleeping with several coeds, but not the girl he was dating. No wonder our discipleship process wasn't going anywhere! Here was his question: "I get tired of sexual partners in a short time. If I married this young Christian virgin, would I also get tired of her in a short time?"

I told him that what he got tired of was sex. People who are bored with sex have depersonalized it. He had no relationship with his partners. They were just sex objects to be conquered and used for his own pleasure. He was not thinking of them, he was thinking of himself. He was trying to satisfy his lust, but it couldn't be satisfied. The more he fed his appetites, the greater they grew. People such as this become obsessed with sexual thoughts. Obsessional sex is always depersonalized, so boredom increases and the obsessive thoughts grow stronger.

One man told me that masturbation was okay for him because he visualized girls without heads! I told him that was precisely the problem with what he was doing. He was depersonalizing sex. That is what pornography does. The sex objects are never presented as people created in the image of God, much less a mother's child. To treat the opposite sex as something less than who they really are is to transgress and defraud them.

GETTING READY FOR MARRIAGE

I used to ask young couples in pre-marital counseling to turn their chairs back to back. I asked them to write their responses to several questions, such as, "How many children do you want to have?" and "When do you want to start having them?" The last question was, "Have you had sexual inter-

WHEN THE RELATIONSHIPS WE HAVE WITH GOD AND OUR SPOUSES ARE THE MOST IMPORTANT IN OUR LIVES, SEX BECOMES THE MOST INTIMATE AND VULNERABLE MEANS OF EXPRESSING LOVE.

course with each other?" Eighteen of the first 20 Christian couples I married had already slept together.

Why did I ask? I wanted to know if that was all they had going for them. Did they believe they had to get married because they had sex together? I wanted to know if she was pregnant, because that would greatly affect the way I discussed sexual adjustment with them. What did they want to tell their children someday? I wanted to know if they would be willing to stop until they got married. Were they bringing a load of guilt to the altar? "God has not called us for the purpose of impurity, but in sanctification" (1 Thess. 4:7, *NASB*). We need to get people ready for marriage by getting them right with God.

When the relationships we have with God and our spouses are the most important in our lives, sex becomes the most intimate and vulnerable means of expressing love. This vulnerability must not be exploited, especially for wives. When women can trust their husbands and know that they will be taken care of, they can abandon themselves to sexual pleasures. In fact, trust may be the most important factor determining orgasmic capacity in women.

For some sick reason our culture is bent on finding the ultimate sexual experience. If they found it, would people be satisfied? Why aren't we bent on finding the ultimate personal relationship? "Blessed are those who hunger and thirst for righteousness, for they shall be satisfied" (Matt. 5:6, *NASB*). What about you? Would you be willing to commit yourself to live a righteous life and pursue the greatest of all relationships, the one every child of God can have with his or her heavenly Father? If so, you will be satisfied, and chances are the sexual relationship you have with your spouse will be satisfying.

A committed Christian couple asked for help at one of my conferences. Because we always try to resolve individual problems first, our lead male counselor, Ron Wormser, met with the husband while I met with the wife. Technically, they were virgins when they got married. However, both had long-term dating relationships with another person, which had included a lot of heavy petting. Ron and I sensed God's leading to have them renounce all the physical contact they had with the other person before marriage. It was as though they had bonded to a first love.

The next day the wife, with tears of joy in her eyes, said to me, "Last night was the most wonderful time my husband and I have ever had together."

That is what God wants for your marriage.

CHAPTER ELEVEN

The Snakebite of Adultery

The Lord said to Moses, "Make a snake and put it up on a pole; anyone who is bitten can look at it and live." So Moses made a bronze snake and put it up on a pole. Then when anyone was bitten by a snake and looked at the bronze snake, he lived.

—NUMBERS 21:8,9

Just as Moses lifted up the snake in the desert, so the Son of Man must be lifted up, that everyone who believes in Him may have eternal life. For God so loved the world that he gave his one and only Son, that whoever believes in him shall not perish but have eternal life. For God did not send his Son into the world to condemn the world, but to save the world through him. Whoever believes in him is not condemned, but whoever does not believe stands condemned already because he has not believed in the name of God's one and only Son.

—JOHN 3:14-18

Perhaps the most intriguing subject for humans to contemplate is God Himself. For many, the next most intriguing subject is sex—which is no accident. Our maleness and our femaleness are part and parcel of being made in God's image.

Our understanding of Genesis 1 shapes our Christian viewpoint about sexuality. Many women, so the story goes, view it this way: God created man. Then He looked at what He had made and said, "I can do better than that." So He created woman!

Men disagree. They say, God created man. All was peaceful and quiet. Too quiet. So He created woman. Neither God nor man has had peace or quiet ever since!

Neither viewpoint is quite biblical. The truth is sex was God's idea, and a good one. Our creation as male or female lies at the center of our humanity as God originally intended it. We were created to live in relationship with God and with each other. Our maleness and our femaleness are linked with our capacity to love and to be loved. This relationship, this capacity to love and be loved, is part of the image of God, and it is stamped within our sexuality. At its best, it reflects the very nature of God.

FOUL CRAVINGS

Why do men and women so often fall into adultery and sexual sins of every sort? Because our sexuality is also fallen, broken and corrupted. Strange creatures, we mortals. From the moment of our conception, such a mix of good and evil swirls within us. From our innermost beings come both God-given longings and foul cravings. We can see it in a small child, even a baby. What is sweeter than a little one who coos and hugs? But at three o'clock in the morning, when the baby is in full bawl, the sweetness is out the window. What becomes obvious to every mother is the rage and selfishness even the smallest child can express. We expect it in little children. The surprise comes when adults, cloaking their foul desires in modern sophistication, give way to anger, rage, malice and endless expressions of selfishness.

The idea of the basic human goodness has been blown out

the window in this century with its world wars, brutal dictators and crime-ridden democracies. We now see what the Bible has always taught—people are made in the image of God, but rebellious and sinful from birth. The Bible states the obvious when it describes a life of disobedience toward God as "gratifying the cravings of our sinful nature and following its desires and thoughts" (Eph. 2:3). We are surprised when good Christians, true believers, are likewise warned about foul cravings and deceitful desires (see Gal. 5:16,17; Eph. 4:22).

Do not misunderstand. These foolish and harmful desires, these foul cravings, belong to our former ways of life before Christ (see Titus 3:3). They have no rightful place in the attitudes and conduct of Christ's followers (see 2 Cor. 5:17). But—and here's the zinger—they must receive brutal treatment, even by Christians. The Bible uses words such as died (not gratified), put aside, put off (see Rom. 6:11-14; 13:14; Gal. 5:16,17; Eph. 4:22).

We miss the point when we think the Bible is merely telling us to "try harder." Putting confidence in our own efforts is a trap, a return to living by man-made rules. It bypasses the grace of God, the work of Christ and the ministry of the Holy Spirit. The grace of God brings salvation that teaches us to say no to worldly passions. Grace teaches us to live self-controlled, upright and godly lives in the present age (see Titus 2:11,12). God's goodness satisfies our God-given longings (see Pss. 63:5; 103:5). The armor of light dispels the darkness—and we put on that armor by clothing ourselves with the Lord Jesus Christ (see Rom. 13:11-14). God's Word leads us to be filled with His Holy Spirit and to live by the Spirit (see Gal. 5:16-18; Eph. 4:29,30; 5:15-20).

AVOIDING THE PITFALLS

Each of us can take responsibility for maintaining our own freedom in Christ. Each can take steps toward obedience, love, faith and maturity. But what about our spouses? No one can live the Christian life for another, not even the closest people in our lives. We live in a day when adultery is common, even among Christians—yes, even among pastors. Mind you, it is still the exception, not the rule. But it is too real a threat to be ignored. So what can caring spouses do to avoid having their marriages fall on the rocks of adultery?

THE PERFECT WIFE

Hardly anyone abandons a perfect wife or a perfect husband for someone else. The problem, however, is that no one is perfect! Let's laugh a little at our imperfections. "Husbands, love your wives," says the Bible (Eph. 5:25). That's easy enough *if* she's always lovable, *and*...

- If she's a great cook, serving delicious desserts, too, and can still fit into her wedding dress.
- If she's active at church, PTA, hospital auxiliary and has unlimited time for her husband and children.
- If she cares for everyone who is sick in the family and never gets sick herself.
- If she has a great sense of humor and never has any bad moods.
- If she admires and praises her husband and never nags him about his faults.
- If she comes home from work, straightens the house, solves the kids' problems, cooks dinner, gets the homework going, cleans up after dinner, starts the laundry, gets the kids back to their homework, runs to the store, irons, gets the kids to bed, talks with her husband, gets the kids back to bed, folds and puts away the laundry, tidies up the house and still brims with so much energy that she slips into some inviting lingerie to entice her husband to bed for a passionate night.
- If she spends an hour each day in prayer and Bible study, yet never appears more knowledgeable than her husband.
- If she runs an on-time taxi service for sports practice, piano lessons, ball games, school plays and church programs, and always joins her husband in his many recreational activities.

- If she plans great birthday parties for children, parents and all the relatives, special social events, fun weekend getaways, surprises for close friends, wonderful vacations—and never exceeds the family budget.
- If she is always improving herself, continuing in education, growing in Bible study, learning computer skills, developing her talents, advancing in her career and always has time to put her husband and children first in everything.
- If she tithes, pays all the bills on time, buys food, clothes, furniture, appliances, cars, a dozen insurance policies and still puts away money in the bank, with cash left in her purse to eat out on demand.
- If she grooms neatly, dresses attractively, smiles genuinely, exercises regularly, eats modestly and weighs in ideally.

Smile. The point here is that no wife is perfect—absolutely none. Perfection is an impossible goal that most often leads to depression. Forget perfection, but pursue progress.

The Perfect Husband

Of course, every wife would love to have the perfect husband. (Impossible goal!) He might live up to your ideal man...

- If he makes lots of money and never becomes a workaholic.
- If he fixes everything around the house and never botches the job.
- If he remembers your anniversary, birthday, kids' birthdays, in-laws' birthdays, engagement day, first date day, special "just for the two of us" days, and every other day.
- If he sends flowers, cards, notes, little gifts, and arranges surprise romantic get-away-alone weekends, and never gives you a can opener for your anniversary.

- If he brags about your cooking and is always ready to take you out for dinner.
- If he is a creative lover—sensitive, romantic, warm but never pushy or demanding—if he's always tuned in to your intimate feelings and never thinks about his own desires.
- If he is capable, competent, responsible, often elevated to positions of leadership and honor, and never works more than 40 hours per week.
- If he goes to all the kids' ball games, plays, lessons, programs, and still spends hours sharing his deepest feelings with you.
- If he has a great sense of humor, is fun to be around and always knows just when to switch to an in-depth conversation.
- If he's strong, courageous, tough when needed and never gets angry.
- If he's kind, tender, gentle, open, honest, vulnerable and never withdraws or gets his feelings hurt.
- If he always cherishes you, showering you with affection and love in all the special ways you dream about, and never, never disappoints you.

I hope you are grinning by now. All husbands are less than perfect. Do you recall the basic lesson? The only successful method for creating an ideal spouse is to become one yourself!

We can help by understanding our spouses' most urgent needs and doing all we can to meet them. These are the felt needs we can meet, not the deep longings only Christ can satisfy. Christ gives us freedom, grace and truth. He satisfies our God-given longings to be accepted, secure and significant. But He commands us to love our spouses, and meeting their felt needs is one of the best ways to show love.

Willard F. Harley, Jr., in *His Needs, Her Needs*, compares meeting needs to making deposits in our spouses' love banks.

Every time we do something good that the other person enjoys we rank a point.[1]

By the way, men and women often calculate differently. Women give one point for each item, no matter how big or small. Men give more points for big items and less for small ones. A woman may award one point for a single rose in a vase, and one point also for a dozen roses. A man may award one point for a gentle response when he expected a lecture, but four points when his wife gives him a surprise weekend getaway in a nice hotel. Of course, the whole idea of a point system is artificial—depositing love units into our spouses' love banks is the important factor.

We can also make withdrawals. Unhappy experiences and disappointing times lead to love units being subtracted from the bank. Continuous effort must be invested to keep each other's love banks overflowing. And that is precisely what Christ's love does for us. It keeps flowing through us to others, and especially to those in our own families. For this reason our adversary focuses on marriages and families for his primary targets. He growls in pleasure when we rack up a lot of withdrawals.

How can we make deposits in our spouses' love banks? We can start by meeting their most urgent needs. Harley suggests 10 of these, 5 for wives and 5 for husbands. The 5 strongest needs of wives are affection, conversation, honesty and openness, financial support and family commitment. The 5 strongest needs of husbands are sexual fulfillment, recreational companionship, an attractive wife, domestic support and admiration. Both men and women have all 10 needs, but the order of urgency varies from person to person. Look over the list of all 10 with your spouse. Then each of you rank them in the order of your personal preference.[2]

We can see by now that prevention is better than cure. Keeping our marriages strong is the best single tactic for making them affair-resistant. Nevertheless, it's not foolproof. Even good marriages are sometimes marred by adultery. Human weakness and moral decline make many spouses vulnerable targets for the evil adversary.

SNAKEBITES

This is earth, not heaven. It is a fallen world, not an ideal one. Every Christian must watch out for "that ancient serpent, who is the devil or Satan" (Rev. 20:2). It is not by accident that the Bible calls Satan a serpent. He is as venomous as a rattlesnake.

When our son Kirk was engaged, Nancy and I (Chuck) were visiting the family of his fiancée, Debbie Sitz, now his wife. From their house on a hill overlooking their eastern Oregon cattle ranch, we were watching deer feed on green pastures far below. Suddenly someone yelled, "It's a rattlesnake!"

A visiting neighbor discovered it under his truck in their driveway. He grabbed a long stick to move the hated reptile into the open. Debbie's dad was confined to a wheelchair as a

---

WHEN WE FIRST BECOME AWARE OF ENTICEMENT TOWARD ADULTERY AND THE DEMONIC SNAKE BEHIND IT, WE NEED TO RUN FOR OUR SPIRITUAL WEAPONS OF RIGHTEOUSNESS.

---

paraplegic; therefore, her mom, Janyce, flew into action. She ran to the garden, grabbed the shovel and raced back to the truck. After three swift blows, she had severed the snake's head. She carefully picked up the rattlesnake head with a shovel, and buried it. (The locals say it can keep biting as a reflex for awhile.) Then she gathered the snake's body with her shovel and threw it over the side of the bluff. We visitors were wary but fascinated.

The picture of coping with a rattlesnake is a good parable for dealing with the devil and his schemes. We need to fly into action and give swift blows that put the satanic temptation to death. Then we put as much distance between ourselves and the temptation itself as possible.

Poisonous snakes may inflict deadly snakebites, as everyone knows. In moral matters we sometimes suffer with the bites, but ignore the snakes.

- Pornography is not the snake, it's the snakebite.
- Abortion is not the snake, but its bite.

- Adultery is not the snake, but its lethal poison.

We all know the snakebites—crime, divorce, out-of-wedlock pregnancy, incest, abortion, homosexual activity, adultery, pornography and violence. We must not forget to include the more subtle sins such as lying, gossip, cheating and many more. Snakebites are so common we forget to attack the snakes. Like our good friends in eastern Oregon, when we first become aware of enticement toward adultery and the demonic snake behind it, we need to run for our spiritual weapons of righteousness (see 2 Cor. 6:7):

- God's armor
- Powerful prayers
- Biblical counsel
- Instant obedience
- Extra precautions

Beware of thinking you can get close to the fire and not get burned. "Bad company corrupts good morals" (1 Cor. 15:33, *NASB*). Snake charmers experience bites, too. In Bangkok, Thailand, I watched a snake show. It was fascinating. The snake charmers appear to risk their lives with deadly cobras. Whether the snakes were really poisonous or had been operated on to remove the deadly glands, I will never know. One thing I do know. I had no intention of getting into the ring with them. The snakepit is no place for me.

What kind of flawed thinking reasons that we can play with deadly snakes without getting bitten? What makes us think we can charm the snakes? Spiritual enemies specialize in deception. They even make people think snakebites happen without snakes! Let's get honest. Snakes are among us and their bites are killing us. We need compassion for those who are bitten by the snakes, but we need something more. We need healing from the snakebites and a hatred for snakes!

Denial and Deception

Why do good Christians sometimes fall into adulterous affairs when they aren't even looking for them? Does it happen? Most certainly! More often than most people think! Too many Christians think to themselves: *This couldn't happen to me! I know God's Word. I teach it [or even preach it] to my friends. I'm outspoken against immorality. There's no way I'm going to fall.*

Once Christians, especially committed believers, believe they are immune, they easily deny that they are being tempted. The greater the denial, the easier the deception. Little compromises sneak up on them. They treat the snakes as if they were domesticated and no threat at all. In fact, they may not even recognize danger until it's too late.

Even strong Christians have vulnerable moments. These moments may come during times of stress, in life transitions such as mid-life crisis or in times when outward circumstances are changing. They may come during business travel alone when a spouse is simply missing a conversational companion. Then along comes a "nice" person who talks and shares, and one thing leads to another until a one-night stand has occurred. The believer hates it later, feeling the guilt of betraying both the Lord and a faithful spouse. Unresolved conflicts from sexual involvement before marriage can give the evil one a foothold. The battle for the mind becomes intense, and sometimes constant.

Couple these vulnerable times with some undetected lust or a hidden pornography habit, often excused as not a serious problem. Suppose that at the same time, neglect is going on in the marriage. Unmet longings are taking their toll. The marriage lacks intimacy, affection, companionship, understanding, communication, admiration, pleasure and especially respect. Then the deceiver moves in.

He attacks at the weakest point and produces *diminishing respect*. He whispers his thoughts into the person's mind, usually in the first person, "I...":

- I'm depressed all the time. I'm so tired of being unhappy.
- I hate this marriage. I don't want to go on like this. Am I going to spend the rest of my life this way?
- It just isn't fair [and all the details why].
- Look at him! [Look at her!] No way can I respect someone like that.

- I just don't want to be married anymore.

When diminishing respect connects with increasing expectations, danger intensifies. One of the subtle dangers in any marriage is that we gradually expect more and more from our spouses. Often the expectations swirl around finances, with demands to earn more or spend less. The expectations may touch other sensitive subjects such as sex, time together, communication, parenting or conflict. As pressures and expectations rise, they are accompanied by the disillusionment that things will never change, now or ever. People begin to rationalize:

- I'm putting more into this marriage than I'm getting out of it.
- I'm tired of living with my nose to the grindstone. When are you going to get a raise? or When will you stop squandering our money?
- You always...!
- You never...!
- Why don't you...?

Within the marriage the couple experiences a breakdown in tender talk and lovemaking. Morning conversations may sound something like the following:

- Please pass the toast.
- What's the weather supposed to be today?
- I'm late for work, so I need to hurry.

The couple is talking, but it's all superficial. No real feelings flow between them. They act more like business partners than lovers. At night their sexual relationship reflects the same neglect, boredom or frustration. They are too busy, too tired, too disinterested or, conversely, too demanding, too demeaning, too dissatisfied.

THE CONVERSATION STAGE

One spouse is feeling trapped in the marriage when along comes a person of the opposite sex, usually separated or divorced, and available. (The enemy is no fool in arranging such casual connections.) This person really listens and gives tender talk. So the two just talk, that's all. What's wrong with that? Both would say they are just friends, nothing more. There's absolutely nothing going on between them. The problem is that tender talk from the opposite sex is occurring *outside* the marriage, but it's not occurring *inside* the marriage. These two naive people have just entered the first of three stages, *the conversation stage.*

The relationship progresses with emotional delight and innocent touching. If he is her friend, she may give him a social hug or an embrace to say good-bye. If she is his secretary, he may put his hand on her shoulder while giving instructions.

A man came to a pastor friend of mine, saying he was feeling strongly attracted to his secretary and feeling absolutely nothing for his wife. The wise pastor asked, "How often are you touching your secretary?"

"Oh, I'm not touching her at all," he replied.

"This week you keep track of any way at all that you touch her," challenged the pastor.

A week later the man reported, "I'm touching her all the time and I'm liking it, too." Emotional delight and innocent touching were happening outside the marriage that were not happening inside the marriage.

There is a time to hug and a time not to hug. A mere social hug may be a good thing. But when the hug is with the person whom the tender talk and emotional delight are also occurring, yellow caution lights should start flashing. As my pastor, C. W. Perry, says, "If you're looking forward to the next hug, you're in trouble!"

THE FRIENDSHIP STAGE

Our imaginary couple just entered the *friendship stage.* If asked, both would say, "We're just good friends." They are still denying and still being deceived. But their story happens repeatedly in real life.

I was privileged to serve on a panel for a Focus on the

Family radio broadcast with Dr. James Dobson. The other panel members included two couples who had rebuilt their marriages after adultery. With one couple, the wife had fallen into an adulterous affair; with the other couple, it was the husband. I was invited because of my book *Running the Red Lights.*

For their children's sakes, the couples preferred not to use their real names. The couple in which the wife had committed adultery went by the names Judy and Peter. Judy's story paralleled the sequence of the three stages described within this chapter.

The couple lived in an upscale neighborhood, attended an evangelical church regularly and knew Christ as Lord and Savior. They were friends and business associates with the couple who lived next door. They played tennis together, had dinners together and were generally the best of friends.

Peter contracted hepatitis, but gradually recovered. Judy did not understand that a period of depression sometimes follows the disease. Although they previously had a good marriage, Peter was not presently much fun to live with, and Judy didn't know why.

Judy and the other man spent more and more time together talking. She even tried to help him talk through some of his marriage problems. The two couples were again having dinner together. In their social circle it was not unusual for husband and wife to be sitting across the table from each other. So Judy was seated beside the other man. During the evening his hand reached over and touched hers, lingering for just a moment.

"In that moment," Judy said, "I knew I loved him." It was not long before their relationship progressed through the final stages and resulted in an adulterous affair.

The Belonging Stage

Let's leave Judy and Peter, and return to our mythical but typical couple. The relationship began in the conversation stage, progressed in the friendship stage and now accelerates in the *belonging stage.* They begin to spend hidden times together. They are making time, or sometimes misusing company time, to be together. These times are unknown to their spouses, covered up, often by lying. They are also making phone calls, sending notes or cards and giving personal gifts to each other. However, because they are not sleeping together, they deny this is an affair. They just know that they are close friends. If you asked them if they were having an emotional affair—and received an honest answer—they might say, "Well, yes, you might call it that."

About this time the woman in the relationship wakes up to what is really going on. If she's married and a Christian, she may say to herself, "I made a mistake about the man I married. He really wasn't God's will for me."

Not too long after (men are slower), the man wakes up. He may say to himself, "I'm in love with two women. I love my wife and I love this woman. What am I supposed to do? But I am responsible for getting her into this relationship, so I can't hurt her [the woman in the emotional affair, not his wife]."

The emotional pressure and physical temptation now feel almost overwhelming. The warning lights are all flashing red, but the couple no longer cares. Only a short time passes until they hop into bed, and full blown physical adultery begins.

That's what happened to Judy and the man next door. That's what happens to thousands of Christians who fall into denial and deception. That's the snakebite!

Usually the adultery stays hidden for awhile, but eventually the two are found out. Sometimes the affair gets broken off, sometimes not. The tragic story ends in divorce court with finances devastated, children emotionally damaged and a cycle of adultery and divorce that will typically become a pattern in the next three or four generations.

BREAKING OFF AN ADULTEROUS AFFAIR

Judy and Peter, the two panelists on Focus on the Family, were among the blessed ones. They saved their marriage. Peter had begun to grow suspicious. He couldn't quite articulate the problem, but things were not right. He thought it strange that Judy spent so much time talking to his neighbor and business partner, although they were best of friends. But then, the neighbor needed some help and Judy was adept at helping people.

Meanwhile, Judy was lying to cover her tracks. The affair and the cover-up that accompanied it were taking an emotional toll on her. She was seeing both her pastor and a psychologist for counseling, although not telling either of them the whole story.

As Peter's suspicions grew, he made an appointment with an attorney friend. He shared with him everything he had seen and felt. The attorney had met countless couples through his practice whose adultery led to divorce. He could easily decipher the signals of adultery. He said, "I don't *think* your wife is having an affair, I *know* she is. Here is my advice. Hire a private investigator to secure the evidence you need before you confront her."

Peter said it was one of the most difficult decisions of his life. Who wants to hire a cop to follow his wife? But he did, and it wasn't long before they had the goods on her.

Peter was a tough kind of guy. He filed for divorce first, then confronted his wife (not a recommended practice). Already having second thoughts about the other man, Judy was devastated. She broke off the adulterous affair and threw herself on Peter's mercy—not a bad strategy.

Judy explained how she felt at that moment, totally broken before God: "I had lied about it until I became so overdosed with lies that I—in absolute brokenness on my knees—said 'I will never lie again about anything, any time, anywhere. I don't care what the consequences are the rest of my life. I don't ever want to tell another lie, live a double life.' I hated the deception."

Judy kept her word. She never lied to Peter again and never returned to the adultery. By God's grace, Judy's repentance, and Peter's faithfulness, they saved their marriage.[3]

What should we do if our spouses are discovered committing adultery? As faithful spouses—not perfect but faithful—experiencing the pain of an adulterous husband or wife, we should immediately seek counsel from an experienced pastor. Emotions are often too gut-wrenching to permit clear thinking, and any action, however foolish, will have consequences.

Every person faced with an adulterous situation should pray before taking any action, search the Scripture, listen to the Holy Spirit and get godly counsel. Then act!

One strategy is to pray hard, remove excuses and become the ideal spouse. Love can sometimes win where anger will lose.[4] Most faithful spouses do not realize that adulterous affairs blow up faster than marriages. Rising expectations also prevail in an affair, and those hopes and dreams are seldom satisfied outside of marriage. Because most adulterous affairs are built on sand, not rock, they will usually collapse. If we turn to the Lord for help during our times of greatest pain, we can become more conformed to His image and more like the people God intended us to be.

ADULTERY VIOLATES THE TEN COMMANDMENTS AND BRINGS THE WRATH OF GOD UPON YOU AND YOUR DESCENDANTS. WHATEVER PLEASURE YOU EXPERIENCE NOW IS NOT WORTH IT IN THE FACE OF ETERNITY.

The faithful spouse should not tolerate a persistent, repeated pattern of adultery. Dr. James Dobson suggests writing a letter to open the cage door and release the partner who feels trapped. With it comes a statement that all services in this marriage will immediately come to an end.[5] Although we never give counsel to divorce, and separation sometimes makes matters worse, there is a place for taking a stand and showing tough love (see 1 Cor. 7:10,11).

ACT NOW

If you are the spouse involved in an adulterous affair, it's past time for you to break it off. Adultery violates the Ten Commandments and brings the wrath of God upon you and upon your descendants. Whatever pleasure you experience now is not worth it in the face of eternity.

"Sooner or later we'll all have to face God, regardless of our conditions. We will appear before Christ and take what's coming to us as a result of our actions, either good or bad. *That* keeps us vigilant, you can be sure. It's no light thing to know that we'll all one day stand in that place of Judgment (2 Cor. 5:10,11, *The Message*).

Ask God to give you the grit and guts to end it once and for all.

Someone will inevitably get hurt by ending the adulterous affair. Allow us to make an appeal. It's never God's will to damage your spouse and children. Your responsibility before God is to protect them and show them sacrificial love. God does not want your spouse and children to scream in pain. Your only responsibility before God to the other adulterer is to leave forever and never go back. The old excuse, I can't hurt her (or him), is one of Satan's favorite lies.

Three steps are needed to end the adulterous affair and recover from its effects. You must *amputate it, grieve from the loss of it* and *heal from the amputation.*

Let's talk brutal facts. Amputation is a painful but fitting action. It means you must sever, once and for all, the one-flesh relationship with your lover (and anyone else except your spouse). Only a total break will do. Freedom in Christ counselors sometimes go with the person to the phone immediately after processing the personal steps (see appendix A). They give prayerful support as the one involved says, "I'm not going to see you again. It's over!"

Find someone to hold you accountable by their presence as you terminate the adulterous relationship; it gives the extra courage so desperately needed. If this approach is impossible, our counsel is not to visit in person. In fact, if no one can support you, don't use the phone at all. It is far better to change your phone number, then write a letter breaking off the affair.

The crucial issue is never to meet the person again. For some people this means changing jobs, or even moving to another location far away.

Amputating an adulterous affair will be painful because the Bible teaches that even sexual intercourse with a prostitute creates a one-flesh bond (see 1 Cor. 6:16). For those who jump from one sexual partner to another without love and commitment, leaving themselves more lonely than ever, the amputations must be total and simultaneous with all of them. At this point the Bible calls for repentance—true remorse and radical change with a dedication to repair the damage. It also calls for a binding promise to live God's way.

Most people who break off an adulterous affair fail to understand the inevitable grieving process. Christians sometimes wrongly believe everything will be all right because the adultery has ended. This myth contains two totally wrong beliefs. One is that the marriage will instantly recover. The problems in the marriage built up over a period of years; they will not disappear overnight. Refilling a spouse's love bank takes time (especially when maximum deposits are 4 units and 1000 or more units may be needed).

The second wrong belief is that grieving over the amputated affair will not be necessary. Although it was completely sinful, it did provide some evil substitute satisfactions for what God intended in marriage. A time of grieving is normal, not abnormal. Bouncing back and forth like a Ping-Pong ball between spouse and the other adulterer never works. The idea of gradual withdrawal simply does not work. It only creates more pain and devastation for everyone involved. It's like trying to run on a broken leg.

During the grieving process, set a cast that will not allow you to return to the adulterous affair. The hardness of the cast is a discipline called 24-hour accountability. This means you give your spouse permission to phone at any time, check up on you anywhere and ask any questions. Your permission should include an agreement to respond honestly and humbly. The cast, the discipline of accountability, means you will call often and give account of all your time, where you've been and what you have been doing. Any lying, even white lies, must immediately be confessed and abandoned. Casts are uncomfortable and clumsy. This discipline will go against your former false sense of freedom. It will irk you, because it's treating you like a child. But as you begin to rebuild trust in your partner's eyes, you will find that it is worth it.

Amputees do heal—so do marriages that survive adultery. Actually they are more common than most people think. For the protection of their children and their reputations, most Christian couples who have survived adultery prefer never to mention it again, other than between themselves. Dr. Dobson had tried for two years to form the panel who told their stories on the broadcast I mentioned earlier in this chapter. Most couples who were asked to publically share their personal experiences with recovery from adultery told him, "No thanks."

Thousands of other couples have rebuilt their marriages after adultery, and so can you. Time, effort and quite possibly some godly counsel will be needed. It will take everything you've got to rebuild what was destroyed. But great effort always pays big dividends. All couples who work wholeheartedly on their marriages, with or without former adultery, will experience a great improvement in their relationships.

Your story will not be the same as the one described in this chapter. It may be that you are a Christian married to an unfaithful non-Christian who lives by this world's standards. It may be that your spouse indulged in a careless one-night fling, and later regretted it deeply. It may be that your spouse is a sexual addict who needs intensive spiritual and psychological counseling. We recommend our books about this subject, A *Way of Escape* by Neil Anderson and *Running the Red Lights* by Charles Mylander.

Freedom in Christ is available for sexual addicts as well as those who are beguiled by their own denial and Satan's deception. Both the "Personal Steps to Freedom" in appendix A and the "Marriage Steps to Freedom" in chapter 14 will prove helpful to both spouses. Offering forgiveness and breaking sexual bondage are vital for marital healing.

The Israelites experienced the judgment of a plague of snakes among them. After Moses prayed for the people, God instructed him to raise up a bronze snake on a pole. Anyone who had the faith to look at God's provision lived. The others died. While talking with Nicodemus, Jesus predicted His coming crucifixion as the cure for spiritual snakebites:

"Just as Moses lifted up the snake in the desert, so the Son of Man must be lifted up, that everyone who believes in him may have eternal life" (John 3:14,15).

- Look at the Cross—Jesus died for you and your snakebites.
- Look at the empty tomb—Jesus rose to give you hope and a future.
- Look at the throne of God—Jesus reigns to crush the head of the serpent, to repel the snakes that threaten you.

Notes

1. Willard F. Harley, Jr., *His Needs, Her Needs, Building an Affair-proof Marriage* (Grand Rapids, Mich.: Fleming H.Revell, 1986, 1994), pp. 18-28.
2. Ibid, pp. 179-185.
3. "Marriages that Survived Infidelity—I" Focus on the Family broadcast, Wednesday, November 1, 1995. Cassette tapes may be ordered from Focus on the Family (1-800-AFAMILY).
4. See Chapter 5, "Help, My Spouse Is Having an Affair," Charles Mylander, *Running the Red Lights* (Ventura, Calif.: Regal Books, 1986), pp. 91-113.
5. Dr. James C. Dobson, *Love Must Be Tough, New Hope for Families in Crisis* (Waco, Tex.: Word Books, 1983), pp. 44-50, 67-69.

CHAPTER TWELVE

Forgive Seventy Times Seven

Then came Peter to him, and said, Lord, how oft shall my brother sin against me, and I forgive him? till seven times? Jesus saith unto him, I say not unto thee, Until seven times: but, Until seventy times seven.

—MATTHEW 18:21,22, KJV

But whom you forgive anything, I forgive also; for indeed what I have forgiven, if I have forgiven anything, I did it for your sakes in the presence of Christ, in order that no advantage be taken of us by Satan; for we are not ignorant of his schemes.

—2 CORINTHIANS 2:10,11, NASB

Forgive us our debts, as we also have forgiven our debtors. For if you forgive men when they sin against you, your heavenly Father will also forgive you. But if you do not forgive men their sins, your Father will not forgive your sins.

—MATTHEW 6:12,14,15

Be kind and compassionate to one another, forgiving each other, just as in Christ God forgave you.

—EPHESIANS 4:32

Bear with each other and forgive whatever grievances you may have against one another. Forgive as the Lord forgave you.

—COLOSSIANS 3:13

When they came to the place called the Skull, there they crucified him, along with the criminals—one on his right, the other on his left. Jesus said, "Father, forgive them, for they do not know what they are doing."

—LUKE 23:33,34

Ask most husbands and wives during the nesting years some simple questions: What's your task in marriage? What's your job, your role? According to my friend Royce Frazier, a marriage and family counselor, most people will respond in terms of parenting:

- "I provide for the family. I work hard to give them the best."
- "I work outside the home—and cook, clean, and take care of the children."
- "I spend a lot of time with the family. The kids' activities really keep us busy."

No doubt, good parenting is blessed by God. Fortunate are the children whose parents love them fully and train them biblically! But parenting alone is never enough. Troubled children are infected by generational sins, and their parents' own dysfunctional marriages. Conflict and crisis in marriage affects the whole family, including the kids. In fact, studies on the children of divorce reveal devastating damage when parents permanently separate.[1]

It is essential that marriage partners resolve problems—easier said than done. Our society teaches us many ways to cope with conflict, but forgiving is not one of them. Run, fight, quit, blame, accuse, give up, get depressed—these are all common ways people cope.

- Running away from problems does not change anyone or anything.
- Endless fighting over the same kinds of problems is useless.
- Quitting is futile, and burying problems is never enough.
- Blaming and accusing each other leads nowhere.
- Giving up and getting depressed is self-destructive.
- Getting even is lethal.
- Communication helps, but only if it actually resolves the problems.

What's missing is forgiveness! Our culture seldom teaches the skills of heartfelt forgiveness—nor, by the way, the practice of loving confrontation to resolve problems. After more than 50 years of secrecy, a woman shared her intensely private story with "Dear Abby":

> I was 20 and he was 26. We had been married two years and I hadn't dreamed he could be unfaithful. The awful truth was brought home to me when a young widow from a neighboring farm came to tell me she was carrying my husband's child. My world collapsed. I wanted to die. I fought an urge to kill her—and him.
>
> I knew that wasn't the answer. I prayed for strength and guidance. And it came. I knew I had to forgive this man, and I did. I forgave her, too. I calmly told my husband what I had learned and the three of us worked out a solution together. (What a frightened little creature she was!) The

baby was born in my home. Everyone thought I had given birth and that my neighbor was "helping me." Actually it was the other way around. But the widow was spared humiliation (she had three other children), and the little boy was raised as my own. He never knew the truth.

REFUSING TO FORGIVE, OR SIMPLY NOT BOTHERING, SENDS A DULL ACHE THROUGH THE SOUL.

Was this divine compensation for my own inability to bear a child? I do not know. I have never mentioned this incident to my husband. It has been a closed chapter in our lives for 50 years. But I've read the love and gratitude in his eyes a thousand times.[2]

REFUSING TO FORGIVE

Forgiveness within marriage starts well, but becomes more difficult if the other partner refuses to change. When our spouses repeatedly sin against us, it is tough to keep on giving forgiveness. Added to that are the struggles and setbacks of daily life—baggage from dysfunctional parents, financial pressures, layoffs from work, too little time alone, sex problems, communication breakdowns, miscarriages, premenstrual syndrome, menopause, surgeries, tragedies, rebellious adolescents, interfering in-laws. It's easy to gather regrets and resentments. No wonder Jesus taught that we should forgive 70 times 7. (If you're counting, you're not forgiving.)

Refusing to forgive, or simply not bothering, sends a dull ache through the soul. Unforgiveness has some nasty consequences. *Refusing to forgive means that God will not forgive us.* After teaching His disciples the Lord's Prayer, Jesus added, "For if you forgive men when they sin against you, your heavenly Father will also forgive you. But if you do not forgive men their sins, your Father will not forgive your sins" (Matt. 6:14,15).

Just kidding, right? Jesus must have had a bad day when He taught this one, don't you think? Maybe He ate some spoiled fish and felt upset in His stomach. Maybe He had a migraine headache that day. Surely, surely, He didn't mean it, did He? But would Jesus lie about something in the Sermon on the Mount? Maybe it's time to read the verses again—and search our hearts for occasions we have not forgiven our spouses, or others.

The tough truth is that Jesus meant it, and the heavenly Father follows through on it. If there is anyone we won't forgive, then we can forget about asking God to forgive us. He turns a deaf ear. Frankly, I want the heavenly Father to forgive my sins, don't you? I don't want anything to foul up the divine chemistry of the Cross that clears my record and cleanses my heart. One more thing—watch out for theological detours that bypass forgiveness. This passage may have more than one explanation, but all informed Bible interpreters agree on one truth: In God's Word forgiveness is a command, not an option.

Refusing to forgive means we will be tormented. Jesus was at it again—hitting hard on forgiving other people. In Matthew 18 He first told Peter to forgive not 7 times but 77 times (see 18:21,22, *KJV*). Then He told a parable about a servant who was forgiven much but wouldn't forgive a little (see vv. 23-35). The punch line of the story hurts. Jesus said the unforgiving servant was turned over to the jailers to be tortured. Then He shared one of the lasting and nasty consequences of not forgiving: "This [being tortured] is how my heavenly Father will treat each of you unless you forgive your brother from your heart" (v. 35).

Would the heavenly Father let someone be tortured just for not forgiving? To find out, simply try not forgiving. It feels like battery acid in the soul. Why would our Father let us go through so much pain? "Because the Lord disciplines those he loves" (Heb. 12:6). If a little pain will lead us to the freedom of forgiveness, He will allow the torment. Psychological problems, depression, restlessness, inner turmoil and dissatisfaction plague the unforgiving.

What's worse, Satan gains an advantage. That's what the Bible teaches (see 2 Cor. 2:10,11, *NASB*). Urging unforgiveness is one of Satan's schemes. He loves to put his thoughts in our heads, again, usually in the first person, "I...":

- I'm not ready to forgive yet.
- I need some counseling first.
- I shouldn't feel this way.
- It's my fault; I don't have anything to forgive.
- It's not that big of a deal; I'll just forget it.
- I'm not going to just let them off my hook!
- Why should I forgive? They're the ones who need to ask my forgiveness.

Refusing to forgive causes us trouble and defiles our own spirits. When we don't forgive, we nurse a little grudge. Give it some time and we feel resentful. Neglect to deal with the resentment and we turn bitter. Here's the bad news. Bitterness pollutes the atmosphere of our lives. Bitter people invite trouble because they blindly cause it. People who keep going in that direction become bitter old men or sour old women. Doesn't that sound like fun?

Do yourself a favor. Grab hold of God's grace and use it to forgive a parent, spouse, friend, associate or neighbor. God gives all the grace you need to forgive every hurtful deed (see Hebrews 12:15). Think of the benefits:

- God forgives our sins.
- God stops our pain.
- God removes our trouble.

Some people misunderstand forgiveness. They believe it is essential to feel good first about the person who hurt them. Nonsense. Forgiveness works best when we get in touch with how bad we feel, or imagine how good we will feel after we've forgiven. Forgiving others does not mean we roll over and play dead, acting like their wrong was okay. We refuse to excuse sin or justify the sinner. Both judgment and salvation are God's business. Our part is simply to take our offenses, hurts and painful memories to the Cross and leave them there. In so doing we agree to live with any consequences God does not remove. We can trust Him! "Never take your own revenge, beloved, but leave room for the wrath of God, for it is written, 'Vengeance is Mine, I will repay, says the Lord'" (Rom. 12:19, *NASB*).

"Forgive as the Lord forgave you" (Col. 3:13). Forgiving others is not a suggestion, it's a command—and a good one! The amazing miracle of forgiving others is that it stops our pain. When we release our offenses, they quit hurting us. When we let go of our grievances, we rid ourselves of the dull aches in our souls. The brackish tastes in our mouths turn sweet again. The overcast skies of dismal feelings become bright and sunny. Why would anyone refuse to forgive?

POWER TO FORGIVE

If I want to forgive I look to the Cross to grasp how the Lord Jesus forgave me. Consider three passages.

1. "When they came to the place called the Skull, there they crucified him, along with the criminals—one on his right, the other on his left. Jesus said, 'Father, forgive them for they do not know what they are doing'" (Luke 23:33,34). On the Cross, Jesus experienced pain and anguish from those who crucified Him. When I forgive as the Lord forgave me, I experience pain from those who have hurt me. It almost sounds like a contradiction. I must experience my pain to stop my pain. However, the pain only quits when the heart releases the offense. Forgiveness takes place within my pain.

I recall an old saying, "Time heals all wounds." True enough if there is not infection or foreign material in the wounds. But if bitterness or resentment infects the spirit, it is more accurate to say, "Time buries all wounds." Time will eventually bury the pain of old grievances that were never forgiven, but it does not heal them. Without warning they will crawl out of the pit of our suppressed memories, pain and all. If we refuse to forgive, they will pop up when we least expect them. Unforgiven hurts rise from the grave to haunt us.

2. *"This is how we know what love is: Jesus Christ laid down his life for us. And we ought to lay down our lives for our brothers" (1 John 3:16).* On the Cross Jesus showed suffering love, laying down His life instead of retaliating against those who hurt Him. When I forgive as the Lord forgave me, I show suffering love, laying down my right to get even with those who have hurt me. In cases of battering and abuse, report it—but still forgive. Justice and forgiveness walk hand in hand. This is possible because we ourselves are forgiven children of a just God. Because we belong to a just God, we call on his human authorities for justice. Because we are children of a forgiving God, we forgive as Christ forgave us.

3. *"For God so loved the world that he gave his one and only Son, that whoever believes in him shall not perish but have eternal life" (John 3:16).* On the Cross Jesus let me off the hook and set me free. When I forgive as the Lord forgave me, I let others off my hook and release them to God's wisdom and judgment. I give up any attempt to get even or settle the score. I leave revenge in God's hands.

When I was a boy my cousin Floyd Hadley and I went fishing. I wasn't good at casting—still learning. On one very bad cast my fishhook stuck in his cheek. Neither Floyd nor I could get it out so we walked to my aunt's house. She couldn't get it out either. Like any concerned mother, she took her son to the doctor. The experienced doctor pushed the tip of the hook on through the cheek, clipped off the barb, then pulled it out.

The hook in Floyd's cheek was a result of my offense, not his. I'm the one who hurt him. But once in his cheek, it was his hook. It would not turn him loose. Suppose he had said, "I'm not going to let you off my hook." Guess who would keep hurting?

Now imagine a gruesome thought. Suppose I continued to hold the line and tugged on it whenever I felt like it. I kept hurting him again and again. I wasn't hurting, he was. The only way for him to get free would be to release the hook. If he refused to let me off his hook, he would keep on hurting. Whoever refuses to forgive prolongs the pain.

I cannot play the martyr role when I forgive—
because Jesus did not forgive me that way.
I cannot settle the score first before I forgive—
because Jesus did not forgive me that way.
I cannot keep a running tally of grievances—
because Jesus did not forgive me that way.
I cannot forgive with my lips and then bring it up again when I need the advantage of some clout—
because Jesus did not forgive me that way.
I cannot forgive and then tell all the right people about it—
because Jesus did not forgive me that way.
I cannot go through all the motions of forgiveness and then harbor resentment for weeks, months, years—
because Jesus did not forgive me that way.
I can forget the score and erase the tally of rights and wrongs—
because Jesus forgave me that way.
I can keep loving and respecting the one who hurt me—
because Jesus forgave me that way.
I can look for signs of genuine repentance—
because Jesus forgave me that way.
I can take the first step to bring about reconciliation—
because Jesus forgave me that way.
I can release all the resentment that clings to the past—
because Jesus forgave me that way.
I can thaw out the frozen bitterness deep inside and begin to relieve the other's pain—
because Jesus forgave me that way.
I can be kind and compassionate, forgiving another—
just as in Christ Jesus God forgave me (see Eph. 4:31,32).

Pray right now. Ask the Lord Jesus to bring to your mind

the names or the faces of every person you need to forgive. The Holy Spirit is amazingly faithful to bring names to our minds, sometimes people we have forgotten for years. The most common names to surface are Mother or Father. (Maybe the Lord is even more concerned than we are that we break the lasting consequences of generational sins.) Jot the names down on a list. Then, one by one, pray this simple forgiveness prayer:

> Lord, I forgive (name) for (specifically identify all offenses and painful memories or feelings).

If the experience was traumatic, such as childhood abuse or adultery in the marriage, you may find forgiveness extremely difficult. In such cases it helps to pray through the following 10 steps, one at a time. Personalize each step by inserting the person's name, or recalling the incident or visualizing what's happening. Even if you do not have a struggle with forgiveness, the following steps are helpful in understanding the forgiveness process.

TEN STEPS TO FORGIVENESS

1. *Feel the pain, hurt, resentment, bitterness and hate (see Matt. 5:4).* Avoid the two extremes of "I shouldn't feel that way" and "I'm not ready to forgive yet."
2. *Submit yourself to God, recalling how Christ forgave you (see Luke 23:33,34; Col. 3:13).* Go to the Cross! You will find the justice and the power there.
3. *Ask for Christ's grace and power to forgive (see Luke 11:9,10).* Sometimes our emotions scream, "I can't forgive! You don't understand what they did to me." True, but Jesus understands, and He will give us everything we need to forgive. When we are willing, God always gives us the grace to obey His commands.
4. *Agree to live with the unavoidable consequences of the other person's sins against you (see Eph. 5:21; Col. 3:13).* If the consequences are avoidable, and it's legal, right and moral to do so, then by all means avoid them! But

if the consequences are unavoidable, then you will have to live with them anyway. Your only choice is between the bondage of bitterness and the freedom of forgiveness.

5. *Release the offense. Tear up the debt the other person owes you (see Matt. 6:12).* When we pray the Lord's prayer, "Forgive us our debts as we forgive our debtors," we are not speaking of finances. Tear up the personal, moral and relational debt you feel the other person owes you. This is the heart of forgiveness.
6. *Never bring it up again as a club (see Rom. 12:17).* In marriage this means, once you forgive, you can never use the information as a weapon during a fight. You never use the information against your spouse. The subject can be discussed to bring resolution or progress. But you can never say, "Well, do you remember when you..." or "I forgave you for....Why can't you...?"
7. *Keep forgiving when your emotions recycle the pain or when the person keeps offending you (see Matt. 18:21,22).* The devil loves to jump on this one. We forgive, we really do. But then the other person keeps hurting our feelings. If it was a major trauma our emotions will cycle to a low period when we don't *feel* like we ever forgave anything in the first place. Then the adversary comes around and says, "Just look at you! What a hypocrite you are! You feel just the same as you did before. You didn't forgive at all. This forgiveness stuff works for other people but it doesn't work for you." What do you do? You submit to God and resist the devil (see Jas. 4:7). Tell him in Jesus' name, "Out of here, evil one! Take a hike, beat it!" (At Freedom in Christ, we recommend you speak out loud or let your lips move.) Then you simply pray the simple forgiveness prayer once again. *"Lord, I forgive ____________ for________________."* Guess what? It will take you about half as long as it did the first time. The next time it will only take half as long as the second time. Soon your emotions will be healed and forgiveness will become a way of life.

8. *Reject the sinful act and tolerate it no longer (see Rom. 12:21).* God does not want you to put up with abuse. Take your stand against the sin. If necessary, find godly allies in your church or get help from someone with governmental authority to stand with you. The God of the Bible is holy and just.
9. *Turn the vengeance over to God and over to God's human authorities (see Rom. 12:19,20; 13:1).* Let God do the disciplining in your marriage. Never try to take His place. Never protect anyone, even a family member, from legitimate church discipline or from impartial civil justice. These authorities are instituted by God for our protection.
10. *Replace the old resentful feelings with the forgiving love of Christ (see Matt. 12:43-45; Eph. 4:31,32).* A spiritual vacuum is dangerous. Anything not controlled by the Holy Spirit will soon attract evil spirits (see Matt. 12:43-45). The result of forgiveness should never be emptiness or defeat, but rather actions of overflowing love.

WHAT YOU DO NOT HAVE TO DO

1. *You do not have to feel good about the person who hurt you—either before or after you forgive.* Forgiveness is not forgetting; forgiveness is an issue between you and God. It does not put a stamp of approval on another's behavior. It does not automatically rebuild trust. It does not make you like someone who has hurt you. It simply releases the offense and lets you focus on the problem, not the problem-producer.
2. *You don't have to tell the other person about your resentful feelings unless Scripture or the Holy Spirit tells you to (see Matt. 5:23-26; 18:15-17).* The need to forgive is between you and God; the need to ask for forgiveness is between you and another person. The Bible tells you to go to someone else when the other person also sees it as a conflict. If the issue is a need for reconciliation between two estranged people, both of whom

are aware of the tension, then go make peace. But if the other person is not aware of it, or it's no big deal to that person, then keep your personal forgiveness between you and God. Every Christian should follow the guidance of the Holy Spirit.

3. *You don't have to wait until you are ready to forgive.* You can obey God's Word right now.

UNLESS YOUR MARRIAGE IS STILL IN ITS EARLIEST STAGES, YOU ARE SURE TO HAVE SOME PAINFUL MEMORIES. ONE OF THE BEST WAYS TO OVERCOME THESE HURTFUL TIMES WITH ONE ANOTHER, OR WITH OTHERS, IS TO FORGIVE.

PAINFUL MEMORIES

Unless your marriage is still in its earliest stages, you are sure to have some painful memories. One of the best ways to deal with these hurtful times with one another, or with others, is to forgive. But don't jump too soon. Seize the opportunity to revisit your past together. In chapter 14 we give the "Marriage Steps to Freedom." Set apart a day to sit down together and process these vital Steps. In Step 5, "Release Old Hurts," you will recall your marriage year by year, decade by decade or stage by stage. First ask the Lord to bring all the good memories to your mind. Jot them down and spend a few moments thanking Him for the good times.

Then ask Him to bring to mind all the painful memories, one life stage at a time. Write these down also, but destroy the list after you have forgiven. It is important at this point to apply forgiveness to yourself, to each other or even to your misguided feelings about God. The explanation in the personal "Steps to Freedom in Christ" (see appendix A) is most helpful.

At the end of your list, write "myself." Forgiving yourself is accepting God's cleansing and forgiveness. Also, write "thoughts against God." Thoughts raised up against the knowledge of God will usually result in angry feelings toward Him. Technically we don't forgive God, because He cannot commit any sin of commission or omission. But we need to specifically renounce false expectations and thoughts about God and agree to release any anger we have toward Him.

Taking time to release the painful memories of our marriages will bring a cleansing and release we cannot experience in any other way. Once we forgive, we burn the lists, or in some way totally destroy it. We need never bring these painful memories up again. They are gone forever.

Notes

1. Barbara Dafoe Whitehead, "Dan Quayle Was Right," *The Atlantic Monthly* 271, no. 4 (April 1993): 47.
2. J. Allan Petersen, *The Myth of the Greener Grass,* (Wheaton, Ill.: Tyndale House Publishers, Inc., 1983), pp. 146-147.

CHAPTER THIRTEEN

When Only One Will Try

To the married I give this command (not I, but the Lord): A wife must not separate from her husband. But if she does, she must remain unmarried or else be reconciled to her husband. And a husband must not divorce his wife.

—1 CORINTHIANS 7:10,11

Have you ever felt like giving in to despair? You've given so much, tried so hard and your marriage partner still does not seem interested. He or she may be a workaholic, alcoholic or sexaholic. Maybe he won't talk. Maybe she won't make love. Maybe he's abusive. Maybe she spends all the money. Or maybe your spouse is responsible but boring, satisfied with this same-o, same-o marriage that leaves you unsatisfied. Does God have answers when only one mate will try? We believe He does.

Most troubled marriages are evidenced by only one spouse willing to work on improving the relationship. Many good marriages sometimes only attest to one marriage partner willing to refine the relationship.

Derek thought to himself, "I'm putting so much more into this marriage than I'm getting out of it. What's the use?" He did not realize that just two years earlier his wife, Kara, had thought the same thing. Theirs was a typical marriage, less than perfect but better than some. It had hope, even from a human point of view. With time, persistence and a big dose of God's grace, it not only survived but flourished.

Doris, however, saw her life with her husband, Drake, go from bad to worse. Both of them were raised in Christian families, but knew nothing about Christ's freedom. They were content as Christians, financially secure and pleased with their wonderful family of three girls, now grown. They were reasonably happy and thought they had a good marriage. Doris, however, had this nagging sense that something was missing.

Drake made a major financial investment that turned into a disaster. Stress hit big time, and for the first time in his life he began to experience panic attacks. His financial stability was going down the drain and the panic attacks persisted. To make matters worse, Doris collapsed while visiting her daughters in another state. She was rushed to the hospital for emergency surgery, and could not travel, even to return home, for four months.

When she did return home, their marriage did not improve. In Doris' own words, "It seemed like all the things on which we had based our value were in jeopardy. Our life appeared to be collapsing before our eyes and we were helpless. Our marriage, which we thought to be so strong, was in serious difficulty. We had never experienced real depression before, but now there seemed to be no respite from it. We didn't understand. We were Christians who had always tried to do the 'right thing.' We felt powerless. Satan also uses circumstances to his own end and he was relentless in his attack. We felt increasingly unhappy."[1]

Along with a close friend, the wife of a former pastor (whose marriage was also in trouble), Doris attended one of Neil's seminars. She found her freedom in Christ and reaffirmed her identity as a child of God. Christ's freedom in her innermost *being* changed her attitude about her *doing*, how she acted. Because she was free on the inside, she gained Christ's confidence on the outside. Life was looking up except for one thing—Drake's attitude. He was pleased that she was encouraged by the Freedom in Christ Conference but felt no need to attend one himself.

Doris played him a video from the conference series[2], but he went to sleep. She tried to get him to read *The Bondage Breaker*. No luck. She even made arrangements with her friend, the former pastor's wife, for the two couples to watch one of Neil's videos together. *Both husbands* went to sleep! What's a wife to do when her husband won't even try? Doris must have been praying, however, because when she reached her wits' end, God took over.

Drake's father, who had been battling cancer, entered the final days of his fight with the dreaded disease. On the flight to visit him, Drake began to read *The Bondage Breaker*, a copy Doris brought along for a mutual friend. He was so impressed he began to tell Doris how good it was. Shock!

On arrival they found Drake's father weak but alert. When Drake told him about the book, he wanted to hear it. This godly man had been a fine Christian for years, so Drake and Doris took turns reading the book to him. He loved it!

With tears streaming down his cheeks, Drake's dad shared how he had needed to hear these truths. Even on his deathbed, Satan was accusing him! He went home to be with the Lord, free in Christ. Needless to say, Drake found his freedom, too. The panic attacks disappeared. In time the Lord restored their marriage and their finances. Best of all, God transformed their relationship with the Lord Jesus; they moved from performance-based Christianity to freedom in Christ.

What happened to the former pastor and his wife? They separated for six weeks until the husband's pride was broken. He then became willing to read *The Bondage Breaker* and take its message to heart. Both he and his wife used their new sense of *being* free in Christ as a basis for *doing* work on their marriage. Drake and Doris eventually had the privilege of standing up with them in a precious time of renewing their marriage vows.

SEPARATE *DOING* AND *BEING*

A theme of this book is that we must separate *doing* from *being*. Many Christian books and speakers give us good advice about what to do. Often, however, they neglect Christ's good news that we can become free in our innermost beings—more whole and healthy than we ever dreamed possible. A subtle form of Christian behaviorism results from an overemphasis on doing: do better, try harder, give more, follow this advice. Many of us try and try, and fail and fail, until we finally give up. Something sinister, something weird, something demonic fouls up our best efforts. Our marriages end in divorce, and our children suffer.

What goes wrong? We try to change what we *do* without Christ's changing who we *are*. None of us can keep up all the right efforts to do better if we are believing Satan's lies in our minds about God and ourselves. Doing without being simply does not work.

Worse yet, health problems escalate. A new report by the National Institute for Healthcare Research shows a significant link between divorce and early death, drug and alcohol use, and various health problems. One discovery found that divorced men face the same risk for cancer as a man who smokes a pack of cigarettes a day. Susan Larson, who cowrote the report, said, "Early death from both cardiovascular disease and strokes doubled for divorced men compared to married men."[3]

Too many of us, including evangelical Christians, consider divorce an option. We rationalize the Bible's truth that God hates divorce (see Mal. 2:13-16; Mark 10:2-12; 1 Cor. 7:10-14) and focus only on the exception clauses (see Matt. 5:31,32; 1 Cor. 7:15). Newspaper columnist Mona Charen explains why so few speak out against this tragic blight on our society:

Divorce is such an accepted part of the national landscape that even cultural crusaders have sometimes held their fire. To condemn divorce is to rebuke not just strangers but your sister, your cousins, your best friend and yourself.

The wreckage divorce has created in the lives of children is too massive to be denied.[4]

What is this massive evidence? In *The Atlantic Monthly*

Barbara Dafoe Whitehead shares some disturbing facts:

According to a growing body of social-scientific evidence, children in families disrupted by divorce and out-of-wedlock birth do worse than children in intact families on several measures of well-being. Children in single-parent families are six times as likely to be poor. They are also likely to stay poor longer. Twenty-two percent of children in one-parent families will experience poverty during childhood for seven years or more, as compared with only two percent of children in two-parent families. A 1988 survey by the National Center for Health Statistics found that children in single-parent families are two to three times as likely as children in two-parent families to have emotional and behavioral problems They are also more likely to drop out of high school, to get pregnant as teenagers, to abuse drugs and to be in trouble with the law. Compared with children in intact families, children from disrupted families are at a much higher risk for physical or sexual abuse.

Contrary to popular belief, many children do not "bounce back" after divorce or remarriage. Difficulties that are associated with family breakup often persist into adulthood. Children who grow up in single-parent or stepparent families are less successful as adults, particularly in the two domains of life—love and work—that are most essential to happiness. Needless to say, not all children experience such negative effects. However, research shows that many children from disrupted families have a harder time achieving intimacy in a relationship, forming a stable marriage or even holding a steady job.[5]

This report is not an isolated instance. *Time* magazine reported the following:

"Almost half of children of divorces enter adulthood as worried, under-achieving, self-deprecating and sometimes angry young men and women," reports Judith Wallerstein, director of the Center for the Family in Transition and author of *Second Chance* (Ticknor & Fields, 1988). Her conclusion is drawn from interviews conducted over a 15-year period with 60 families, mostly white middle class. It included 131 children, who were 2 to 18 years old at the time of the divorce. Other Wallerstein findings:

- Three out of five youngsters felt rejected by at least one parent.
- Half grew up in settings in which the parents were warring with each other even after the divorce.
- Two-thirds of the girls, many of whom had seemingly sailed through the crisis, suddenly became deeply anxious as young adults, unable to make lasting commitments and fearful of betrayal in intimate relationships.
- Many boys, who were overly troubled in the post-divorce years, failed to develop a sense of independence, confidence or purpose. They drifted in and out of college and from job to job.[6]

THE TRADITIONAL WISDOM THAT IT IS WORTH SAVING A MARRIAGE OR STAYING WITH A BAD ONE FOR THE SAKE OF THE CHILDREN SEEMS WISER THAN EVER BEFORE.

The traditional wisdom that it's worth saving a marriage or staying with a bad one for the sake of the children, seems wiser than ever before. But moving a marriage from divorce to freedom is never easy.

It takes more than trying harder, more than good techniques, more than advanced relationship skills to save a troubled marriage. It takes sacrifice, dedication, commitment. It takes putting our hands into the hand of the Holy Spirit and allowing Him to lead us in light of God's Word, even to the Cross. It takes adjusting our lives to God's ways and believing His truth.

NOT DIVORCE, BUT FREEDOM

Only one person in some marriages is willing to go through the "Marriage Steps." The good news is that most of the spiritual bondage in the marriage can be broken by one Christian spouse. God hears and answers prayer, even if only one will pray. What's the worst thing that could happen? The spouse who finds freedom becomes a better person! And the best? The committed one may indeed save the marriage without a word being spoken. Is this not similar to what Peter counseled Christian wives with unbelieving husbands? "Your beauty...should be that of your inner self, the unfading beauty of a gentle and quiet spirit, which is of great worth in God's sight" (1 Pet. 3:3,4). Your spouse may be "won over without words" (see v. 1) by your behavior.

With this in mind, we have adapted "Marriage Steps" in appendix A into the "Marriage Steps for One Spouse." (They are available through Freedom in Christ, 491 E. Lambert Rd., La Habra, CA 90631. Phone 310/691-9128 or FAX 310/691-4035.) If you really want freedom, begin with the personal "Steps to Freedom in Christ." If you find difficulty at any point, ask a trusted pastor and Christian prayer partner to lead you through them. Another person's prayer power and personal encouragement make a remarkable difference. Within the next week go through the "Marriage Steps," seeking Christ's cleansing of your marriage relationship. However, even after processing the "Marriage Steps for One Spouse," a long and difficult road may yet lie ahead.

Lance and Wendy are friends of mine (Chuck). (We've changed their names to provide privacy, although they have gone public on Christian television with their story.) Although it was only two years since their wedding, Lance (an unbeliever) and Wendy (a half-hearted believer) were living like married singles. He was deeply involved in sports and she was busy at work. Wendy was not getting the attention she needed, so she began to look for it at work. It didn't take long to find an attentive male—and an adulterous affair.

Lance, however, was so busy between work and sports that it was easy for Wendy to hide her time away with her illicit lover. She played the role of a normal wife, and Lance suspected nothing. Then one night she did not come home, and a big red flag started waving.

Lance confronted Wendy, much to her relief. Finally her double life was out in the open so they could deal with the problems. But instead of resolving anything, they only fought. Wendy left home for the other man. Lance was deeply upset and spent a lot of time crying—although he was not normally a crier by nature. The days of separation turned into weeks, and weeks into months. In fact, after five months Wendy filed for divorce, which in time became final.

Although he was now divorced, Lance did not give up. He turned to the church and received Christ as His Lord and Savior. He wanted Wendy back, so he decided to go to work, not on her but on himself. He pursued Christ with a passion, making every possible change for the better. Near the end of 10 months of separation, seeing the changes in Lance, Wendy rededicated her life to Christ. Once Jesus was again allowed His rightful Lordship, she became intensely uncomfortable with her adultery and, although divorced, returned home to Lance.

The two forgave each other—for neglect, for adultery—and opened a new chapter in their lives. They agreed to close the book on their past sins and look ahead to their new life in Christ. They remarried. It's now years later and Lance and Wendy have helped many other couples find hope when everything seemed hopeless.

"I learned to forgive Wendy," Lance said. "Even years later it still hurts, but I have learned to forgive."

LIVING WITH PAIN

If you are the only one who will try in your marriage, and if the marriage is deeply flawed, then you may be living with constant pain. During such a time, turn to the Psalms. Many were written in times of pain, and they cry out to God for help against one's enemies. The Psalms help us during our times of trouble as well:

> I am in pain and distress; may your salvation, O God, protect me (Ps. 69:29).

> He heals the brokenhearted and binds up their wounds (Ps. 147:3).

> Keep me safe, O God, for in you I take refuge (Ps. 16:1).

Let's face the tough questions. How does a faithful Christian spouse live with pain? How do you tolerate the spouse who keeps on hurting you again and again? How can you be responsible without becoming a sick controller or a co-dependent? What if your spouse is an addict, a thief, an adulterer or a credit card junkie? In my book *Running the Red Lights* (Regal Books), I wrote the following about being responsible or irresponsible:

- I will *let* you be responsible. And I will not knowingly contribute to your being irresponsible.
- I will not try to force you to be responsible by nagging, condemning, scolding, moralizing.
- I will not knowingly let you be irresponsible by removing the consequences when you do what is wrong.
- I will stand by you, care for you, cry with you; but I will not bail you out time after time after time.
- I will not personally judge you, pretending I am your judge instead of God.
- Neither will I personally provide a shelter for your sin, pretending I am your Savior instead of Christ.
- I will love you, accept you, forgive you and give you a fresh start whenever you ask for it.[7]

Begin to put these principles into practice, and your pain will increase—at least at first. Sometimes things get worse before they get better. Never forget that Jesus lived with pain. The prophet Isaiah predicted the suffering of the Messiah: "He was despised and rejected by men, a man of sorrows, and familiar with suffering" (53:3). Hebrews tells us, "Although he was a son, he learned obedience from what he suffered" (Heb. 5:8). Jesus said to his disciples, "You are those who have stood by me in my trials" (Luke 22:28). When no one else under stands your pain, Jesus does.

How did Jesus treat those who mistreated Him? How did He treat Judas Iscariot, one of the Twelve, who betrayed Him? The Bible reveals that although He warned Judas, He also protected him from the anger of the disciples. He appealed to

WHEN ONLY ONE SPOUSE WILL TRY, GOD'S WISDOM IS NEEDED. PRAY FOR WISDOM, SEEK WISDOM, LIVE IN WISDOM.

Judas to change, but also treated him as a friend until the moment of betrayal. He was neither deceived nor fooled by Judas's hypocrisy. But neither did Jesus use His knowledge against Judas to do him in.

Jesus suffered for the sins of the whole world, but His crucifixion came directly from Judas' treachery. Instead of attacking Judas, exposing him or even protecting Himself, Jesus considered Judas' evil acts as part of the Father's perfect plan for His life. Yet Jesus did not allow Judas to sway him from God's best, nor did He pay attention to his criticism (see John 12:4-8). What a model for us on how to treat the one who betrays us, even if it's a spouse!

WISDOM

When only one spouse will try, God's wisdom is needed. Pray for wisdom, seek wisdom, live in wisdom. One of the great Bible promises for wisdom links it with trouble and trials (see Jas. 1:2-7). Sometimes we develop the most character and gain the wisest insights in the worst of relationships. Read Eugene H. Peterson's paraphrase in *The Message* with your marriage in mind:

Consider it a sheer gift, friends, when tests and

> challenges come at you from all sides. You know that under pressure, your faith-life is forced into the open and shows its true colors. So don't try to get out of anything prematurely. Let it do its work so you become mature and well-developed, not deficient in any way.
>
> If you don't know what you're doing, pray to the Father. He loves to help. You'll get his help, and won't be condescended to when you ask for it. Ask boldly, believingly, without a second thought. People who "worry their prayers" are like wind-whipped waves. Don't think you're going to get anything from the Master that way, adrift at sea, keeping all your options open (Jas. 1:2-8).

Wisdom is the bridge between being and doing. Wisdom takes who we are and who God is, and applies that knowledge to a real-life situation. Wisdom takes God's truth and puts it to work in our marriages.

Our focus in this chapter has been on being, on becoming the kind of person who can save or improve a marriage. From this point on our focus in this chapter will be on doing. Recall the analogy of a hub and spokes at the beginning of this book. We spend time making sure we are connected to Christ, our hub. Then the spokes connect us from Christ to our marriage partner and the specific trials we encounter.

HIDDEN CREATIVITY

What if you could become more creative in your marriage? What if the Holy Spirit would lead you to the very thoughts, words and acts that would put your marriage back together, healthy and whole? Would you adjust your life to His leading? Would you really work at your marriage? Would you determine to become, by God's grace, the best possible marriage partner within His will? If your answers are yes, we have good news for you.

All who have received Christ and live in Him are united

with His creativity. That's a fact! We share in the "fullness" of God that is our inheritance in Christ. (Stick with us now. This is a little deep, but it unlocks great potential within you when you really grab hold of its truth). Notice what Colossians says about God's fullness—in Christ and in you. "For in Christ all the *fullness* of the Deity lives in bodily form, and you have been given *fullness* in Christ" (Col. 2:9,10, italics added).

The first half of the verse makes sense to those who understand that Christ is God the Son, the second Person of the Trinity. All the fullness of God lives in the resurrected, risen and reigning Lord Jesus. So far, so good. But next comes the surprise. Because Christ lives in us, and He has all the fullness of God, it follows that the fullness of God lives in us, too. Think this through biblically. We are crucified, buried, made alive, raised up and seated with Christ at the right hand of God (see Rom. 6:3-5; Gal. 2:20; Eph. 2:4-6; Col. 3:1-3). The spiritual results of these truths are staggering. Because we are united with Christ (see Phil. 2:1), His fullness lives in us. That does not make us God, but it does mean that God Himself *and His character qualities* live within us.

We don't pretend to exhaust all the meaning of the fullness of Christ within us, but one thing is obvious from the context: it includes His authority and His creativity (see Col. 1:16; 2:8,9). Let this sink in. As *The Message* puts it in Colossians 2:8,9: "You don't need a telescope, a microscope, or a horoscope to realize the fullness of Christ." We are united with Christ, so in Him we have spiritual authority and creativity.

Some people object to that concept. "Not me. I'm just not creative at all." Wait a minute, maybe you are misunderstanding creativity. Some people think creativity is only for artsy-craftsy types, or only for geniuses in their chosen fields or only for those who make totally new breakthroughs in music, art, science, literature or architecture. Frankly, there's more to it than that. Your hidden creativity shows up when:

- Christ gives you an idea that works in your marriage.
- Christ inspires a thought that is helpful to your spouse.
- Christ puts the right words in your mouth (maybe

with your children or grandchildren), just when you need them.
- Christ leads you to an appreciated way to show you care.
- Christ does anything fresh and new through you that you had not done or thought of before.

With this more accurate description of creativity, every Christian qualifies. Thank Him and praise Him that it includes you! We never know when Christ's creativity will show up in us. But because we share in His fullness, *it will happen.* It may even be in unexpected moments in your troubled marriage, so look for it, pray for it, expect it. And when it comes, use it for His glory. Acknowledge Christ as the source, and love Him for it.

Hidden creativity is our present possession, a cherished part of being united with Christ. Not only does He make us creative—Christ Himself is creative in re-creating us (see Phil. 1:6; 2:12,13). Enjoy Him! No matter how bad a marriage may be, Christ can fulfill the deepest longings of both spouses. His creativity is at work within us to fulfill all of His promises. He never promises us a great marriage, but He does promise His fullness, including His authority in prayer and His creativity in our actions.

JANICE AND TED

Janice was 26, with two children and a husband, Ted, who was committing adultery. Each night Ted came home for dinner, then went to his girlfriend's house where he slept until morning. Janice was desperate, and turned to a biblical counselor for help.

The counselor asked Janice if she was willing to fight for her marriage. She assured him that she was willing to do anything. Sensing her eagerness and Christian attitude, he gave her a tough assignment. He recommended that she treat her husband just like she would treat Jesus. He challenged her to love and serve him, even for the short time he was home, just the way she would care for Jesus if He were visiting her home.

Janice reminded the counselor that Ted was nothing like Jesus. He was sleeping with another woman, and doing nothing to build their marriage. The counselor outlined her options: continue what she's now doing (which was making her miserable); yell and scream and threaten; divorce him; or take the biblical approach and let her actions match her prayers. Assured that Janice was praying for Ted, the counselor again asked her to love and serve Ted for one week just as if he were Jesus. She agreed to try.

Janice dressed her best each night, fixed Ted's favorite meal, put the paper beside his favorite chair and did everything she could think of to treat him like Jesus Himself. The first night Ted muttered under his breath and left as usual. The second night he said a few civil words to Janice, then left for his girlfriend's house. The third night he asked Janice what was going on. She explained she was treating him the way she always should have. That night he did not go to his girlfriend's but slept in a separate bedroom at home. By the end of the week, he was seeing his girlfriend less often and staying in the house more often.

When Janice returned to talk with the counselor, she knew, for the first time in many months, she had Ted's attention. The counselor suggested, when the timing was right, Janice share with Ted that a man at church was teaching her to how to treat her husband, and that this man wanted to meet Ted, too. The moment came, and Ted agreed to talk with the man whose input had so dramatically altered his wife's attitudes and actions.

In talking with the counselor, Ted openly admitted he was "messing around" with another woman. The counselor asked how the relationship was going. Ted indicated that although they had a sexual relationship, he really didn't love her. She was putting a lot of pressure on him to leave Janice and marry her. However, he was thinking about breaking off the affair and trying to work things out with Janice.

By the time the session was over, Ted had not only committed to coming home, but had received Christ as his Lord and Savior. The counselor led both of them in repenting before God and forgiving each other. (This is one of the purposes of the "Marriage Steps" in appendix A.)

Janice and Ted met with the counselor for many months on a weekly basis. Some times were helpful, others painful. But they kept growing in Christ and remained faithful in their new attitudes toward one another. They both became active in the church, growing in Christ and maturing in their marriage. Not all stories turn out as well as this one, but many do.[8]

REMOVE EXCUSES

When only one spouse will try, a good strategy is to remove the other spouse's excuses. Wayward husbands and wives most often feel the need to justify their actions. Often they will engage in blame-shifting. They say, "Well, you always..." or "You never..." or "What about the time that you..." or "You're not so perfect either, because you do..." or "It's hopeless because you...." An alert spouse can compile a list of excuses and begin to remove them. The process of removing the excuses builds the character of the one who tries, and improves conditions in the marriage.

Surprisingly, the marriage partner who is not trying usually is neither pleased nor impressed with this change. A second list of new excuses most often emerges. It's good to know this ahead of time so no one will be surprised and give up hope. A new set of excuses is normal, not abnormal—par for the course. Simply begin removing the second list—and expect a third. By the time the third set of excuses is removed, there will almost always be a visible change in the indifferent partner's behavior. Once in awhile it's for the worse, but most often it's for the better. Meanwhile, concentrate on meeting the other's needs (and keep meeting them). Specialize in your spouse's love language. (Get really good at it!)

WINNING THROUGH LOSING

Jesus taught an interesting principle about losing to win. "For whoever wants to save his life will lose it, but whoever loses his life for me will save it" (Luke 9:24). This principle applies in a hurting marriage. The person who loses life by following

Jesus' teaching and example in a troubled marriage wins real life in Christ. The world system says, "Don't put up with that garbage. You have rights, too. I know this single person who is really lonely. Let me introduce you." Your friends will say, "Get out. Haven't you had enough? Here's the name of a good divorce attorney."

Jesus teaches us to love our enemies, stand by our marriages and sacrifice ourselves in love. It's not easy, but often it's effective. If you are free in Christ, living in the Spirit *and supported by a group of caring Christian people,* you will become a better person—and you might save your marriage. Don't miss the support of other Christians committed to saving marriages; their encouragement and prayers are essential to your success.

Never confuse winning through losing—what the Bible calls humility—with becoming a doormat or a pushover. The one who finds freedom in Christ becomes stronger in the Lord, not weaker. The humble spouse, the one who is committed to winning by losing, also learns to communicate feelings, desires and requests in a compelling way. When Christ is energizing us and His creativity is at work within us, we count on His help. He will help us *win* through losing, not lose through winning. He will help us attain our true goal of becoming a man or woman of God. He may rescue the marriage as well.

MAKING AN APPEAL

A painful marriage always sends the faithful spouse to prayer. And prayer, sometimes coupled with fasting, leads to fresh power. Prayer leads to God's plan of action. If the plan is big enough to call for a change in your role or your marriage relationship, it will require an appeal to your spouse. The spouse who is trying, who is praying and working on the marriage, can make an appeal to the one who is not. An appeal is a call for a change, or for help or for a specific request. A good appeal communicates something intensely desired in a way most likely to be heard.

Watch for just the right moment to speak up. If possible, try to catch a time when everyone's mood seems right. Appeals made in the heat of anger or with the cutting sarcasm of a critical spirit seldom carry much weight. If necessary, make an appointment or create a "right" time to share the burden of your heart. When the right moment comes, breathe a quick prayer and seize the opportunity. The grave danger is backing off when you should move ahead. Tact and sensitivity will help. So will healthy eye contact, warm non-verbal signals, kind words, carefully worded phrases and good questions.

When you make the appeal, let your loyalty show. Express appreciation for anything positive the uncaring spouse may have done. Clearly show your respect for your spouse's position, as well as any sensitivity or support ever shown in any way. A rebellious spirit always wounds and never heals. With tact and sensitivity, tell your story and share your feelings, including the desired change God has laid on your heart. If possible, tie your appeal to your spouse's interests and desires. Ask yourself, "How does this plan, idea or feeling tie in with my spouse's best intentions?"

Make a clear, polite request for what you would like. If your spouse agrees to your request, take action at the proper time. If it is denied, don't argue. In a cheery voice, respond with, "That's okay," or "No problem." If it's something really serious and the denial is a major blow, respond calmly: "I'm sorry you feel that way, but you have a right to your own opinion."

When you are alone, pray and ask some penetrating questions. Why was my appeal denied? Was it loyal, tactful, clear? Had I earned the right to be heard? Did I speak in a good spirit and with God's timing? Is this answer God's message to me? Should I accept it or regroup and look for the right chance to make a new appeal? What does God want me to do next? Let's sum up a good appeal.

1. Know your limits. Only God can budge your spouse.
2. Prepare your plan. Think it through in prayer.
3. Appeal with feeling. Keep courtesy and respect in the forefront.
4. Move ahead. Obeying God is more important than pleasing people.

A good appeal can touch a human spirit, change a convinced mind and reach for a great goal. Persist in making heartfelt appeals for specific changes. Space these appeals at least four months apart. Each time pray hard, look for the right moment, and follow the Holy Spirit's guidance. Remember, it took a long time to develop the problems you face, and it will take what seems like forever to resolve them. Never give up—never! God delights in the impossible. In the meantime, wear the full armor of God, submit to Him daily and resist the devil (see Jas. 4:6-10; 1 Pet. 5:8,9).

PROTECTED

When your marriage is in trouble, when you are the only one who will try, wear the full armor of God (see Eph. 6:10-20). Take your stand against the devil's schemes to destroy your marriage. Put on the belt of truth and make honesty and integrity your way of life. Never tell lies. Wear the breastplate of righteousness, the bulletproof vest around your chest, receiving Christ's righteousness and living in right relationship with God and, as much as possible, with your spouse.

Lift the shield of faith, which stops the enemy's surprise bullets. Put on the helmet of salvation, the full deliverance from sin and from lasting damage to your mind. Grasp the sword of the Spirit, the spoken Word of God that gives you just the right words at the time you most need them. Buckle on the boots of readiness, always ready to move into spiritual battle with the gospel of peace. Let peace in your marriage be the good news of Christ you bring. Let the peace flow from your forgiveness, your repentance, your identity in Christ and your freedom. Then pray always, in every way the Holy Spirit leads.

You can achieve your goal to become a godly man or a godly woman. You may become God's instrument to restore and rebuild your marriage. If you do, three or four generations to come will thank you. And when you stand before the judgment seat of Christ, Jesus will praise you (see 2 Cor. 5:10).

Notes

1. Letter mailed to Neil Anderson.
2. Dr. Neil T. Anderson, "Resolving Personal Conflicts" and "Resolving Spiritual Conflicts," 1992, available from Freedom in Christ, 491 E. Lambert Road, La Habra, CA 90631. Phone (310) 691-9128 or FAX (310) 691-4035.
3. Dan Davidson, ed., *The Pastor's Weekly Briefing* 3, no. 36 (September 8, 1995): 2. Pastoral Ministries, Focus on the Family, Colorado Springs, CO 80995.
4. Mona Charen, syndicated columnist, "We can't separate divorce and social chaos," *The Orange County Register*, Monday, 19 June 1995, Metro 7.
5. Barbara Dafoe Whitehead, "Dan Quayle Was Right," *The Atlantic Monthly* 271, no. 4 (April, 1993): 47.
6. Anastasia Toufexis, Reported by Georgia Harbison/New York, "The Lasting Wounds of Divorce," *Time* 133, no. 6 (February 6, 1989): 61.
7. Charles Mylander, *Running the Red Lights, Putting the Brakes on Sexual Temptation* (Ventura, Calif.: Regal Books, 1986), pp. 215-216.
8. Jimmy Evans, *Marriage on the Rock, Creating Your Dream Marriage Through God's Principles* (New York: McCracken Press, an imprint of Multi Media Communicators, Inc., 1994), pp. 203-212.

CHAPTER FOURTEEN

Steps to Setting Your Marriage Free

This final chapter presents the actual process for setting your marriage free. Our intention is not to help you manage your conflicts, rather we believe your conflicts can be resolved in Christ. The Lord will be your wonderful counselor, and the Holy Spirit will guide you into all truth. That truth and the truth of God's Word will set you free. If you have a relatively mature relationship with mutual trust and respect, you can work through this process without outside assistance. We (Chuck and Neil) have taken the time to do so with our wives.

The personal "Steps to Freedom" in appendix A must be processed first. We estimate about 85 percent of the Christian community can process them on their own. Set aside an evening when you can be alone, in a location where you wouldn't be embarrassed to read and process the Steps out loud. If you cannot get through them on your own, call someone who has been trained to help others. Both the personal Steps and the Steps to Setting Your Marriage Free are available from the Freedom in Christ Ministries office. If your spouse is unwilling to participate, you can obtain a modification of these marriage Steps through our office. They have been developed for those who desire to be totally honest and responsible before God, even though their spouses are not willing to process the Steps. Assuming personal responsibility is the best way to save the marriage and will eventually win the trust of a rebellious spouse. These individual Steps can also be used in conjunction with the inductive study for premarital counseling.

Is your desire to walk in the light, and speak the truth in love? Are you willing to allow God to show you anything He desires? If so, share your intentions with each other before you begin. God's will is to reveal blockages in intimacy within your marriage and to make it even better. Certainly He wants the life of Christ to display His glory in you and your marriage.

You must both agree to assume personal responsibility and not attack the other person's character or family. Allow the Holy Spirit to bring understanding and conviction. This process will not work unless you speak the truth in love and walk in the light. The Lord loves you and wants to see you free from your past, alive in Him and committed to one another. If your relationship is experiencing difficulty, then we suggest you have a responsible person assist you. It would have to be a person whom you both can trust.

TIPS FOR GROUPS

If you have completed the first 13 chapters in your small group and desire to complete the Steps at a weekend retreat, we suggest Friday evening be spent in corporate prayer and fellowship. If you have not worked through the individual Steps to Freedom in Christ, then Friday night would be the time to do so. The accommodations must allow privacy for each couple. In a group setting, each Step should begin with instruction by the facilitator, followed by the prayer that begins each section. Each couple should then finish the Step together in a private location. We have (Neil and Chuck) conducted a Setting Your Marriage Free Conference with the above schedule using hotels and churches. The process was incredibly resolving for those who successfully worked through the individual Steps first.

If you intend to use these Steps in your church, we strongly suggest you use this book and Study Guide or cover the same material in your preaching and teaching before you attempt to go through the process. Sunday School classes, discipleship groups and small group ministries that are reading this book and using the Study Guide can process these Steps in their weekly scheduled meetings. We suggest you take one Step per week. Each Step would be completed by every couple in their own home on their own.

We would prefer you first work through the material taught in *Victory Over the Darkness* (Regal Books), and *The Bondage Breaker* (Harvest House Publishers). If you wish to start a Christ-centered discipleship/counseling ministry in your church to set people free, see appendix B.

Are you ready to begin? If so, start the process by praying the following prayer together:

PRAYER OF COMMITMENT BY HUSBAND AND WIFE:

Dear heavenly Father,

We love You and we thank You for Your grace, truth, love, power, forgiveness and blessings in Christ. We can love each other because You first loved us. We can forgive because we have been forgiven, and we can accept one another just as You have accepted us. We desire nothing more than to know and do Your will. We ask for Your divine guidance and protection during this time of seeking freedom in our marriage. We give ourselves emotionally to You and each other, and ask You to free us so we can share from our hearts.

We buckle on the belt of Your truth, put on the breastplate of Your righteousness and commit ourselves to the gospel of peace. We hold up the shield of faith, and stand against the flaming arrows of the enemy. We commit ourselves to take every thought captive in obedience to You. We put on the helmet of salvation which assures us of Your forgiveness, Your life and our freedom in You. We put off the old self, and put on the new self which is being renewed in Your image. We take the sword of the Spirit, the spoken Word of God, to defend ourselves against the father of lies. We acknowledge our dependence upon You, and understand that apart from Christ we can do nothing.

We pray You will grant us genuine repentance and living faith. We desire our marriage to become a beautiful picture of Your relationship with us. We ask You to fill us with Your Holy Spirit, lead us into all truth and set us free in Christ.

In Jesus' precious name, we pray. Amen.

Have a Bible present and a pad of paper to record issues you are seeking to resolve. Before you proceed through the Steps to Setting Your Marriage Free, one small but important exercise will help you to get started. To resolve conflicts, you must look at all the problems, and that can be quite negative. So take the time to answer the following two questions; then share your answers with your spouse:

What five character qualities do you most appreciate about your spouse?

1.
2.
3.
4.
5.

What five things does your spouse do that you really appreciate?

1.
2.
3.
4.
5.

ESTABLISH GOD'S PRIORITY FOR MARRIAGE

Step One

The first Step is to seek the Lord's wisdom concerning how completely we have left father and mother and have bonded to one another. Remember the words of Jesus, "He who loves father or mother more than Me is not worthy of Me. And he who loves son or daughter more than Me is not worthy of Me" (Matt. 10:37, *NASB*). This does not mean we don't honor father and mother, but it does mean we can have only one Lord in our lives. It means our spiritual heritage must take precedence over our natural heritage.

In what ways could we be holding on to some unhealthy ties that are keeping us from committing ourselves fully to the Lord and then to each other? Those ties might be physical, emotional, spiritual, or financial. Ask the Lord to reveal to your mind the ways you have not yet left father and mother and have not cleaved only to one another.

> Dear heavenly Father,
>
> We humbly submit ourselves to You and ask for Your divine guidance. We ask that You reveal to our minds any way that we have allowed our physical heritage to be more important than our spiritual heritage. Show us anything in our lives that has taken on a greater sense of importance to us than our relationship to You. We also ask You to show us in what ways we have not honorably left our mothers and our fathers physically, spiritually, mentally, emotionally, or financially. We desire to be spiritually bonded to You in order that we can be fully bonded to each other.
>
> In Jesus' name, we pray. Amen.

Both spouses should sit silently before the Lord to individually and honestly consider their relationship with God and with their own parents. Do not consider your spouse's relationship with your mother-in-law and father-in-law. Let the Lord be the judge and allow your spouse to assume responsibility for his/her parents. Each one can consider these questions:

1. Does the approval of relatives mean more to me than the approval of God?
2. Am I still trying to live up to the expectations of my relatives?

3. Is my relationship with God the most important relationship in my life?
4. Is my relationship with my spouse the second most important relationship in my life?
5. Would I be willing to sever any other relationship that would threaten my relationship with God and my spouse even if it included my physical family?

Leaving father and mother cannot mean dishonoring them. Being disrespectful to your parents cannot lead to freedom. Consider these questions:

1. Have you gone against your parents' counsel in getting married?
2. If so, have you prayerfully tried to reconcile your differences and receive their blessing?
3. In what ways have you been disrespectful of your parents or not shown appreciation for what they have done?

Note: If you feel your parents have wronged you, you will be given an opportunity to forgive them later in the Steps.

Write down any ungodly way you are still bonded to your own parents or stepparents:

Physically:

Spiritually:

Mentally:

Emotionally:

Financially:

When you have both finished your lists, privately confess it to God. Then share with each other what you have learned. If it has affected your relationship with each other in a negative way, then ask each other for forgiveness. If you have been unduly critical of your in-laws, you should ask your spouse to forgive you.

Conclude this Step with the following prayer together:

> Dear heavenly Father,
>
> We thank You for revealing these important issues to us. We rededicate our lives to You and to each other. Our desire is to become one flesh and one spirit in Christ. May Your Holy Spirit bond us together in love for You and for each other. Show us how we can rightly relate to our earthly parents and other relatives. Forgive us for any way that we have dishonored our parents, and show us how we can honor them according to Your will.
>
> In Jesus' precious name, we pray. Amen.

Note for those who previously have been married:
You may want to ask the Lord if any unhealthy bonding remains between ex-spouses and their families. The process would be the same as above.

Break Cycles of Abuse

Step Two
In this Step you will be asking the Lord to reveal the family sins and iniquities that have been passed on to you from previous generations. First, however, realize that most Christian families are just doing the very best they can, and it would be wrong to see only their sins and iniquities. Take the time to share with your spouse the answer to the following:

> What habits, customs, traditions and values have you observed in your spouse's family that you really appreciate?

Because of one man (Adam), sin entered into the world and consequently all have sinned. This transmission of sin has affected every generation and every people group of the world. The fact that generational cycles of abuse exist is a well-attested social phenomena. This is an opportunity to find freedom in Christ by breaking the curse of ancestral sins and by making a concerted effort to stop the cycles of abuse. If we do not face these issues, we will teach what we have been taught, discipline our children the way we have been disciplined and relate to our spouses the way our parents did. Scripture teaches that those who are fully trained will be like their teachers. Childhood training isn't just based on what was said; it is also based on what was modeled. Family values are more caught than taught.

When we were born physically alive but spiritually dead, we had neither the presence of God in our lives nor the knowledge of His ways. We were pre-programmed by sin to live our lives independently from God. During those formative years of our lives, we learned how to cope, survive and succeed without God. When we came to Christ, nobody pushed the clear buttons in the marvelous computers we call our minds. That is why Paul said we must no longer be conformed to this world, but be transformed by the renewing of our minds (see Rom. 12:2).

We have all developed many defense mechanisms to protect ourselves. Denial, projection, blaming and many other self-protective behaviors are no longer necessary now that we are in Christ. We are accepted for who we are and that gives us the freedom to be real and honest. Jesus is our defense. We can walk in the light and speak the truth in love.

We can't fix our pasts, but we can be free from them by the grace of God. Trying not to be like our parents or other role models in our lives is still letting those people determine who we are and what we are doing. Thank God for the good lessons learned, but let the Lord renew your mind and free you from your past.

Strongholds have primarily been erected in our minds from the environments in which we were raised and the traumatic experiences in our pasts. Those strongholds affect our temperaments and the way we relate to our spouses and children. They will remain unless we renew our minds according to the Word of God. They result in behavior patterns we have learned over time.

Start this Step by asking the Lord to mentally reveal the iniquities and family sins of your ancestors passed on spiritually and environmentally.

Pray together the following prayer:

> Dear heavenly Father,
>
> You are the only perfect parent that we have. We thank You for our natural parents who brought us into this world. We acknowledge they were not perfect, nor were our families and communities where we grew up. We ask that You reveal to our minds the dysfunctional patterns and family sins of our ancestors that have been going on for generations. Reveal to us the strongholds in our minds that have kept us from fully honoring You and embracing the truth. Give us the grace to face the truth and not to be defensive. Only You can meet our deepest needs of acceptance, security, significance and sense of belonging. We thank You that You have made us new creations in Christ. We desire to be free from our pasts, so we can be all You want us to be.
>
> In Jesus' name, we pray. Amen.

Allow the Lord to reveal any and all family sins of your ancestors. Each spouse should consider first his or her own upbringing and family heritage. Individually and honestly address the following issues and write your answers down on paper:

1. What sins seemed to be repeated again and again in your family, such as lying, criticizing, drinking, compulsive gambling, cheating, pride, bitterness, adultery, divorce, etc.?
2. How did the family deal with conflict? How do you now deal with it?
3. How did each member of your family communicate? Can you speak the truth in love?
4. How did your parents discipline their children? How do you?

5. Where did your parents get their significance? Security? Acceptance? Where do you?
6. Did your parents exhibit the spiritual fruit of self-control or were they controllers or enablers? Which are you?
7. What was their religious preference? What non-Christian beliefs (cultic or occultic) or idols did they embrace? (An "idol" can be anything that has greater prominence in their lives than Christ.)
8. What lies did they believe? How has this affected you?
9. What other ancestral sins has God revealed to your mind?

After making your individual lists, share what you have learned with each other. Remember, "there is now no condemnation for those who are in Christ Jesus" (8:1), and we are to accept one another as Christ has accepted us (see 15:7). Mutual sharing allows both to understand and accept each other.

We are not responsible for our parents' sins, but because our parents sinned we have been taught, trained and disciplined in ways that may not be healthy. Denial and cover-up will only perpetuate the sins of our ancestors and the curse upon us and upon our children. It is our responsibility to face these issues and stop the cycle of abuse so it is not passed on to the next generation. The Lord instructs us to confess our iniquity and the iniquity of our forefathers (see Lev. 26:40).

Both spouses should now pray individually and out loud in each other's presence, the following prayer for every family sin of their ancestors.

> Dear heavenly Father,
>
> I confess (name every sin) as sinful and displeasing to You. I turn from it, reject it, and ask You to break its hold on our marriage.
>
> In Jesus' name. Amen.

We are to confess not only the family sins of our ancestors, but also our own sins. Individual and personal sins are dealt with in the personal Steps to Freedom in Christ. However, marriages also have corporate sins that must be confessed and forsaken. Corporate sins are patterns of behavior in marriage that are displeasing to God and contrary to His revealed will.

A PATTERN OF SINFULNESS WITHIN A MARRIAGE CALLS FOR HUSBAND AND WIFE TO DEAL WITH IT TOGETHER.

They do not differ from individual sins in nature. Sin is still sin whether practiced by an individual or a married couple. A pattern of sinfulness within a marriage, however, calls for husband and wife to deal with it together.

Examples of corporate sins within marriage might be:

1. Engaging in sinful activities together that displease God or damage others.
2. Taking part together in non-Christian religious rituals or any cult or occult ceremonies or practices.
3. Agreeing together on any sin: covering up for each other, lying, theft, adultery, divorce, cheating on taxes, drunkenness, child abuse, etc.
4. Withholding tithes and offerings from God.
5. Falling into patterns of gossip, slander, filthy language or other sins of the tongue in *conversations with each other.*
6. Tolerating sinful behavior on the part of our children, especially while they live under our roof, such as swearing, foul language, sex outside of marriage, gambling, alcohol, drugs or anything that contradicts God's written Word.
7. Reading or viewing pornographic material or anything produced by psychics, mediums, occult practitioners, cults or false religions.

Pray the following prayer together:

> Dear heavenly Father,
>
> As we seek You, bring to our minds all the corporate sins that we have committed in our marriage and family. Remind us of the sins of our ancestors and their families. Open our eyes to any tendency to repeat the same dysfunctional patterns. Give us discernment to identify and renounce the corporate sins in our marriage we have tolerated or have not dealt with adequately. Then grant us grace that we may confess them, renounce them, turn away from them and commit ourselves never to return to them.
>
> In Jesus' cleansing name, we pray. Amen.

Begin to identify your marriage's corporate sins. Usually this Step starts slowly but gradually gains momentum. Be patient and work for general agreement. Write down on paper only those items which have consensus between husband and wife that they are corporate marriage sins.

In each other's presence confess all the Lord has revealed to you. Then each of you should ask your spouse's forgiveness for the ways your involvement in these sins has hurt the other and damaged your marriage.

When you both are finished, make the following declaration:

> We confess and renounce our own corporate sins and all those sins of our ancestors. We declare by the grace of God that we are new creations in Christ. We commit ourselves and our marriage to the Lord Jesus Christ. We take our place in Christ, and by His authority, we command Satan to flee from us, our marriage and our family. We belong to God, and we are a part of His family and under His protection. We put on the armor of God and commit ourselves to stand firm in our relationship to our heavenly Father.

Satan's grip from generational sins and cycles of abuse can be broken instantly. However, it will take time to renew our minds and overcome patterns of the flesh. An experienced pastor or committed Christian counselor can often help in this process.

We must accept one another and build up one another. Growth in character will also take time, and we must be patient with each other. Unconditional love and acceptance frees individuals so they can accept themselves and grow in the grace of the Lord.

Conclude this Step with the following prayer:

> Dear heavenly Father,
>
> Thank You for Your unconditional love and acceptance. We give ourselves and each other to You. Enable us by Your grace to accept each other as You have accepted us, and to be merciful as You have been merciful. Show us how we can build up one another, encourage one another and forgive one another. We acknowledge we have not attained the full stature of Christ, but we desire to be like You in our marriage and in all we do.
>
> We face up to our own corporate sins, as well as the family sins of our ancestors. We honestly confess our participation in them and agree this behavior is unacceptable to You. We disown them and repudiate them. In Jesus' name we break all the influence of their dysfunctional patterns upon us and our marriage. We cancel out all advantages, schemes and other works of the devil that have been passed from our ancestors to us and to our marriage. We break any foothold or stronghold built from the enemy's influence, and we give our hearts to You for the renewing of our minds.
>
> We invite the Holy Spirit to apply the shed blood of the Lord Jesus on calvary's cross to our corporate sins and to our ancestral sins. Through God's grace, by faith, we claim the work of Christ in His death and resurrection as our ransom from sin, release from guilt and removal of shame.
>
> In Jesus' precious name, we pray. Amen.

BALANCE RIGHTS AND RESPONSIBILITIES

Step Three

In this Step you will be asking the Lord to reveal to your minds any ungodly ways you have related to each other. We are responsible for our own character and the needs of each other. Scripture teaches us to be submissive to one another, love one another, accept one another and respect one another. Pray together the following prayer, asking the Lord to reveal any ways self-centered living and demanding your own rights have kept you from assuming your responsibilities to love and accept one another.

Pray together out loud:

> Dear heavenly Father,
>
> We thank You for Your full and complete love and acceptance. Thank you that the unselfish sacrifice of Christ's death on the Cross and His resurrection met our greatest need for forgiveness and life. We ask You to reveal to our minds any ways we have been selfish in our relationship with each other. Show us how we have not loved each other, not accepted each other, not respected each other and have not been submissive to the needs of each other in the fear of Christ. Show us how we have been angry, jealous, insecure, manipulative or controlling.
>
> In Jesus' name, we pray. Amen.

Sit silently before the Lord and allow Him to reveal every way you have not:

1. Loved your spouse as you should have:

2. Accepted your spouse as you should have:

3. Respected your spouse as you should have:

4. Submitted to your spouse as you should have:

5. Appreciated your spouse as you should have:

6. Trusted God to bring conviction and self-control in your spouse:

When you have finished completing the above, verbally confess what the Lord has shown you, and ask your spouse's forgiveness for not being what God called you to be. Do not overlook the times and ways that you have communicated rejection, disrespect and lack of appreciation.

Now share with each other your personal needs that you feel are not being met without attacking the other person's character. It is legitimate to share a need; it is not legitimate to attack another's character. Then share the times and ways your spouse has shown love, respect and acceptance to you.

Conclude this Step with the following prayer of commitment.

Dear heavenly Father,

We have fallen short of Your glory and have not lived up to our responsibilities. We have been selfish and self-centered. Thank You for Your forgiveness. We commit ourselves to an increasing pattern of love, acceptance and respect for each other. We will submit to each other's needs in reverence to Christ. Restore to us our first love.

In Jesus' name, we pray. Amen.

Break Sexual Bondage

Step Four

Note: Individual freedom from sexual bondage coming from your own past must be achieved before continuing with this step. You should have already dealt with this in the individual Steps to Freedom in Christ. If not, you will need to pray individually first, asking the Lord to reveal to your mind every sexual use of your body as an instrument of unrighteousness. As God reveals, renounce each use by saying, "Lord, I renounce (name the specific use of your body) with (name the person), and I ask You to break that bond." Don't bypass anything God brings to your mind, including sensual touching of another or sexual fantasies of another person. (Please refer to the individual Steps for the complete process.)

Scripture teaches we do not have authority over our own bodies, but our spouses do (see 1 Cor. 7:1-5). However, our spouses cannot resolve our problems of lust; only Christ can break those bondages. It may be necessary to read *A Way Of Escape* if either or both have been struggling with sexual bondage. However, we can and should meet one another's sexual needs.

Pray the following out loud together:

> Dear heavenly Father,
>
> We know You desire for us to be free from sexual bondage, and to be responsive and respectful of each other's needs. Free us from our lust, and may our sexual union be one of honest love and respect for each other. We now ask You to reveal to our minds any way we have sexually violated our marital commitment to each other. Give us the grace to speak the truth in love and the desire to be intimately bonded together sexually. If we have not been honest about our sexual needs and desires, show us how. Give us the freedom to communicate in such a way that our love for each other can be fully expressed.
>
> In Jesus' precious name, we pray. Amen.

Sit silently before the Lord and allow Him to guide you. Ask Him to cover the next few minutes with grace. Sex is a very intimate expression of love and can be a tremendous cause for guilt and insecurity when experienced outside the will of God.

1. In what way have you been dishonest about your sexual relationship together?
2. What have you been doing together that you now believe to be wrong?
3. How have your consciences been violated or have either of you violated the conscience of the other?

These questions need to be honestly answered and forgiveness sought of each other. The best way to find out if we have violated the other person's conscience is to ask!

After you have done this, then complete this Step with the following prayer:

> Dear heavenly Father,
>
> We stand naked before You. You know the thoughts and intentions of our hearts. We desire to be sexually free before You and with each other. We acknowledge that we have sinned. Thank You for Your forgiveness and cleansing. We now give our bodies to You and to each other. Fill us with Your Holy Spirit and bond us together in love. May our sexual relationship be holy in Your sight, and may it be an expression of our love for each other.
>
> In Jesus' name, we pray. Amen.

Then declare:

> In the name and authority of the Lord Jesus Christ, we command Satan to leave our presence. We present our bodies to the Lord Jesus Christ and reserve the sexual use of our bodies for each other only. We renounce the lie of Satan that sex is dirty or that our bodies are dirty. We stand naked and unashamed before God and each other.

RELEASE OLD HURTS

Step Five

Forgiveness sets us free from our past. It is routinely necessary in any marriage because we don't live with perfect people. Resentment and bitterness will tear us apart. Forgiveness is the first step in reconciliation, which is essential for bonding together. We also need to forgive others so Satan cannot take advantage of us (see 2 Cor. 2:10,11). We are to be merciful just as our heavenly Father is merciful (see Luke 6:36). We are to forgive as we have been forgiven (see Eph. 4:31,32).

Start this Step by making a time line, beginning with the day you first met and ending with today as shown below. Above the line list all the good memories that you have had together in your marriage. Below the line, list all the painful memories.

GOOD MEMORIES

First Met ________________________________Today

Thank the Lord, out loud in the presence of each other, for the good memories that have been especially meaningful in your relationship.

> "Lord, I thank you for (name the good memory)...."

PAINFUL MEMORIES

After thanking the Lord aloud for the good memories of your marriage, pray together the following prayer. Then follow with a few moments of silent prayer, allowing the Lord to help you recall the painful experiences and traumatic events of your marriage.

> Dear heavenly Father,
>
> Sometimes pain has come to us through circumstances, sometimes from other people, sometimes from each other. Whatever the cause, surface in our minds all the pain that You want us to deal with at this time. Let us get in touch with the emotional core of hurt and heartache, trauma and threat, that have damaged our marriage. Show us where we have allowed a root of bitterness to spring up, causing trouble and defiling many (see Heb. 12:15).

In Jesus' precious name, we pray. Amen.

Caution! This step is not a time for blame-casting but for pain-sharing.

Individually make lists of painful memories the Lord brings to your minds. Use real names, places and dates as much as possible. It is nearly impossible to get in touch with the emotional core of pain without using people's names and

FORGIVENESS MAY LEAD TO FORGETTING, BUT TRYING TO FORGET WILL ONLY COMPLICATE FORGIVENESS.

recalling specific events. We easily pick up each other's offenses. We also easily turn bitter toward those we perceive have wrongly influenced our spouses (even when our spouses don't see it). Jealousy can also create bitterness. One word of caution: Everything is to be spoken in love and respect. This is not a time for malicious talk. It is a time to bring healing to damaged emotions and to free yourself from your past. Simply record what happened and how you felt about it. Each spouse can say amen when finished. Understand that forgiveness is not forgetting. Forgiveness may lead to forgetting, but trying to forget only complicates forgiveness. Before you start the forgiveness process, please recall these 10 steps to forgiveness:

1. Allow yourself and your spouse to feel the pain, hurt, resentment, bitterness and hate (see Matt. 5:4).
2. Submit to God, recalling how Christ forgave you (see Matt. 18:21-35; Eph. 4:32; Col. 3:13; Jas. 4:7,8).
3. Ask for Christ's grace and power to forgive (see Luke 11:9,10).

4. Agree to live with the unavoidable consequences of the other person's sin against you (see Eph. 5:21).
5. Release the offense. Tear up the moral, personal or relational debt the other person owes you (see Matt. 6:12).
6. Never bring it up again as a weapon against them (see Rom. 12:17).
7. Keep forgiving when your emotions recycle the pain or when the other person keeps offending you (see Matt. 18:21,22).
8. Reject the sinful act and tolerate it no longer (see Rom. 12:21).
9. Turn the vengeance over to God and over to God's human authorities (see Rom. 19,20; 13:1).
10. Replace the old resentful feelings with the forgiving love of Christ (see Eph. 4:31,32).

Do not make forgiveness more difficult than it already is. Some things we do *not* have to do:

1. We don't have to feel good about the person who hurt us either before or after we forgive.
2. We don't have to tell other people about our resentful feelings unless the Holy Spirit guides us to do so. Matthew 5:23-26 does tell us to seek forgiveness and be reconciled to those we have offended, as the Holy Spirit guides.
3. We don't have to wait until we are ready to forgive. We can obey God's Word right now.

Each person should lift the painful memories before the Lord, asking for courage to face the pain honestly and for the grace to forgive fully. Releasing the offenses results in relieving the pain. Item by item, individually forgive each person you recall and release the offenses as follows:

> "Lord, I forgive (name) for (specifically identify all offenses and painful memories)."

Prayerfully focus on each person until every remembered pain has surfaced. Be sure to include your husband or wife and every painful memory in your marriage. Both spouses should also ask the Lord's forgiveness and forgive themselves as needed. Bitterness hardens the heart, but forgiveness softens it. After you have completed the above, pray the following prayer, and make the following declaration together out loud:

> Dear heavenly Father,
>
> We thank You for Your unconditional love and forgiveness. It is Your kindness and patience that have led us to forgiveness. In the name of Jesus and with His kindness and tenderness, we forgive every person who has ever hurt us, our family, or our marriage. We forgive each other for the pain that has come through weakness, poor judgment, and outright sin. We accept Your forgiveness of ourselves for the pain and damage caused in our marriage.
>
> By Your grace, bring healing, help, and hope to those who have hurt us, and to those who have been hurt by us. We bless them all in the name of our Lord Jesus Christ, who taught us, "Love your enemies, do good to those who hate you, bless those who curse you, pray for those who mistreat you" (Luke 6:27,28). According to Your Word, we pray for those who have hurt us.
>
> In the precious name of Jesus Christ, we pray. Amen.

Together make the following declaration:

> By the authority of the Lord Jesus Christ, Who is seated at the heavenly Father's right hand, we assume our responsibility to resist the devil. We declare that we are crucified, buried, made alive, raised up and seated with Christ at the right hand of God. In union with Christ and with His authority, we command Satan to release any foothold on our lives or any influence on our marriage. Satan, in the all-powerful name of the crucified, risen and reigning Lord Jesus Christ, leave our presence and

our marriage. Do not come back. Take away with you all of your lingering effects upon our memories, upon our relationships, upon our present thoughts and upon our future together.

UNMASK SATAN'S DECEPTIONS

Step Six

The goal of Satan is to discredit the work of Christ and tear apart your marriage and family. His primary weapons are deception, temptation and accusation. He also uses harassment, discouragement and disillusionment. When we buy his little lies, we turn against God and each other. Our homes become a battle ground instead of a proving ground. The desire is for every member of the family to be a part of the building crew, rather than the wrecking crew. The tongue is the instrument he uses most. We either become tongue tied and refuse to speak the truth in love or we allow the tongue to become a destructive weapon.

If only one member of the family pays attention to the Holy Spirit, it will have strengthening effects upon every other member. On the other hand, if only one member of the family pays attention to a deceiving spirit, it will have weakening effects upon every other member. The purpose of this Step is to unmask the evil one's deceptions and stand against his attacks in the power of the Holy Spirit.

Satan uses real people to mount his attacks. They may be coming from deceived or evil people inside or outside the family. For example, a friend or coworker may lead your spouse into an adulterous affair. The attacks may come through relatives or neighbors who use their tongues as a destructive weapon. They may come from people who give us bad counsel to leave our marriage or abandon our children. They may even possibly come through Satanists who use occultic rituals or blood sacrifices in an evil attempt to destroy our families and, therefore, our testimonies. Ask the Lord to show you the nature of these attacks so you can stand against them and be united as one family under the Lordship of Christ.

Dear heavenly Father,

We stand under Your authority. We give thanks that You are our hiding place, our protection and our refuge. We clothe ourselves and our marriage with the Lord Jesus Christ and with the full armor of God. We choose to be strong in You, Lord, and in the power of Your might. We stand firm in our faith, submit to You, God, and resist the devil.

Open our eyes to see the attacks of the evil one against us, our marriage and our family. Give us spiritual discernment to become aware of Satan's schemes, not ignorant of them. Open our eyes to the reality of the spiritual world in which we live. We ask You for the ability to discern spiritually so we can judge rightly between good and evil.

As we wait silently before You, reveal to us the attacks of Satan against us, our marriage, our family and our ministries so we may stand against them and expose the father of lies.

In Jesus' discerning name, we pray. Amen.

Make a list of whatever God brings to your mind that may be due to:

1. Repetitive thoughts that cause you to close your spirit toward God and each other (1 Tim. 4:1; 2 Cor. 10:3-5).
2. Recurring times and situtations that cause distractions, confusion and disorder in your marriage and in your home—usually during family discussions, devotions and times surrounding church and ministry (1 Thess. 2:18).
3. Improper stewardship (1 Cor. 4:1,2).
    a. Sins that have been tolerated in the home.
    b. Anti-Christian material brought into the home.

Sinful activities need to be renounced. Attacks from the enemy because of our obedience to Christ need to be understood so we can recognize them and stand against them in the future. As a family, we need to understand that we wrestle not against flesh and blood, but against the powers of darkness (see Eph. 6:12). We don't want to be blindfolded warriors who strike out at ourselves or each other.

When you tear down an established Satanic stronghold in your family, you may have some resistance. To walk free from past influences and present attacks, verbally make the following declaration, then pray together the following prayer:

Declaration:

> As children of God who have been delivered from the power of darkness and translated into the kingdom of God's dear Son, we submit to God and resist the devil. We cancel out all demonic working passed on to us from our ancestors. We have been crucified and raised with our Lord Jesus Christ, and we now sit enthroned with Him in heavenly places. We renounce all Satanic assignments directed toward us, our marriage, our family and our ministry. We cancel every curse Satan and his deceived, misguided or evil workers have put on us and our marriage. We announce to Satan and all his forces that Christ became a curse for us when He died on the Cross. We reject any and every way in which Satan may claim ownership of us. We belong to the Lord Jesus Christ who purchased us with His own blood. We reject all other occultic rituals and blood sacrifices whereby Satan may claim ownership of us, our marriage, and our children. We declare ourselves to be eternally and completely signed over and committed to the Lord Jesus Christ. By the authority we have in Jesus Christ, we now command every familiar spirit and every enemy of the Lord Jesus Christ to leave our presence and our home forever. We commit ourselves to our heavenly Father to do His will from this day forward.

Prayer:

> Dear heavenly Father,
>
> We come to You as Your children, purchased by the blood of the Lord Jesus Christ. You are the Lord

of the universe and the Lord of our lives. We yield our rights to You as the Lord of our marriage. We submit our bodies to You as instruments of righteousness, a living sacrifice, that we may glorify You in our bodies and in our marriage. We reserve the sexual use of our bodies for each other only. We now ask You to fill us with Your Holy Spirit. We commit ourselves to the renewing of our minds to prove that Your will is good, perfect and acceptable for us. We commit ourselves to take every thought captive to the obedience of Christ.

All this we do in the name and authority of the Lord Jesus Christ. Amen.

Next, commit your home to the Lord. Have you brought any foreign objects into your home that could serve as an idol or were ever used for a non-Christian religious purpose? These could provide grounds for Satan to have access to your home. Are there any pornographic videos, magazines or books? Occult or false-religion materials? Anything else that needs to be cleansed from your home? Ask the Lord to reveal any such sins or articles in your home. Covenant before the Lord to remove all these items from your home and burn or destroy them. Then commit your home to the Lord as follows:

Dear heavenly Father,

We acknowledge that You are the Lord of all. All things You have created are good, and You have charged us to be good stewards of all You have entrusted to us. Thank You for all You have provided for our family. We claim no ownership of what You have entrusted to us. We dedicate our home to You, our living quarters, our work space and all the property, possessions and finances you have entrusted to us. We promise to remove from our home anything and everything displeasing to you.

We renounce any attacks, devices or ceremonies of the enemy or his people designed to claim any ownership of that with which we have been entrusted. We have been bought and purchased by the blood sacrifice of our Lord Jesus Christ. We claim our home for our family as a place of spiritual safety and protection from the evil one. We renounce anything and everything that has taken place in our home by us, or by those who have lived in our house before us, that does not please our heavenly Father. We ask for Your divine protection around our home and our family. We desire to honor You in all our ways. Thank You for Your protection.

Dear Lord, you are the King of our lives and our marriage and we exalt You. May all that we do bring honor and glory to You.

In Jesus' holy name, we pray. Amen.

Then declare:

As children of God, seated with Christ in the heavenly places, we command every evil spirit to leave our presence and our home. We renounce all curses and spells against our house, property, possessions and our very selves. We announce to Satan and all his workers that our marriage, our family and all that our heavenly Father has entrusted to us belongs to the Lord Jesus Christ. We submit it all to the direction and control of the Holy Spirit.

RENEW CHRISTIAN MARRIAGE

Step Seven

All who marry, whether Christian or not, become part of God's creation order of marriage (see Gen. 1:26-28; 2:18-25). A *creation order* is a God-given longing built into the fabric of human life. As a result of this God-given longing, every culture and all people groups on earth practice marriage in some form. No exceptions! Violating marriage breaks the order of creation and always brings terrible consequences.

When one partner (or both) knows Jesus Christ as Lord and Savior, the marriage becomes sanctified or set apart as holy, part of God's new Christian order (see 1 Cor. 7:14). They commit themselves to Christ's new creation in marriage and enter a marriage covenant before God and one another. Christian marriage far exceeds a mere social contract. Marriage as a social contract is only a legal agreement between two parties. Christian marriage is a lifelong covenant with binding vows, spoken before God and human witnesses. If the vows are broken, they bring God's judgment. If they are kept, they bring God's rewards.

Satan's lie is that we are married singles, bound only by a human relationship and a social contract. That means marriage can be broken whenever either party feels the partners have irreconcilable differences. In Christ, there are no irreconcilable differences. We have been reconciled to Him, and we have been given the ministry of reconciliation.

God's truth is that the marriage vows bind us into the organic union of Christian marriage. A new creation lasts until the death of one of the spouses. A contract can be canceled, but a new creation lasts a lifetime. Contracts can be broken or renegotiated, but a new creation either grows toward fulfillment or is violated.

Living in obedience to God's Word in Christian marriage (or any other part of life) brings the Lord's shelter of protection (see Ps. 91). It results in God's blessings, including children who are set apart for God's purposes (see 1 Cor. 7:14). By God's grace His blessings extend not only to those who are faithful to Him, but also to their descendants for many generations to come (see Exod. 20:6; Deut. 7:9; Luke 1:50). Violating marriage brings God's curse, not only upon ourselves, but also upon our descendants for three or four more generations (see Exod. 20:5; 34:7; Num. 14:18; Jer. 32:18).

Verbally make the following declaration by speaking aloud in unison. Then pray the prayer that follows.

Declaration:

> Satan, we renounce you in all your works and all your ways. We submit ourselves and our marriage to God, and we resist the devil. In the all-powerful name of the Lord Jesus Christ, we command you to leave our marriage. Take all of your deceitful spirits, evil demons and fallen angels with you, and go

to the place where the Lord Jesus Christ sends you. Leave us and our marriage and don't come back. Take with you all of your temptations to violate our marriage vows. Take with you all of your accusing and demeaning thoughts we could have against each other. Take with you all of your deceptions that contradict God's written Word. The Lord Jesus Christ has torn down your demonic authority, and we stand against your influence and activity toward our lives and our marriage.

You are a defeated foe, disarmed of your weapons, and made a public spectacle by the cross of Christ (see Col. 2:15). Greater is He who is in us than he who is in the world (see 1 John 4:4). The prince of this world now stands condemned (see John 16:11). Christ has the supremacy over every evil throne, power, rule, or authority (see Col. 1:16). Jesus shared our humanity that by His death He might destroy him who holds the power of death, that is, the devil (see Heb. 2:14). We resist you by the authority of Christ and because we are alive in Him; therefore, you must flee from us (see James 4:7).

Pray aloud together:

Dear heavenly Father,

We gladly acknowledge that You created marriage and family life for Your glory. Thank You for designing marriage as a *creation order*, woven into the fabric of human society. We commit ourselves anew to a covenant of Christian marriage with all its blessings.

We renounce the devil's lie that we are married singles, bound only by a human relationship and a social contract. We recall that our marriage is binding as long as we both shall live. We acknowledge that we can never violate our marriage vows without bringing lasting damage upon ourselves, upon our children and upon our descendants for three or four generations to come.

We confess we have not perfectly lived up to our marriage vows. We confess we have not always lived as one in Christ. We have fallen short of Your perfect will by our own selfishness and sin. We gladly accept Your forgiveness of our sins through the blood of Christ on the Cross (see 1 John 2:1,2). By grace through faith we receive Christ's abundant life into our hearts and His holiness into our marriage (see John 10:10; 1 Cor. 7:14).

We crucify our own fleshly lusts and sinful desires which tempt us to ignore or violate our marriage vows (see 1 Pet. 2:11; Gal. 5:24). We clothe ourselves and our marriage with the Lord Jesus Christ and His armor of light (see Rom. 13:12-14; Gal. 3:26,27). We give ourselves to live by the Spirit in daily obedience to Christ (see Gal. 5:16; 1 Pet. 1:2).

We announce that in Christ we have all the spiritual blessings we need to live out our new creation. We affirm that we are one in Christ Jesus—one marriage, one flesh, one family (see Eph. 1:3; 3:14-15; Gen. 2:24; Mark 10:6-9). We submit ourselves and our marriage to the ownership of our heavenly Father, to the lordship of Jesus Christ and to the power of the Holy Spirit. From this day forward, we ask You to use our marriage to display Your splendor before our children. We invite You to work through us to show Your glory in the midst of a corrupt and wicked generation.

In Jesus' glorious name. Amen.

When you were first married, you spoke vows that said, I take thee as my lawful wedded wife or husband. In this renewal of vows, become a giver instead of a taker. Please note the slight change in wording from I *take you* as my wedded husband or wife to I *give myself to you* to be your husband or wife. As you hold hands and face each other, first the husband, and then the wife, repeat the following. In a group setting a minister of the gospel can lead this renewal of marriage vows.

I (name) give myself to you, (name), to be your wedded (husband or wife), to have and to hold from this day forward, for better or for worse, for richer or for poorer, in sickness and in health, to love and to cherish, until death do us part, according to God's holy Word; and hereto, I pledge you my faithfulness.

LIVING FREE IN CHRIST

Freedom must be maintained. You have won a very important battle in an ongoing war. Freedom is yours as long as you keep choosing truth and standing firm in the strength of the Lord. If more painful memories should surface, or if you become aware of lies you have been living, renounce them and choose the truth. Some couples have found it helpful to go through these steps again.

If you haven't already done so, please read *Victory Over the Darkness* and *The Bondage Breaker*. If you are a parent, we suggest reading *The Seduction of Our Children. Walking in the Light* was written to help people understand God's guidance so they are able to discern counterfeit guidance. To maintain your freedom, we suggest the following:

1. Become active together in a Christ-centered church, a small Christian group and a ministry for Christ. Build healthy allies for your marriage. Step outside of yourselves for Christ.
2. Study your Bible daily, pray and be sensitive to the leading of the Holy Spirit. We also suggest reading one chapter together every day of *Living Free in Christ* for the next 36 days. Then use the devotional, *Daily in Christ*, by Neil and Joanne Anderson.
3. Review and apply your personal freedom in Christ. Remind yourselves of your identity in Christ, winning the battle for the mind, and processing the Steps to Freedom in Christ (personal freedom) as an ongoing personal inventory. The Lord uses marriage to reveal more layers of the onion of our selfishness which He wants to peel off.
4. Take every thought captive to the obedience of

Christ. Assume responsibility for private thoughts, reject the lies, choose the truth and stand firm in your identity in Christ.

5. Don't drift away! It is very easy to get lazy in your thoughts and revert back to old habit patterns of thinking. Share struggles openly with each other.
6. Don't expect your spouse to fight your battle. Although you can help each other, no one else can think, pray or read the Bible for you.
7. If serious problems still prevail, seek out a competent Christian pastor or counselor who is committed to the biblical institution of marriage, and not just to the individual apart from marriage.

Pray with confidence as follows:

Dear heavenly Father,

We honor You as our sovereign Lord. We acknowledge that You are always present with us. You are the only all-powerful and all-knowing God. You are kind and loving in all Your ways. We love You. We thank You that we are united together with Christ, and we are spiritually alive in Him. We choose not to love the world, and we crucify the flesh and all its sinful desires.

We thank You that we are children of God, new creations in Christ Jesus, full of eternal life in Christ. We ask You to fill us with Your Holy Spirit that we may live our lives free from sin. We declare our dependence upon You, and we take our stand against Satan and all his lying ways. We choose to believe the truth and we refuse to be discouraged, or to give up hope for our marriage. You are the God of all hope, and we are confident that You will meet our needs as we seek to live according to Your Word. We express with confidence that we can live a responsible life and be faithful in our marriage through Christ Who strengthens us.

We ask these things in the precious name of our Lord and Savior, Jesus Christ. Amen.

Declaration:

> We now take our stand in Christ and we put on the whole armor of God. In union with Christ, we command Satan and all his evil spirits to depart from us. We submit our bodies to God as living sacrifices and renew our minds by the living Word of God that we may prove the will of God is good, acceptable and perfect.

(Please see the following identity list.)

WE ARE ONE IN CHRIST

We Are Accepted in Christ:

John 1:12	We are God's children.
John 15:15	We are Christ's friends.
Romans 5:1	We have been justified.
1 Corinthians 6:17	We are united with the Lord and one with Him in spirit.
1 Corinthians 6:20	We have been bought with a price; we belong to God.
1 Corinthians 12:27	We are members of Christ's body.
Ephesians 1:1	We are saints.
Ephesians 1:5	We have been adopted as God's children.
Ephesians 2:18	We have direct access to God through the Holy Spirit.
Colossians 1:14	We have been redeemed and forgiven of all our sins.
Colossians 2:10	We are complete in Christ.

We Are Secure in Christ:

Romans 8:1,2	We are free from condemnation.
Romans 8:28	We are assured that all things work together for good.
Romans 8:33,34	We are free from any condemning charges against us.
Romans 8:35	We cannot be separated from the love of God.

2 Corinthians 1:21	We have been established, anointed and sealed by God.
Colossians 3:3	We are hidden with Christ in God.
Philippians 1:6	We are confident that the good work God has begun in us will be perfected.
Philippians 3:20	We are citizens of heaven.
2 Timothy 1:7	We have not been given a spirit of fear, but of power, love and a sound mind.
Hebrews 4:16	We can find grace and mercy in time of need.
1 John 5:18	We are born of God and the evil one cannot touch us.

We Are Significant in Christ:

Matthew 5:13,14	We are the salt and light of the earth.
John 15:1,5	We are a branch of the true vine, a channel of His life.
John 15:16	We have been chosen and appointed to bear fruit.
Acts 1:8	We are personal witnesses of Christ's.
1 Corinthians 3:16	We are God's temple.
2 Corinthians 5:17-20	We are ministers of reconciliation.
2 Corinthians 6:1	We are God's coworkers.
Ephesians 2:6	We are seated with Christ in the heavenly realm.
Ephesians 2:10	We are God's workmanship.
Ephesians 3:12	We may approach God with freedom and confidence.
Philippians 4:13	We can do all things through Christ who strengthens us.

APPENDIX A

Steps to Freedom in Christ

It is my deep conviction that the finished work of Jesus Christ and the presence of God in our lives are the only means by which we can resolve our personal and spiritual conflicts. Christ in us is our only hope (see Col. 1:27), and He alone can meet our deepest needs of life, acceptance, identity, security and significance. The discipleship counseling process upon which these steps are based should not be understood as just another counseling technique that we learn. It is an encounter with God. He is the Wonderful Counselor. He is the One who grants repentance that leads to a knowledge of the truth which sets us free (see 2 Tim. 2:24-26).

The "Steps to Freedom in Christ" do not set you free. *Who* sets you free is Christ, and *what* sets you free is your response to Him in repentance and faith. These steps are just a tool to help you submit to God and resist the devil (see Jas. 4:7). Then you can start living a fruitful life by abiding in Christ and becoming the person He created you to be. Many Christians will be able to work through these steps on their own and discover the wonderful freedom that Christ purchased for them on the cross. Then they will experience the peace of God which surpasses all comprehension, and it shall guard their hearts and their minds (see Phil. 4:7).

Before You Begin

The chances of that happening and the possibility of **maintaining that freedom will be greatly enhanced if you read *Victory Over the Darkness* and *The Bondage Breaker* first.**

Many Christians in our western world need to understand the reality of the spiritual world and our relationship to it. Some can't read these books or even the Bible with comprehension because of the battle that is going on for their minds. They will need the assistance of others who have been trained. The theology and practical process of discipleship counseling is given in my book, Helping Others Find Freedom in Christ, and the Study Guide that accompanies it. The book attempts to biblically integrate the reality of the spiritual and the natural world so we can have a whole answer for a whole person. In doing so, we cannot polarize into psychotherapeutic ministries that ignore the reality of the spiritual world or attempt some kind of deliverance ministry that ignores developmental issues and human responsibility.

You May Need Help

Ideally, it would be best if everyone had a trusted friend, pastor or counselor who would help them go through this process because it is just applying the wisdom of James 5:16: "Therefore, confess your sins to one another, and pray for one another, so that you may be healed. The effective prayer of a righteous man can accomplish much." Another person can prayerfully support you by providing objective counsel. I have had the privilege to help many Christian leaders who could not process this on their own. Many Christian groups all over the world are using this approach in many languages with incredible results because the Lord desires for all to come to repentance (see 2 Pet. 3:9), and to know the truth that sets us free in Christ (see John 8:32).

Appropriating and Maintaining Freedom

Christ has set us free through His victory over sin and death on the cross. However, appropriating our freedom in Christ through repentance and faith and maintaining our life of freedom in Christ are two different issues. It was for freedom that Christ set us free, but we have been warned not to return to a yoke of slavery which is legalism in this context (see Gal. 5:1) or to turn our freedom into an opportunity for the flesh (see Gal. 5:13). Establishing people as free in Christ makes it possible for them to walk by faith according to what God says is true and live by the power of the Holy Spirit and not carry out the desires of the flesh (see Gal. 5:16). The true Christian life avoids both legalism and license.

If you are not experiencing freedom, it may be because you have not stood firm in the faith or actively taken your place in Christ. It is every Christian's responsibility to do whatever is necessary to maintain a right relationship with God and mankind. Your eternal destiny is not at stake. God will never leave you nor forsake you (see Heb. 13:5), but your daily victory is at stake if you fail to claim and maintain your position in Christ.

Your Position in Christ

You are not a helpless victim caught between two nearly equal but opposite heavenly super-powers. Satan is a deceiver. Only God is omnipotent, omnipresent and omniscient. Sometimes the reality of sin and the presence of evil may seem more real than the presence of God, but that's part of Satan's deception. Satan is a defeated foe and we are **in Christ**. A true knowledge of God and knowing our identity and position in Christ are the greatest determinants of our "mental health." A false concept of God, a distorted understanding of who we are as children of God and the misplaced deification of Satan are the greatest contributors to "mental illness."

Many of our illnesses are psychosomatic. When these issues are resolved in Christ our physical bodies will function better, and we will experience greater health. Other problems are clearly physical, and we need the services of the medical profession. Please consult your physician for medical advice and the prescribing of medication. We are both spiritual and physical beings who need the services of both the church and the hospital.

Winning the Battle for Your Mind

The battle is for the mind, which is the control center of all that we think and do. The opposing thoughts you may experience as you go through these steps can control you only if you believe them. **If you are working through these steps alone, don't be deceived by any lying, intimidating thoughts in**

your mind. If a trusted pastor or counselor is helping you find your freedom in Christ, he or she must have your cooperation. You must share any thoughts you are having in opposition to what you are attempting to do. As soon as you expose the lie, the power of Satan is broken. The only way that you can lose control in this process is if you pay attention to a deceiving spirit and believe a lie.

You Must Choose

The following procedure is a means of resolving personal and spiritual conflicts which have kept you from experiencing the freedom and victory Christ purchased for you on the cross. Your freedom will be the result of what you choose to believe, confess, forgive, renounce and forsake. No one can do that for you. The battle for your mind can only be won as you personally choose truth. As you go through this process, understand that Satan is under no obligation to obey your thoughts. Only God has complete knowledge of your mind because He is omniscient (all-knowing). So we can submit to God inwardly, but we need to resist the devil by reading aloud each prayer and by verbally renouncing, forgiving, confessing, etc.

This process of reestablishing our freedom in Christ is nothing more than a fierce moral inventory and a rock-solid commitment to truth. It is the first step in the continuing process of discipleship. There is no such thing as instant maturity. It will take you the rest of your life to renew your mind and conform to the image of God. If your problems stem from a source other than those covered in these steps, you may need to seek professional help.

May the Lord grace you with His presence as you seek His face and help others experience the joy of their salvation.

Neil T. Anderson

PRAYER

Dear Heavenly Father,

We acknowledge Your presence in this room and in our lives. You are the only omniscient (all-knowing), omnipotent (all-powerful) and omnipresent (always present) God. We are dependent upon You, for apart from You we can do nothing. We stand in the truth that all authority in heaven and on earth has been given to the resurrected Christ, and because we are in Christ, we share that authority in order to make disciples and set captives free. We ask You to fill us with Your Holy Spirit and lead us into all truth. We pray for Your complete protection and ask for Your guidance. In Jesus' name. Amen.

DECLARATION

In the name and authority of the Lord Jesus Christ, we command Satan and all evil spirits to release (name) in order that (name) can be free to know and choose to do the will of God. As children of God seated with Christ in the heavenlies, we agree that every enemy of the Lord Jesus Christ be bound to silence. We say to Satan and all your evil workers that you cannot inflict any pain or in any way prevent God's will from being accomplished in (name's) life.

PREPARATION

Before going through the *Steps to Freedom,* review the events of your life to discern specific areas that might need to be addressed.

Family History

_______ Religious history of parents and grandparents

_______ Home life from childhood through high school
_______ History of physical or emotional illness in the family
_______ Adoption, foster care, guardians

Personal History

_______ Eating habits (bulimia, bingeing and purging, anorexia, compulsive eating)
_______ Addictions (drugs, alcohol)
_______ Prescription medications (what for?)
_______ Sleeping patterns and nightmares
_______ Rape or any sexual, physical, emotional abuse
_______ Thought life (obsessive, blasphemous, condemning, distracting thoughts, poor concentration, fantasy)
_______ Mental interference in church, prayer or Bible study
_______ Emotional life (anger, anxiety, depression, bitterness, fears)
_______ Spiritual journey (salvation: when, how and assurance)

Now you are ready to begin. The following are seven specific steps to process in order to experience freedom from your past. You will address the areas where Satan most commonly takes advantage of us and where strongholds have been built. Christ purchased your victory when He shed His blood for you on the cross. Realizing your freedom will be the result of what you choose to believe, confess, forgive, renounce and forsake. No one can do that for you. The battle for your mind can only be won as you personally choose truth.

As you go through these *Steps to Freedom*, remember that Satan will only be defeated if you confront him verbally. He cannot read your mind and is under no obligation to obey your thoughts. Only God has complete knowledge of your mind. As you process each step, it is important that you submit to God inwardly and resist the devil by reading aloud each prayer—verbally renouncing, forgiving, confessing, etc.

You are taking a fierce moral inventory and making a rock-solid commitment to truth. If your problems stem from a source other than those covered in these steps, you have nothing to lose by going through them. If you are sincere, the only thing that can happen is that you will get very right with God!

Step 1

COUNTERFEIT VS. REAL

The first step to freedom in Christ is to renounce your previous or current involvement with satanically-inspired occult practices and false religions. You need to renounce any activity and group which denies Jesus Christ, offers guidance through any source other than the absolute authority of the written Word of God or requires secret initiations, ceremonies or covenants.

In order to help you assess your spiritual experiences, begin this step by asking God to reveal false guidance and counterfeit religious experiences.

> **Dear Heavenly Father,**
> **I ask You to guard my heart and my mind and reveal to me any and all involvement I have had either knowingly or unknowingly with cultic or occult practices, false religions or false teachers. In Jesus' name, I pray. Amen.**

Using the "Non-Christian Spiritual Experience Inventory" on the following page, carefully check anything in which you were involved. This list is not exhaustive, but it will guide you in identifying non-Christian experiences. Add any additional involvement you have had. Even if you "innocently" participated in something or observed it, you should write it on your list to renounce, just in case you unknowingly gave Satan a foothold.

Non-Christian Spiritual Experience Inventory

(Please check those that apply.)

- ☐ Astral-projection
- ☐ Ouija board
- ☐ Table or body lifting
- ☐ Dungeons and Dragons
- ☐ Speaking in trance
- ☐ Automatic writing
- ☐ Magic eight ball
- ☐ Telepathy
- ☐ Using spells or curses
- ☐ Seance
- ☐ Materialization
- ☐ Clairvoyance
- ☐ Spirit guides
- ☐ Fortune telling
- ☐ Tarot cards
- ☐ Palm reading
- ☐ Astrology/ horoscopes
- ☐ Rod & pendulum (dowsing)
- ☐ Self-hypnosis
- ☐ Mental manipulations or attempts to swap minds
- ☐ Black and white magic
- ☐ New Age medicine
- ☐ Blood pacts or cutting yourself in a destructive way
- ☐ Fetishism (objects of worship, crystals, good luck charms)
- ☐ Incubi and succubi (sexual spirits)
- ☐ Other ____________

- ☐ Christian Science
- ☐ Unity
- ☐ The Way International
- ☐ Unification Church
- ☐ Mormonism
- ☐ Church of the Living Word
- ☐ Jehovah's Witnesses
- ☐ Children of God (Love)
- ☐ Swedenborgianism
- ☐ Unitarianism
- ☐ Masons
- ☐ New Age
- ☐ The Forum (EST)
- ☐ Spirit worship
- ☐ Other ____________

- ☐ Buddhism
- ☐ Hare Krishna
- ☐ Bahaism
- ☐ Rosicrucian
- ☐ Science of the Mind
- ☐ Science of Creative Intelligence
- ☐ Transcendental Meditation
- ☐ Hinduism
- ☐ Yoga
- ☐ Echkankar
- ☐ Roy Masters
- ☐ Silva Mind Control
- ☐ Father Divine
- ☐ Theosophical Society
- ☐ Islam
- ☐ Black Muslim
- ☐ Religion of Martial Arts
- ☐ Other ____________

1. Have you ever been hypnotized, attended a New Age or parapsychology seminar, consulted a medium, Spiritist, or channeler? Explain.

   ____

2. Do you or have you ever had an imaginary friend or spirit guide offering you guidance or companionship? Explain.

   ____

3. Have you ever heard voices in your mind or had repeating and nagging thoughts condemning you or that were foreign to what you believe or feel, like there was a dialogue going on in your head? Explain.

   ____

4. What other spiritual experiences have you had that would be considered out of the ordinary?

   ____

5. Have you ever made a vow, covenant, or pact with any individual or group other than God?

   ____

6. Have you been involved in satanic ritual or satanic worship in any form? Explain.

   ____

When you are confident that your list is complete, confess and renounce each involvement, whether active or passive, by praying aloud the following prayer, repeating it separately for each item on your list:

> Lord,
> I confess that I have participated in ______
> ____
> and I renounce ______________________________.
> Thank You that in Christ I am forgiven.

If there has been any involvement in satanic ritual or heavy occult activity, you need to state aloud the following special renunciations which apply. Read across the page, renouncing the first item in the column on the Kingdom of Darkness and then affirming the first truth in the column on the Kingdom of Light. Continue down the page in this manner.

All satanic rituals, covenants, and assignments must be specifically renounced as the Lord allows you to recall them. Some who have been subjected to satanic ritual abuse may have developed multiple personalities in order to survive. Nevertheless, continue through the *Steps to Freedom* in order to resolve all that you consciously can. It is important that you resolve the demonic strongholds first. Every personality must resolve his/her issues and agree to come together in Christ. You may need someone who understands spiritual conflict to help you maintain control and not be deceived into false memories. Only Jesus can bind up the broken-hearted, set captives free and make us whole.

Special Renunciations for Satanic Ritual Involvement

Kingdom of Darkness	Kingdom of Light
I renounce ever signing my name over to Satan or having had my name signed over to Satan.	I announce that my name is now written in the Lamb's Book of Life.
I renounce any ceremony where I may have been wed to Satan.	I announce that I am the bride of Christ.
I renounce any and all covenants that I made with Satan.	I announce that I am a partaker of the New Covenant with Christ.
I renounce all satanic assignments for my life, including duties, marriage and children.	I announce and commit myself to know and do only the will of God and accept only His guidance.
I renounce all spirit guides assigned to me.	I announce and accept only the leading of the Holy Spirit.
I renounce ever giving of my blood in the service of Satan.	I trust only in the shed blood of my Lord Jesus Christ.
I renounce ever eating of flesh or drinking of blood for satanic worship.	By faith I eat only the flesh and drink only the blood of Jesus in Holy Communion.
I renounce any and all guardians and Satanist parents who were assigned to me.	I announce that God is my Father and the Holy Spirit is my Guardian by which I am sealed.
I renounce any baptism in blood or urine whereby I am identified with Satan.	I announce that I have been baptized into Christ Jesus and my identity is now in Christ.
I renounce any and all sacrifices that were made on my behalf by which Satan may claim ownership of me.	I announce that only the sacrifice of Christ has any hold on me. I belong to Him. I have been purchased by the blood of the Lamb.

Step 2

DECEPTION VS. TRUTH

Truth is the revelation of God's Word, but we need to acknowledge the truth in the inner self (see Ps. 51:6). When David lived a lie, he suffered greatly. When he finally found freedom by acknowledging the truth, he wrote: "How blessed is the man...in whose spirit there is no deceit" (Ps. 32:2). We are to lay aside falsehood and speak the truth in love (see Eph. 4:15, 25). A mentally healthy person is one who is in touch with reality and relatively free of anxiety. Both qualities should characterize the Christian who renounces deception and embraces the truth.

Begin this critical step by expressing aloud the following prayer. Don't let the enemy accuse you with thoughts such as: "This isn't going to work" or "I wish I could believe this but I can't" or any other lies in opposition to what you are proclaiming. Even if you have difficulty doing so, you need to pray the prayer and read the Doctrinal Affirmation.

> Dear Heavenly Father,
>
> I know that You desire truth in the inner self and that facing this truth is the way of liberation (John 8:32). I acknowledge that I have been deceived by the father of lies (John 8:44) and that I have deceived myself (1 John 1:8). I pray in the name of the Lord Jesus Christ that You, Heavenly Father, will rebuke all deceiving spirits by virtue of the shed blood and resurrection of the Lord Jesus Christ. By faith I have received You into my life and I am now seated with Christ in the heavenlies (Eph. 2:6). I acknowledge that I have the responsibility and authority to resist the devil, and when I do, he will flee from me. I now ask the Holy Spirit to guide me into all truth (John 16:13). I ask You to "Search me, O God, and know my heart; try me and know my anxious thoughts; and see if there be any hurtful way in me, and lead me

in the everlasting way" (Ps. 139:23-24). In Jesus' name, I pray. Amen.

You may want to pause at this point to consider some of Satan's deceptive schemes. In addition to false teachers, false prophets and deceiving spirits, you can deceive yourself. Now that you are alive in Christ and forgiven, you never have to live a lie or defend yourself. Christ is your defense. How have you deceived or attempted to defend yourself according to the following?

Self-deception

_______ Hearing God's Word but not doing it (see Jas. 1:22; 4:17)
_______ Saying we have no sin (see 1 John 1:8)
_______ Thinking we are something when we aren't (see Gal. 6:3)
_______ Thinking we are wise in our own eyes (see 1 Cor. 3:18-19)
_______ Thinking we will not reap what we sow (see Gal. 6:7)
_______ Thinking the unrighteous will inherit the Kingdom (see 1 Cor. 6:9)
_______ Thinking we can associate with bad company and not be corrupted (see 1 Cor. 15:33)

Self-defense

(defending ourselves instead of trusting in Christ)
_______ Denial (conscious or subconscious refusal to face the truth)
_______ Fantasy (escaping from the real world)
_______ Emotional insulation (withdrawing to avoid rejection)
_______ Regression (reverting back to a less threatening time)
_______ Displacement (taking out frustrations on others)
_______ Projection (blaming others)
_______ Rationalization (making excuses for poor behavior)

For those things that have been true in your life, pray aloud:

Lord,

I agree that I have been deceived in the area of

> ______________________________. Thank You for forgiving me. I commit myself to know and follow Your truth. Amen.

Choosing the truth may be difficult if you have been living a lie (been deceived) for many years. You may need to seek professional help to weed out the defense mechanisms you have depended upon to survive. The Christian needs only one defense—Jesus. Knowing that you are forgiven and accepted as God's child is what sets you free to face reality and declare your dependence on Him.

Faith is the biblical response to the truth, and believing the truth is a choice. When someone says, "I want to believe God, but I just can't," they are being deceived. Of course you can believe God. Faith is something you decide to do, not something you feel like doing. Believing the truth doesn't make it true. It's true; therefore, we believe it. The New Age movement is distorting the truth by saying we create reality through what we believe. We can't create reality with our minds; we face reality. It is what, or who you believe in that counts. Everybody believes in something, and everybody walks by faith according to what he or she believes. But if what you believe isn't true, then how you live (walk by faith) won't be right.

Historically, the church has found great value in publicly declaring its beliefs. The Apostles' Creed and the Nicene Creed have been recited for centuries. Read aloud the following affirmation of faith, and do so again as often as necessary to renew your mind. Experiencing difficulty in reading this affirmation may indicate where you are being deceived and under attack. Boldly affirm your commitment to biblical truth.

DOCTRINAL AFFIRMATION

I recognize that there is only one true and living God (Ex. 20:2-3) who exists as the Father, Son and Holy Spirit and that He is worthy of all honor, praise and glory as the Creator, Sustainer and Beginning and End of all things (Rev. 4:11; 5:9-10; Is. 43:1, 7, 21).

I recognize Jesus Christ as the Messiah, the Word who became flesh and dwelt among us (John 1:1, 14). I believe that He came to destroy the works of Satan (1 John 3:8), that He disarmed the rulers and authorities and made a public display of them, having triumphed over them (Col. 2:15).

I believe that God has proven His love for me because when I was still a sinner, Christ died for me (Rom. 5:8). I believe that He delivered me from the domain of darkness and transferred me to His kingdom, and in Him I have redemption, the forgiveness of sins (Col. 1:13-14).

I believe that I am now a child of God (1 John 3:1-3) and that I am seated with Christ in the heavenlies (Eph. 2:6). I believe that I was saved by the grace of God through faith, that it was a gift, and not the result of any works on my part (Eph. 2:8-9).

I choose to be strong in the Lord and in the strength of His might (Eph. 6:10). I put no confidence in the flesh (Phil. 3:3) for the weapons of warfare are not of the flesh (2 Cor. 10:4). I put on the whole armor of God (Eph. 6:10-20), and I resolve to stand firm in my faith and resist the evil one.

I believe that apart from Christ I can do nothing (John 15:5), so I declare myself dependent on Him. I choose to abide in Christ in order to bear much fruit and glorify the Lord (John 15:8). I announce to Satan that Jesus is my Lord (1 Cor. 12:3), and I reject any counterfeit gifts or works of Satan in my life.

I believe that the truth will set me free (John 8:32) and that walking in the light is the only path of fellowship (1 John 1:7). Therefore, I stand against Satan's deception by taking every thought captive in obedience to Christ (2 Cor. 10:5). I declare that the Bible is the only authoritative standard (2 Tim. 3:15-16). I choose to speak the truth in love (Eph. 4:15).

I choose to present my body as an instrument of righteousness, a living and holy sacrifice, and I renew my mind by the living Word of God in order that I may prove that the

will of God is good, acceptable and perfect (Rom. 6:13; 12:1 2). I put off the old self with its evil practices and put on the new self (Col. 3:9-10), and I declare myself to be a new creature in Christ (2 Cor. 5:17).

I trust my Heavenly Father to fill me with His Holy Spirit (Eph. 5:18), to lead me into all truth (John 16:13) and to empower my life that I may live above sin and not carry out the desires of the flesh (Gal. 5:16). I crucify the flesh (Gal. 5:24) and choose to walk by the Spirit.

I renounce all selfish goals and choose the ultimate goal of love (1 Tim. 1:5). I choose to obey the two greatest commandments: to love the Lord my God with all my heart, soul and mind, and to love my neighbor as myself (Matt. 22:37-39).

I believe that Jesus has all authority in heaven and on earth (Matt. 28:18) and that He is the head over all rule and authority (Col. 2:10). I believe that Satan and his demons are subject to me in Christ since I am a member of Christ's body (Eph. 1:19-23). Therefore, I obey the command to submit to God and to resist the devil (Jas. 4:7), and I command Satan in the name of Christ to leave my presence.

Step 3

BITTERNESS VS. FORGIVENESS

We need to forgive others in order to be free from our pasts and to prevent Satan from taking advantage of us (see 2 Cor. 2:10-11). We are to be merciful just as our Heavenly Father is merciful (see Luke 6:36). We are to forgive as we have been forgiven (see Eph. 4:31-32). Ask God to bring to mind the names of those people you need to forgive by expressing the following prayer aloud:

Dear Heavenly Father,
I thank You for the riches of Your kindness,

forbearance, and patience, knowing that Your kindness has led me to repentance (Rom. 2:4). I confess that I have not extended that same patience and kindness toward others who have offended me, but instead I have harbored bitterness and resentment. I pray that during this time of self-examination You would bring to my mind those people that I need to forgive in order that I may do so (Matt. 18:35). I ask this in the precious name of Jesus. Amen.

As names come to mind, make a list of only the names. At the end of your list, write "myself." Forgiving yourself is accepting God's cleansing and forgiveness. Also, write "thoughts against God." Thoughts raised up against the knowledge of God will usually result in angry feelings toward Him. Technically, we can't forgive God because He cannot commit any sin of commission or omission. But we need to specifically renounce false expectations and thoughts about God and agree to release any anger we have toward Him.

Before you pray to forgive these people, stop and consider what forgiveness is, what it is not, what decision you will be making, and what the consequences will be. In the following explanation, the main points are in bold print:

Forgiveness is not forgetting. People who try to forget find they cannot. God says He will remember our sins "no more" (see Heb. 10:17), but God, being omniscient, cannot forget. Remember our sins "no more" means that God will never use the past against us (see Ps. 103:12). Forgetting may be the result of forgiveness, but it is never the means of forgiveness. When we bring up the past against others, we are saying we haven't forgiven them.

Forgiveness is a choice, a crisis of the will. Since God requires us to forgive, it is something we can do. However, forgiveness is difficult for us because it pulls against our concept of justice. We want revenge for offenses suffered. However, we are told never to take our own revenge (see Rom. 12:19). You say, "Why should I let them off the hook?" That is precisely the problem. You are still hooked to them, still bound by your past. **You will let them off your hook, but**

they are never off God's. He will deal with them fairly, something we cannot do.

You say, "You don't understand how much this person hurt me!" But don't you see, they are still hurting you! How do you stop the pain? **You don't forgive someone for their sake; you do it for your own sake so you can be free. Your need to forgive isn't an issue between you and the offender; it's between you and God.**

Forgiveness is agreeing to live with the consequences of another person's sin. Forgiveness is costly. You pay the price of the evil you forgive. You're going to live with those consequences whether you want to or not; your only choice is whether you will do so in the bitterness of unforgiveness or the freedom of forgiveness. Jesus took the consequences of your sin upon Himself. All true forgiveness is substitutionary, because no one really forgives without bearing the consequences of the other person's sin. God the Father "made Him who knew no sin to be sin on our behalf, that we might become the righteousness of God in Him" (2 Cor. 5:21). Where is the justice? It's the cross that makes forgiveness legally and morally right: "For the death that He died, He died to sin, once for all" (Rom. 6:10).

Decide that you will bear the burdens of their offenses by not using that information against them in the future. This doesn't mean that you tolerate sin. You must set up scriptural boundaries to prevent future abuse. Some may be required to testify for the sake of justice but not for the purpose of seeking revenge from a bitter heart.

How do you forgive from your heart? You acknowledge the hurt and the hate. If your forgiveness doesn't visit the emotional core of your life, it will be incomplete. Many feel the pain of interpersonal offenses, but they won't or don't know how to acknowledge it. Let God bring the pain to the surface so He can deal with it. This is where the healing takes place.

Don't wait to forgive until you feel like forgiving; you will never get there. Feelings take time to heal after the choice to forgive is made and Satan has lost his place (see Eph. 4:26-27). **Freedom is what will be gained, not a feeling.**

As you pray, God may bring to mind offending people and experiences you have totally forgotten. Let Him do it even if it is painful. Remember, you are doing this for your sake. God wants you to be free. Don't rationalize or explain the offender's behavior. Forgiveness is dealing with your pain and leaving the other person to God. Positive feelings will follow in time; freeing yourself from the past is the critical issue right now.

Don't say, "Lord, please help me to forgive," because He is already helping you. Don't say, "Lord, I want to forgive," because you are bypassing the hard-core choice to forgive which is your responsibility. Stay with each individual until you are sure you have dealt with all the remembered pain—what they did, how they hurt you, how they made you feel (rejected, unloved, unworthy, dirty, etc.).

You are now ready to forgive the people on your list so you can be free in Christ, with those people no longer having any control over you. For each person on your list, pray aloud:

> **Lord,**
>
> **I forgive (name the person) for (verbally share every hurt and pain the Lord brings to your mind and how it made you feel).**

After you have forgiven every person for every painful memory, then finish this step by praying:

> **Lord,**
>
> **I release all these people to You, and my right to seek revenge. I choose not to hold on to my bitterness and anger, and I ask You to heal my damaged emotions. In Jesus' name, I pray. Amen.**

Step 4

REBELLION VS. SUBMISSION

We live in rebellious times. Many believe it is their right to sit in judgment of those in authority over them. Rebelling against God and His authority gives Satan an opportunity to attack. As our commanding general, the Lord says, "Get into ranks and follow Me. I will not lead you into temptation, but I will deliver you from evil" (see Matt. 6:13).

We have two biblical responsibilities regarding authority figures: Pray for them and submit to them. The only time God permits us to disobey earthly leaders is when they require us to do something morally wrong before God or attempt to rule outside the realm of their authority. Pray the following prayer:

Dear Heavenly Father,

You have said that rebellion is as the sin of witchcraft and insubordination is as iniquity and idolatry (1 Sam. 15:23). I know that in action and attitude I have sinned against You with a rebellious heart. Thank you for forgiving my rebellion, and I pray that by the shed blood of the Lord Jesus Christ all ground gained by evil spirits because of my rebelliousness will be canceled. I pray that You will shed light on all my ways that I may know the full extent of my rebelliousness. I now choose to adopt a submissive spirit and a servant's heart. In the name of Christ Jesus, my Lord. Amen.

Being under authority is an act of faith. You are trusting God to work through His established lines of authority. There are times when employers, parents and husbands are violating the laws of civil government which are ordained by God to protect innocent people against abuse. In these cases, you need to appeal to the state for your protection. In many states, the law requires such abuse to be reported.

In difficult cases, such as continuing abuse at home, further counseling help may be needed. And, in some cases, when earthly authorities have abused their position and are requiring disobedience to God or a compromise in your commitment to Him, you need to obey God, not man.

We are all admonished to submit to one another as equals in Christ (see Eph. 5:21). However, there are specific lines of authority in Scripture for the purpose of accomplishing common goals:

Civil Government (see Rom. 13:1-7; 1 Tim. 2:1-4; 1 Pet. 2:13-17)
Parents (see Eph. 6:1-3)
Husband (see 1 Pet. 3:1-4) or Wife (see Eph. 5:21; 1 Pet. 3:7)
Employer (see 1 Pet. 2:18-23)
Church Leaders (see Heb. 13:17)
God (see Dan. 9:5, 9)

Examine each area and confess those times you have not been submissive by praying:

> **Lord,**
> **I agree I have been rebellious toward ______________________. I choose to be submissive and obedient to your Word. In Jesus' name, Amen.**

Step 5
PRIDE VS. HUMILITY

Pride is a killer. Pride says, "I can do it! I can get myself out of this mess without God or anyone else's help." Oh no, we can't! We absolutely need God, and we desperately need each other. Paul wrote: "We worship in the Spirit of God and glory in Christ Jesus and put no confidence in the flesh" (Phil. 3:3). Humility is confidence properly placed. We are to be "strong in the Lord and in the strength of His might" (Eph. 6:10). James 4:6-10 and 1 Peter 5:1-10 reveal that spiritual conflict follows pride. Use the following prayer to express your commitment to live humbly before God:

> **Dear Heavenly Father,**
> **You have said that pride goes before destruction and an arrogant spirit before stumbling (Prov. 16:18). I confess that I have lived independently and have not denied myself, picked up my cross daily and followed You (Matt. 16:24). In so doing,**

I have given ground to the enemy in my life. I have believed that I could be successful and live victoriously by my own strength and resources. I now confess that I have sinned against You by placing my will before Yours and by centering my life around myself instead of You. I now renounce the self-life and by so doing cancel all the ground that has been gained in my members by the enemies of the Lord Jesus Christ. I pray that You will guide me so that I will do nothing from selfishness or empty conceit, but with humility of mind I will regard others as more important than myself (Phil. 2:3). Enable me through love to serve others and in honor prefer others (Rom. 12:10). I ask this in the name of Christ Jesus, my Lord. Amen.

Having made that commitment, now allow God to show you any specific areas of your life where you have been prideful, such as:

_______ Having a stronger desire to do my will than God's will;
_______ Being more dependent upon my strengths and resources than God's;
_______ Too often believe that my ideas and opinions are better than others;
_______ Being more concerned about controlling others than developing self-control;
_______ Sometimes consider myself more important than others;
_______ Having a tendency to think that I have no needs;
_______ Finding it difficult to admit that I was wrong;
_______ Having a tendency to be more of a people-pleaser than a God-pleaser;
_______ Being overly concerned about getting the credit I deserve;
_______ Being driven to obtain the recognition that comes from degrees, titles and positions;
_______ Often thinking I am more humble than others;
_______ These other ways: ______________________.

For each of these that has been true in your life, pray aloud:

Lord,
I agree I have been prideful by: ____________
____.
I choose to humble myself and place all my confidence in You. Amen.

Step 6
BONDAGE VS. FREEDOM

The next step to freedom deals with habitual sin. People who have been caught in the trap of sin-confess-sin-confess may need to follow the instructions of James 5:16, "Confess your sins to one another, and pray for one another, so that you may be healed. The effective prayer of a righteous man can accomplish much." Seek out a righteous person who will hold you up in prayer and to whom you can be accountable. Others may only need the assurance of 1 John 1:9: "If we confess our sins, He is faithful and righteous to forgive us our sins and to cleanse us from all unrighteousness." Confession is not saying "I'm sorry"; it's saying "I did it." Whether you need the help of others or just the accountability to God, pray the following prayer:

Dear Heavenly Father,
You have told us to put on the Lord Jesus Christ and make no provision for the flesh in regard to its lust (Rom. 13:14). I acknowledge that I have given in to fleshly lusts which wage war against my soul (1 Pet. 2:11). I thank You that in Christ my sins are forgiven, but I have transgressed Your holy law and given the enemy an opportunity to wage war in my physical body (Rom. 6:12-13; Eph. 4:27; Jas. 4:1; 1 Pet. 5:8). I come before Your presence to acknowledge these sins and to seek Your cleansing (1 John 1:9) that I may be freed from the bondage of sin. I now ask You

to reveal to my mind the ways that I have transgressed Your moral law and grieved the Holy Spirit. In Jesus' precious name, I pray. Amen.

The deeds of the flesh are numerous. Many of the following issues are from Galatians 5:19-21. Check those that apply to you and any others you have struggled with that the Lord has brought to your mind. Then confess each one with the concluding prayer. Note: sexual sins, eating disorders, substance abuse, abortion, suicidal tendencies, perfectionism and fear will be dealt with later.

____ stealing
____ lying
____ fighting
____ jealousy
____ envying
____ outbursts of anger
____ complaining
____ criticizing
____ lusting
____ cheating
____ gossiping
____ controlling
____ procrastinating
____ swearing
____ greediness
____ laziness
____ divisiveness
____ gambling
____ other____________

Dear Heavenly Father,

I thank You that my sins are forgiven in Christ, but I have walked by the flesh and therefore sinned by________________________. Thank You for cleansing me of all unrighteousness. I ask that You would enable me to walk by the Spirit and not carry out the desires of the flesh. In Jesus' name, I pray. Amen.

It is our responsibility not to allow sin to reign in our mortal bodies by not using our bodies as instruments of unrighteousness (see Rom. 6:12,13). If you are or have struggled with sexual sins (pornography, masturbation, sexual promiscuity, etc.) or are experiencing sexual difficulty in your marriage, pray as follows:

Lord,

I ask You to reveal to my mind every sexual

use of my body as an instrument of unrighteousness. In Jesus' precious name, I pray. Amen.

As the Lord brings to your mind every sexual misuse of your body, whether it was done to you (rape, incest or other sexual abuse) or willingly by you, renounce every occasion:

Lord,
I renounce (name the specific misuse of your body) with (name the person) and ask You to break that bond.

Now commit your body to the Lord by praying:

Lord,
I renounce all these uses of my body as an instrument of unrighteousness and by so doing ask You to break all bondages Satan has brought into my life through that involvement. I confess my participation. I now present my body to You as a living sacrifice, holy and acceptable unto You, and I reserve the sexual use of my body only for marriage. I renounce the lie of Satan that my body is not clean, that it is dirty or in any way unacceptable as a result of my past sexual experiences. Lord, I thank You that You have totally cleansed and forgiven me, that You love and accept me unconditionally. Therefore, I can accept myself. And I choose to do so, to accept myself and my body as cleansed. In Jesus' name. Amen.

SPECIAL PRAYERS FOR SPECIFIC PROBLEMS

Homosexuality

Lord,
I renounce the lie that You have created me or

anyone else to be homosexual, and I affirm that You clearly forbid homosexual behavior. I accept myself as a child of God and declare that You created me a man (woman). I renounce any bondages of Satan that have perverted my relationships with others. I announce that I am free to relate to the opposite sex in the way that You intended. In Jesus' name. Amen.

Abortion

Lord,

I confess that I did not assume stewardship of the life You entrusted to me. I choose to accept your forgiveness, and I now commit that child to You for Your care in eternity. In Jesus' name. Amen.

Suicidal Tendencies

Lord,

I renounce suicidal thoughts and any attempts I have made to take my own life or in any way injure myself. I renounce the lie that life is hopeless and that I can find peace and freedom by taking my own life. Satan is a thief, and he comes to steal, kill, and destroy. I choose to be a good steward of the physical life that You have entrusted to me. In Jesus' name, I pray. Amen.

Eating Disorders or Self-Mutilation

Lord,

I renounce the lie that my value as a person is dependent upon my physical beauty, my weight or size. I renounce cutting myself, vomiting, using laxatives or starving myself as a means of cleansing myself of evil or altering my appearance. I announce that only the blood of the Lord Jesus Christ cleanses me from sin. I accept the reality that there may be sin present in me due to the lies I have believed and the wrongful use of my body, but I renounce the lie that I am evil or that any part of my body is evil. My body is the temple of the Holy Spirit and I belong to You, Lord. I receive Your love and acceptance of me. In Jesus' name. Amen.

Substance Abuse

Lord,

I confess that I have misused substances (alcohol, tobacco, food, prescription or street drugs) for the purpose of pleasure, to escape reality or to cope with difficult situations—resulting in the abuse of my body, the harmful programming of my mind and the quenching of the Holy Spirit. I ask Your forgiveness. I renounce any satanic connection or influence in my life through my misuse of chemicals or food. I cast my anxiety onto Christ Who loves me, and I commit myself to no longer yield to substance abuse, but to the Holy Spirit. I ask You, Heavenly Father, to fill me with Your Holy Spirit. In Jesus' name. Amen.

Drivenness and Perfectionism

Lord,

I renounce the lie that my self-worth is dependent upon my ability to perform. I announce the truth that my identity and sense of worth are found in who I am as Your child. I renounce seeking the approval and acceptance of other

people, and I choose to believe that I am already approved and accepted in Christ because of His death and resurrection for me. I choose to believe the truth that I have been saved, not by deeds done in righteousness, but according to Your mercy. I choose to believe that I am no longer under the curse of the law because Christ became a curse for me. I receive the free gift of life in Christ and choose to abide in Him. I renounce striving for perfection by living under the law. By Your grace, Heavenly Father, I choose from this day forward to walk by faith according to what You have said is true by the power of Your Holy Spirit. In Jesus name. Amen.

Plaguing Fears

Dear Heavenly Father,

I acknowledge You as the only legitimate fear object in my life. You are the only omnipresent (always present) and omniscient (all-knowing) God and the only means by which all other fears can be expelled. You are my sanctuary. You have not given me a spirit of timidity, but of power and love and discipline. I confess that I have allowed the fear of man and the fear of death to exercise control over my life, instead of trusting in You. I now renounce all other fear objects and worship You only. I pray that You would fill me with Your Holy Spirit that I may live my life and speak Your Word with boldness. In Jesus' name, I pray. Amen.

Prejudice and Bigotry

Dear heavenly Father,

I know that You love everyone equally and that You do not show favoritism, but You accept people from every nation who fear You and do what

is right (Acts 10:34). You do not judge people based on race, gender, culture, economic or social status (Gal. 3:28). I confess that I have too often prejudged others or regarded myself superior because of these things. I have not always been a minister of reconciliation, but have been a proud agent of division through my attitudes, words and deeds. I repent of all hateful bigotry and proud prejudice and I ask You, Lord, to reveal to my mind all the specific ways in which this form of pride has corrupted my heart and mind. I confess and renounce the prideful sin of prejudice against (name the group). I thank You for Your forgiveness, Lord, and ask You to change my heart and make me a loving agent of reconciliation with (name the group). In Jesus' name. Amen.

After you have confessed all known sin, pray:

Dear Heavenly Father,

I now confess these sins to You and claim my forgiveness and cleansing through the blood of the Lord Jesus Christ. I cancel all ground that evil spirits have gained through my willful involvement in sin. I ask this in the wonderful name of my Lord and Savior, Jesus Christ. Amen.

Step 7

ACQUIESCENCE VS. RENUNCIATION

Acquiescence is passively giving in or agreeing without consent. The last step to freedom is to renounce the sins of your ancestors and any curses which may have been placed on you. In giving the Ten Commandments, God said: "You shall not make for yourself an idol, or any likeness of what is in heaven above or on the earth beneath or in the water under the earth. You shall not worship them or serve them; for I, the Lord your God, am a jealous God, visiting the iniquity of the fathers on the children, on the third and fourth generations of those who hate Me" (Ex. 20:4,5).

Familiar spirits can be passed on from one generation to the next if not renounced and if your new spiritual heritage in Christ is not proclaimed. You are not guilty for the sin of any ancestor, but because of their sin, Satan may have gained access to your family. This is not to deny that many problems are transmitted genetically or acquired from an immoral atmosphere. All three conditions can predispose an individual to a particular sin. In addition, deceived people may try to curse you, or satanic groups may try to target you. You have all the authority and protection you need in Christ to stand against such curses and assignments. Ask the Lord to reveal to your mind the sins and iniquities of your ancestors by praying the following prayer:

Dear Heavenly Father,

I thank You that I am a new creation in Christ. I desire to obey Your command to honor my mother and my father, but I also acknowledge that my heritage has not been perfect. I ask you to reveal to my mind the sins and iniquities of my ancestors in order to confess, renounce and forsake them. In Jesus' name, I pray. Amen.

Now claim your position and protection in Christ by making the following declaration verbally, and then by humbling yourself before God in prayer.

Declaration

I here and now reject and disown all the sins and iniquities of my ancestors, including (name them). As one who has been delivered from the power of darkness and translated into the kingdom of God's dear Son, I cancel out all demonic working that has been passed on to me from my ancestors. As one who has been crucified and raised with Jesus Christ and who sits with Him in heavenly places, I renounce all satanic assign-

ments that are directed toward me and my ministry, and I cancel every curse that Satan and his workers have put on me. I announce to Satan and all his forces that Christ became a curse for me (Gal. 3:13) when He died for my sins on the cross. I reject any and every way in which Satan may claim ownership of me. I belong to the Lord Jesus Christ who purchased me with His own blood. I reject all other blood sacrifices whereby Satan may claim ownership of me. I declare myself to be eternally and completely signed over and committed to the Lord Jesus Christ. By the authority I have in Jesus Christ, I now command every spiritual enemy of the Lord Jesus Christ to leave my presence. I commit myself to my Heavenly Father to do His will from this day forward.

Prayer

Dear Heavenly Father,

I come to You as Your child purchased by the blood of the Lord Jesus Christ. You are the Lord of the universe and the Lord of my life. I submit my body to You as an instrument of righteousness, a living sacrifice, that I may glorify You in my body. I now ask You to fill me with Your Holy Spirit. I commit myself to the renewing of my mind in order to prove that Your will is good, perfect and acceptable for me. All this I do in the name and authority of the Lord Jesus Christ. Amen.

Once you have secured your freedom by going through these seven steps, you may find demonic influences attempting reentry, days or even months later. One person shared that she heard a spirit say to her mind "I'm back" two days after she had been set free. "No, you're not!" she proclaimed aloud. The attack ceased immediately. One victory does not constitute winning the war. Freedom must be maintained. After completing these steps, one jubilant lady asked, "Will I always be like this?"

I told her that she would stay free as long as she remained in right relationship with God. "Even if you slip and fall," I encouraged, "you know how to get right with God again."

One victim of incredible atrocities shared this illustration: "It's like being forced to play a game with an ugly stranger in my own home. I kept losing and wanted to quit, but the ugly stranger wouldn't let me. Finally I called the police (a higher authority), and they came and escorted the stranger out. He knocked on the door trying to regain entry, but this time **I recognized his voice and didn't let him in.**" What a beautiful illustration of gaining freedom in Christ. We call upon Jesus, the ultimate authority, and He escorts the enemy out of our lives. Know the truth, stand firm and resist the evil one. Seek out good Christian fellowship, and commit yourself to regular times of Bible study and prayer. God loves you and will never leave or forsake you.

Aftercare

Freedom must be maintained. You have won a very important battle in an ongoing war. Freedom is yours as long as you keep choosing truth and standing firm in the strength of the Lord. If new memories should surface or if you become aware of "lies" that you have believed or other non-Christian experiences you have had, renounce them and choose the truth. Some have found it helpful to go through the steps again. As you do, read the instructions carefully.

For your encouragement and further study, read *Victory Over the Darkness* (or youth version *Stomping Out the Darkness*), *The Bondage Breaker* (adult or youth version), and *Released from Bondage*. If you are a parent, read *Spiritual Protection for Your Children*. *Walking in the Light* was written to help people understand God's guidance and discern counterfeit guidance. Also, to maintain your freedom, we suggest the following:

1. Seek legitimate Christian fellowship where you can walk in the light and speak the truth in love.

2. Study your Bible daily. Memorize key verses.
3. Take every thought captive to the obedience of Christ. Assume responsibility for your thought life, reject the lie, choose the truth and stand firm in your position in Christ.
4 Don't drift away! It is very easy to get lazy in your thoughts and revert back to old habit patterns of thinking. Share your struggles openly with a trusted friend. You need at least one friend who will stand with you.
5. Don't expect another person to fight your battle for you. Others can help, but they can't think, pray, read the Bible or choose the truth for you.
6. Continue to seek your identity and sense of worth in Christ. Read *Living Free in Christ* and the devotional, *Daily in Christ*. Renew your mind with the truth that your acceptance, security and significance is in Christ by saturating your mind with the following truths. Read the entire list of who you are "in Christ" and the Doctrinal Affirmation (in Step 2) aloud morning and evening over the next several weeks (and look up the verses referenced).
7. Commit yourself to daily prayer. You can pray these suggested prayers often and with confidence:

Daily Prayer

Dear Heavenly Father,

I honor You as my sovereign Lord. I acknowledge that You are always present with me. You are the only all-powerful and wise God. You are kind and loving in all Your ways. I love You and thank You that I am united with Christ and spiritually alive in Him. I choose not to love the world, and I crucify the flesh and all its passions.

I thank You for the life that I now have in Christ, and I ask You to fill me with Your Holy Spirit that I may live my life free from sin. I declare my dependence upon You, and I take my

stand against Satan and all his lying ways. I choose to believe the truth, and I refuse to be discouraged. You are the God of all hope, and I am confident that You will meet my needs as I seek to live according to Your Word. I express with confidence that I can live a responsible life through Christ who strengthens me.

I now take my stand against Satan and command him and all his evil spirits to depart from me. I put on the whole armor of God. I submit my body as a living sacrifice and renew my mind by the living Word of God in order that I may prove that the will of God is good, acceptable, and perfect. I ask these things in the precious name of my Lord and Savior, Jesus Christ. Amen.

Bedtime Prayer

Thank You, Lord, that You have brought me into Your family and have blessed me with every spiritual blessing in the heavenly realms in Christ. Thank You for providing this time of renewal through sleep. I accept it as part of Your perfect plan for Your children, and I trust You to guard my mind and my body during my sleep. As I have meditated on You and Your truth during this day, I choose to let these thoughts continue in my mind while I am asleep. I commit myself to You for Your protection from every attempt of Satan or his emissaries to attack me during sleep. I commit myself to You as my Rock, my Fortress and my Resting Place. I pray in the strong name of the Lord Jesus Christ. Amen.

Cleansing Home/Apartment

After removing all articles of false worship from home/apartment, pray aloud in every room, if necessary:

> **Heavenly Father, we acknowledge that You are Lord of heaven and earth. In Your sovereign power and love, You have given us all things richly to enjoy. Thank You for this place to live. We claim this home for our family as a place of spiritual safety and protection from all the attacks of the enemy. As children of God seated with Christ in the heavenly realm, we command every evil spirit claiming ground in the structures and furnishings of this place, based on the activities of previous occupants, to leave and never return. We renounce all curses and spells utilized against this place. We ask You, Heavenly Father, to post guardian angels around this home (apartment, condo, room, etc.) to guard it from attempts of the enemy to enter and disturb Your purposes for us. We thank You, Lord, for doing this, and pray in the name of the Lord Jesus Christ. Amen.**

Living in a Non-Christian Environment

After removing all articles of false worship from your room, pray aloud in the space allotted to you:

> **Thank You, Heavenly Father, for my place to live and be renewed by sleep. I ask You to set aside my room (portion of my room) as a place of spiritual safety for me. I renounce any allegiance given to false gods or spirits by other occupants, and I renounce any claim to this room (space) by Satan based on activities of past occupants or me. On the basis of my position as a child of God and a joint-heir with Christ who has all authority in heaven and on earth, I command all evil spirits to leave this place and never to return. I ask You, Heavenly Father, to appoint guardian angels to protect me while I live here. I pray this in the name of the Lord Jesus Christ. Amen.**

Who I Am in Christ

I Am Accepted

John 1:12	I am God's child.
John 15:15	I am Christ's friend.
Rom. 5:1	I have been justified.
1 Cor. 6:17	I am united with the Lord, and I am one spirit with Him.
1 Cor. 6:19,20	I have been bought with a price. I belong to God.
1 Cor. 12:27	I am a member of Christ's body.
Eph. 1:1	I am a saint.
Eph. 1:5	I have been adopted as God's child.
Eph. 2:18	I have direct access to God through the Holy Spirit.
Col. 1:14	I have been redeemed and forgiven of all my sins.
Col. 2:10	I am complete in Christ.

I Am Secure

Rom. 8:1,2	I am free forever from condemnation.
Rom. 8:28	I am assured that all things work together for good.
Rom. 8:31-34	I am free from any condemning charges against me.
Rom. 8:35-39	I cannot be separated from the love of God.
2 Cor. 1:21,22	I have been established, anointed and sealed by God.
Col. 3:3	I am hidden with Christ in God.
Phil. 1:6	I am confident that the good work that God has begun in me will be perfected.
Phil. 3:20	I am a citizen of heaven.
2 Tim. 1:7	I have not been given a spirit of fear but of power, love and a sound mind.

Heb. 4:16	I can find grace and mercy to help in time of need.
1 Jn. 5:18	I am born of God and the evil one cannot touch me.

I Am Significant

Matt. 5:13,14	I am the salt and light of the earth.
John 15:1,5	I am a branch of the true vine, a channel of His life.
John 15:16	I have been chosen and appointed to bear fruit.
Acts 1:8	I am a personal witness of Christ.
1 Cor. 3:16	I am God's temple.
2 Cor. 5:17-21	I am a minister of reconciliation for God.
2 Cor. 6:1	I am God's coworker (1 Cor. 3:9).
Eph. 2:6	I am seated with Christ in the heavenly realm.
Eph. 2:10	I am God's workmanship.
Eph. 3:12	I may approach God with freedom and confidence.
Phil. 4:13	I can do all things through Christ who strengthens me.

APPENDIX B

Materials and Training for You and Your Church

Christ is the answer and truth will set you free. I (Neil) have never been more convinced of this truth. Jesus is the bondage breaker, and He is the wonderful counselor. The following material will benefit both you and your marriage. It will most likely result in your freedom in Christ and help you to become the person God wants you to be. That would be tremendous, but I think the Lord has something far bigger in mind. Let me explain.

Crystal Evangelical Free Church hosted our "Resolving Personal and Spiritual Conflicts" conference. Immediately afterward, they began their own "Freedom Ministry" by training encouragers. Within three years they had led more than 1,500 hurting and desperate people to freedom in Christ. They have also hosted their own conference to show other churches how to do it. Ninety-five percent of their trained encouragers are laypeople. Because there are not enough professional pastors or counselors in our country to reach more than 5 percent of our population, we must equip the saints to do the work of ministry.

Suppose your church carefully chose 20 people and trained them, as I will outline shortly. If each person agreed to help just one other person every other week, by the end of one year, your church would have helped 520 people. And the ministry won't stop there! These people would become witnesses without even trying. Your church would become known in the community as a place that really cares for its people and has an answer for the problems of life. How can people witness if they are in bondage? But children of God who are established free in Christ will naturally (and supernaturally) be witnesses as they glorify God by bearing fruit.

The material for training encouragers includes books, study guides and tape series (both video and audio). The tape series all have corresponding syllabi. The training will best be facilitated if the trainees watch the videos, read the books and complete the study guides. The study guides will greatly increase the learning process and help people to personalize and internalize the message. The cost prohibits some from using the videos. In such cases, the books and study guides can still be effective.

The basic and advanced materials are given as follows in the order they should be taught:

BASIC-LEVEL TRAINING

First Four Weeks

Purpose:	To understand who we are in Christ, how to walk by faith and win the battle for our minds, to understand our emotions and the means by which we relate to one another.
Video/Audio Series:	"Resolving Personal Conflicts."
Reading:	*Victory over the Darkness* and accompanying study guide.
Youth Edition:	*Stomping Out the Darkness* and accompanying study guide.
Supplemental Reading:	*Living Free in Christ*: The purpose of this book is to establish us complete in Christ and to show how He meets the most critical needs of our lives: identity, acceptance, security and significance. This is the first book we have people read after they go through the Steps or pray to receive Christ.

Second Four Weeks

Purpose:	To understand the nature of the spiritual world; to know the position, authority, protection and vulnerability of the believer; to know how to set captives free.
Video/Audio Series:	"Resolving Spiritual Conflicts."
Reading:	*The Bondage Breaker* and accompanying study guide.
Youth Edition:	*The Bondage Breaker Youth Edition* and accompanying study guide.
Supplemental Reading:	*Released from Bondage:* This book contains chapter-length personal testimonies of people who have found freedom in Christ from depression, incest, lust, panic attacks, eating disorders, etc., with explanatory comments by Neil Anderson.

Note: *Breaking Through to Spiritual Maturity* is an adult curriculum for teaching the previous material. *Busting Free* is the youth curriculum for teaching the youth editions.

Third and Fourth Four Weeks

Purpose:	To understand the theology and practical means by which we can help others find freedom in Christ with a discipleship/counseling approach.
Video/Audio Series:	"Spiritual Conflicts and Counseling" and "How to Lead a Person to Freedom in Christ."
Reading:	*Helping Others Find Freedom in Christ* plus the training manual and accompanying study guide. The study guide also details how your church can establish a discipleship/counseling ministry, and it has answers for the most commonly asked questions.
Youth Edition:	*Helping Our Children Find Freedom in Christ* (in process).

Supplemental Reading: *Daily in Christ:* This is a one-year devotional that we encourage individuals as well as families to read annually.

The following are prerequisites to successfully complete the basic training:

1. Complete the "Steps to Freedom" with an encourager.
2. Complete two or more freedom appointments as a prayer partner.
3. Be recommended by the director of the Freedom ministry and meet the qualifications established by his or her church.

In addition to our basic training, Freedom in Christ Ministries has appropriate materials available for advanced training for specific issues. The topics can be covered by offering additional training, special meetings or regularly scheduled encourager meetings. We strongly suggest that your team of encouragers meet regularly for prayer, instruction and feedback. It has been our experience that cases become more difficult as the group matures. On-the-job training is essential for any ministry. None of us have arrived. About the time we think we have heard it all, along comes a case that shatters all stereotypes and doesn't fit into any mold. This unpredictability keeps us from falling into patterns of complacency and relying on our own cleverness, rather than relying on God. The advanced training material should be studied in the order given:

ADVANCED-LEVEL TRAINING

First Four Weeks

Purpose: To discern counterfeit guidance from divine guidance; to explain fear, anxiety, how to pray by the Spirit and how to walk by the Spirit.

Book: *Walking in the Light.*

Youth Edition: *Know Light, No Fear.*

Second Four Weeks

Purpose:	To understand the culture in which our children are being raised; what is going on in their minds; how to be the parents they need; and how to lead them to freedom in Christ.
Book and Video Series:	*The Seduction of Our Children*
Supplemental Reading For Adults:	*Protecting Your Family from the Enemy* by Neil Anderson and Pete and Sue Vander Hook.
For Youth:	*To My Dear Slimeball* by Rich Miller.

Third Four Weeks

Purpose:	To understand how people get into sexual bondage and how they can be free in Christ.
Book:	*A Way of Escape.*
Youth Edition:	*Purity Under Pressure.*

Fourth Four Weeks (can include one of the following):

Book:	*Freedom from Addiction.*
Subjects Include:	The nature of substance abuse and how the bondage can be broken in Christ.
Book:	*The Christ-Centered Marriage.*
Book and Video Series:	*Setting Your Church Free*: This book and video series by Neil Anderson and Charles Mylander is for Christian leaders. It teaches a biblical pattern of leadership and shows how churches can resolve their corporate conflicts and establish Christ as the head of their ministries.
Book:	*Spiritual Warfare* by Dr. Timothy Warner.
Video/Audio Series:	"Resolving Spiritual Conflicts and Cross-Cultural Ministry," also by Dr. Timothy Warner.

Schedules for Basic-Level Training

A 16-week format requires meeting one night each week for two to three hours. Viewing two video lessons each night, it will take about 12 weeks to view the first three video series. The last 4 weeks, use the video "How to Lead a Person to Freedom in Christ." It provides four one-hour segments. Showing a one-hour video each evening allows ample time for discussion. This schedule does not include much time for discussing the books and inductive studies or the content of the video series. Another meeting could be scheduled for that purpose, such as Sunday morning. If necessary, the material could be discussed after the video has been shown. A summary of the schedule is as follows:

Week #1	**Week #2**	**Week #3**
Resolving Personal Conflicts	Resolving Spiritual Conflicts	Spiritual Conflicts and Counseling and How to Lead a Person to Freedom in Christ.
Two video lessons each night	Two video lessons each night; last tape shows the "Steps to Freedom," which can be done as a group in the class or separately with an encourager.	Two video lessons each night for four weeks, then one hour per night for four weeks.

Although these meetings can be open to all who will commit the time, it should be made clear that attending the seminars does not automatically qualify anyone to participate in the ministry. Another possible schedule would be showing one video series on a Friday night/Saturday format each month. This will require only one facilitator giving one weekend each month. It would be possible to cover all the material in four weekends. There is generally less time for discussion of the videos in this schedule, but you can meet Sunday morning or one night a week to discuss the books and the inductive studies.

Weekend #1	**Weekend #2**	**Weekend #3**
Resolving Personal Conflicts	Resolving Spiritual Conflicts	Spiritual Conflicts and Counseling
Friday Night-Video Lessons: 1-2	Friday Night-Video Lessons: 1-2	Friday Night-Video Lessons: 1-2
Saturday: Lessons: 3-8	Saturday: Lessons: 3-7 and the "Steps to Freedom"	Saturday: Lessons: 3-8

The fourth weekend could be completed on Saturday only, using the shorter video series "How to Lead a Person to Freedom in Christ." We realize it is a lot of material to cover, but there are no shortcuts. I cover almost all of this material when I conduct a "Resolving Personal and Spiritual Conflicts" conference in a week. These materials can be purchased from:

Freedom in Christ Ministries
491 E. Lambert Rd.
La Habra, California 90631
(562)691-9128
(562)691-4035 FAX

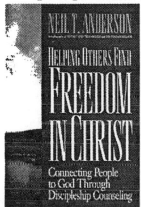

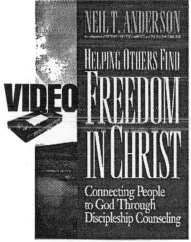

FREEDOM IN CHRIST SPECIAL RESOURCES

VIDEO SEMINARS

Resolving Personal Conflicts PART I reveals the power of your identity in Christ in 8 messages covering: The Search for Identity and Meaning, Faith Renewal, Walking by Faith, Strongholds, The Battle for our Minds, Relational Perspectives, Healing Damaged Emotions, Forgiving from the Heart.

Workbook 1-884284-02-7

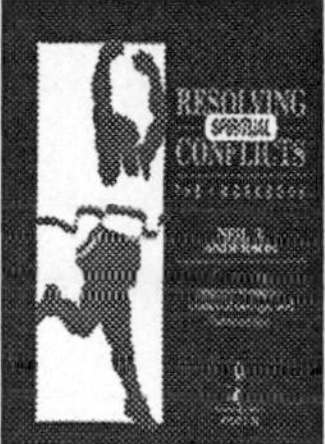

Resolving Spiritual Conflicts PART II reveals the powerful truth that will break even the most stubborn habits or private sins in 8 messages covering: The Position of the Believer, The Authority of the Believer, The Protection of the Believer, The Vulnerability of the Believer, Temptation, Accusation, Deception, Steps to Freedom.

Workbook • ISBN 1-884284-07-8

Walking in the Light–
Thomas Nelson Publishing
Neil T. Anderson
Learn to discern God's guidance in an age of spiritual counterfeits. Dr. Anderson explains the spiritual dimension of divine guidance and exposes the nature of counterfeit guidance.

Paperback • ISBN 08407.43866

RESOURCES FOR PEOPLE AT-RISK

A Way of Escape–Harvest House
Neil T. Anderson
We've all faced sexual struggles. For those who feel caught by unwanted thoughts, compulsive habits, or a painful past, **A Way of Escape** provides concrete steps to overcome the bondage of sexual strongholds battling in your mind.

Paperback • ISBN 15650.71700

Purity Under Pressure–Harvest House
Neil T. Anderson and Dave Park
In this book, you'll find out the difference between being friends, dating and having a relationship. You'll see how the physical stuff fits in. And you'll get answers to the questions you're asking.

Paperback • ISBN 15650 72928

The Seduction of Our Children – Harvest House
Neil T. Anderson and Steve Russo
A battle is raging for the minds of our children. It's a battle parents must win! This book will prepare parents to counter Satan's assault by understanding his strategies and warring against them.

Paperback • ISBN 08908.18886
Video • 1-884284-15-9

SPECIAL READING

To My Dear Slimeball–Harvest House
Rich Miller
In the spirit of C.S. Lewis, Rich creates the secret world of Slimeball and Spitwad–two demons intent on making life miserable for 15-year-old David. As you gain access to their private plans, you'll see how to detect their crafty schemes in your own life.

Paperback • ISBN 15650.71875

Released from Bondage–
Thomas Nelson Publishing
Neil T. Anderson
Released from Bondage contains gripping true stories of freedom from obsessive thoughts, compulsive behavior, childhood abuse and many more.

Paperback • ISBN 08407.43882

FOR CHURCHES

Setting Your Church Free
Neil T. Anderson and Charles Mylander
Spiritual battles can effect entire churches as well as individuals. **Setting Your Church Free** shows pastors and church leaders how they can apply the powerful principles from **Victory Over the Darkness** to lead their churches to freedom.

Hardcover • ISBN 08307.16556

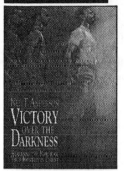

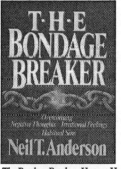

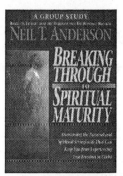

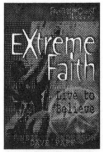